MILITARY WASTE

MILITARY WASTE

THE UNEXPECTED CONSEQUENCES
OF PERMANENT WAR READINESS

Joshua O. Reno

 UNIVERSITY OF CALIFORNIA PRESS

University of California Press
Oakland, California

Library of Congress Cataloging-in-Publication Data

Names: Reno, Joshua, author.
Title: Military waste : the unexpected consequences of
    permanent war readiness / Joshua O. Reno.
Description: Oakland, California : University of California Press,
    [2020] | Includes bibliographical references and index.
Identifiers: LCCN 2019019315 (print) | ISBN 9780520974128
    (e-book) | ISBN 9780520316010 (cloth : alk. paper) |
    ISBN 9780520316027 (pbk. : alk. paper)
Subjects: LCSH: Military supplies—Environmental aspects. |
    Military supplies—Social aspects.
Classification: LCC UC260 .R39 2020 (print) | DDC 363.72/8—dc23
LC record available at https://lccn.loc.gov/2019019315
LC ebook record available at https://lccn.loc.gov/2019980770

Manufactured in the United States of America

28   27   26   25   24   23   22   21   20   19
10   9   8   7   6   5   4   3   2   1

This book is dedicated to my parents, James and Barbara Reno. One taught me about machines, the other about the environment. Both taught me to value peace over war.

CONTENTS

Acknowledgments   *ix*

Introduction   *1*
1. Worth the Waste   20
2. Flight or Fight   49
    Coauthored with Priscilla Bennett
3. Sunk Cost   83
    Coauthored with Priscilla Bennett
4. The Wrong Stuff   *108*
5. Domestic Blowback   *140*
6. Island Erasure   *174*
    Conclusion   *202*

Notes   *215*
Reference List   *237*
Index   *265*

ACKNOWLEDGMENTS

There are many people to thank for their help with this book. First and foremost, there are the people who welcomed Priscilla Bennett and me into their lives to share their experiences of military waste, especially: Drew Deskur and the Kopernik Observatory & Science Center, as well as members of the Kopernik Astronomical Society; James Stemm and the staff at the Pima Air & Space Museum; Terry Shelton and Arizona Aircraft Recovery and Restoration; Eric Firestone and Carlo McCormick; the incomparable Susan Sherwood and the volunteers at TechWorks who agreed to speak with me; the incredible Joe Weatherby, as well as the History of Diving Museum, Valeo Films, and Mote Marine Laboratory. Special thanks are due to Jeremy and the Getman family, to Kathy Lippincott and Richard Rich for trusting me to carry out my very first ever ethnographic project in Elmira in 2001 and 2002, portions of which are finally appearing in print all these years later.

The following people provided helpful commentary at critical times in the development of this project: Catherine Alexander, Dominic Boyer, Jamie Cross, Darcie DeAngelo, Gökçe Günel, Britt Halvorson, Gay Hawkins, Gabriel Hecht, David Henig, Doug Holmes, Cymene Howe, Rachelle Jereza, Eleana Kim, BrieAnna Langlie, Josh Lepawsky, Carl Lipo, Peter Little, Katherine Martineau, Oana Mateescu, Randy McGuire, David Mixter, David Pedersen, Sabina Perrino, Lisa Ruth Rand, Vilma Santiago-Irizarry, Daniel Sosna, Ruth Van Dyke, Vasiliki Touhouliotis, Matthew Wolf-Meyer, and Leah Zani. I also have to acknowledge generous support from fellow participants in the Indian Ocean Energies workshops organized in Johannesburg in

2015 and 2016 by WiSER, especially Sharad Chari, Jamie Cross, Jatin Dua, Isabel Hofmeyr, Pamila Gupta, Sarah Nutall, Meg Samuelson and Jennifer Wenzel; participants in the "Putting Dirt in Its Place" conference in Cambridge in 2017, especially Catherine Alexander and Patrick O'Hare; participants in the "Everybody Is Fixing Something" salon in Edinburgh (also in 2017), especially Jamie Cross, Jamie Furniss, Rachel Harkness, Lara Houston, Declan Murray, and Peter Redfield. Thank you also to the organizers of the Mellon Foundation's EcoCritical Sawyer Seminar on Wastelands at Washington University in St. Louis, for inviting me to present sample book chapters, with special thanks to Heather O'Leary, Nancy Reynolds, Vasiliki Touhouliotis, and all those who participated in the incredibly productive workshop that followed the talk. Thanks also are due to Robin Nagle and Rozy Fredericks for organizing a discard studies workshop where a draft chapter of this book was discussed, as well as participants Rebeca Cuntala, Jacob Doherty, Cassie Fennell, Julie Livingstone, Emma Park, Nicole Ramirez, Jennifer Wenzel, and Amy Zhang, all of whom offered helpful commentary. Finally, thanks to the organizers of the RATS 2016 "Radical Ontologies for the Contemporary Past" conference in Binghamton in 2016, specifically Maura Bainbridge and Rui Gomes Coelho.

Several kind souls commented on specific chapters or proposal drafts, including Catherine Alexander, Kim De Wolff, Siobhan Hart, Laura Jeffrey, and Kearbey Robinson. Ema Grama deserves special recognition for reading and providing invaluable feedback on more than one chapter. I am solely responsible for what resulted from these dialogues (except where Priscilla Bennett is listed as coauthor). Funding for this research came courtesy of Binghamton University and the Harpur College Dean's Office. Thanks to Chris Reiber for helping to ensure I received funding for this research at an early stage. While only two chapters bear her name as coauthor, my collaboration with Priscilla Bennett ultimately made this project possible. I am deeply thankful, both for her impeccable skills as an ethnographer and her commitment to seeing the research through to the end. As always, Reed Malcolm was a helpful guide throughout the life of this project, for which I am very grateful. Thanks also are owed to the anonymous peer reviewers for providing supportive and constructive feedback.

Writing a book means making sacrifices. Since I would always rather spend time with Charlie Reno than write about anything, I am thankful to him for refusing my company at crucial times in the writing process. Sharing a life with Jeanne Reno means watching in admiration as she keeps people safe and protects the environment with unmatched, unflappable perseverance. She is a constant source of inspiration to try and do something similarly worthwhile, even if I know I'm bound to fail.

This book is dedicated to my parents, Jim and Barb Reno. Anyone can give life; not everyone teaches you right from wrong and the moves to the Time Warp.

Introduction

Wars are wasteful. They lay waste to landscapes and lives and leave destructive traces behind in the pain of personal loss, injury, and trauma, the hazard of hidden and unexploded ordnance, and the slow violence of toxic contamination. But preparing for a war you never fight is also wasteful. Even if shots are never fired, bombs never dropped, permanent preparation for war diverts natural resources, productive forces, and political focus away from other pressing concerns. It can also be just as destructive for human health and the environment. World War III never happened, and yet material evidence of this contest is strewn everywhere: resting at the bottom of the ocean, rusting in deserts, floating in near-Earth orbit, circulating in radioactive bloodstreams.[1]

The United States is permanently ready for large-scale wars that may never come. This may one day end, meaning it was not really permanent but temporary. By saying it is permanent, I am not making a prediction about the future, but calling attention to the present state of American industry, politics, and the military, and how they related in the past. Despite occasional reductions in spending, since the world wars American defense spending has tended to steadily increase. And yet, it was not only with the national security state established during the Cold War that war preparation became a permanent investment, seemingly detached from whether the nation was actually at war or not. Permanent war-readiness was realized one piece at a time, not all at once: from the nation's very first navy, built just after the Revolution (chapter 3), to the reconstitution of the military after the Civil War (chapter 5), to the first planes used in combat in World War I (chapter 2), to the creation of a civilian space agency, the National Aeronautics and Space Administration (NASA), alongside its counterparts in the Department of Defense (DoD), the Advanced Research Projects Agency (ARPA), and the National Reconnaissance Office (NRO) (chapter 4). At the same time, a belief in permanent war-readiness was never guaranteed and never universally supported. Moments of collective opposition to unchecked military growth represent an ironic consequence of this history. In fact, there have been many unintended consequences of America's unprecedented military buildup, including antiwar and environmentalist resistance, as many civilians used the threat of apocalyptic conflagration and the knowledge it generated to create transnational countermovements.[2] Other consequences have received far less attention. In the chapters that follow, I document American civilians confronted with by-products of exponential military growth, unexpectedly and accidentally, outside the designs of the US defense establishment. Unlike the wastes of actual warfare, these obstacles and opportunities would present themselves whether or not any specific war ever took place.

Waste is a very flexible term with moral, economic, and ecological dimensions to it.[3] It may refer to a lost and irredeemable expenditure, one that is the opposite of economic productivity or biological fecundity. This sense of the term is in tension with another, which depicts waste instead as a productive ingredient to ecologies and economies—as a necessary element of capitalism, for instance (see Gidwani and Reddy 2011; Yates 2011; Gidwani 2013). In this book I draw on both meanings of waste in order to capture some of the many ways in which people interact with America's permanent war apparatus. Pursuing military waste in this way leads to experiences and stories far from official military actions, involving people who struggle to represent and reimagine fragments of the military they have come across. These fragments are sometimes literal objects, whether humble devices, hulks of warcraft, or bits of debris. But I also find surprising by-products of permanent war preparation elsewhere, like mass shootings and small islands converted into wilderness areas. Each chapter takes on distinct objects with more or less distance from clearly militarized sites or actors. The overall goal of the book, and its structure, is to reveal lines of continuity between American life and the military, to trace connections even where none are apparent.[4]

My argument is based on ethnographic and archival research undertaken from 2015–18, with the exception of chapter 5, which was completed from 2001–2. My research assistant Dr. Priscilla Bennett and I got to know civilians throughout the United States who work and live with different forms of military waste. Following Hugh Gusterson, each chapter considers a *microworld* of distinct actors and wastes, offering an anthropological investigation into "the ways in which these worlds clash and fit together" (2004, xxi). While most have not experienced war directly for themselves, their lives have been impacted in some way by permanent war preparation. By examining how civilians manage and imagine relations with permanent war-readiness, this book follows others that challenge the presumed purification of military from civilian worlds.[5]

While virtual, the separation between military and civilian life in the United States is not merely symbolic. Imagine an alien anthropologist landing in Fort Bragg, North Carolina, and taking it to be representative of American society. The visitor would see people with government-issued clothes, haircuts, food, weapons, housing, education, and health care, following a strictly hierarchical division of duties with little room for questioning authority, let alone disobeying orders. What would our alien conclude about this society's system of government or mode of production? Nothing remotely resembling how Americans tend to think of themselves, their values, and institutions. It would be as if an authoritarian and communist subculture were subsisting within and generously and enthusiastically supported by a society celebrated for its alleged democratic and market freedoms. As Kenneth MacLeish argues, "The military is frequently figured from both within and without as an institution apart from the nation as a whole, existing to protect the public yet exceeding it in discipline, virtue and moral authority" (2013, 188; cf. Mills 1956, 175–76). This virtual divide arguably has further expression in the analytical distinction between militarism and militarization, where the former may suggest the discourse, ideology, or culture associated with being a nation at war and the latter the more practical and material considerations of actual, state-based warfare.[6]

Such compartmentalization is never complete, however, and military and civilian worlds inevitably leak into and shape one another.[7] Unintended and unruly by-products, or wastes, make permanent war preparation visible in new ways, introducing microworlds of social action where these simple binaries collapse. Exploring diverse interactions with and conceptions of military waste challenge divides between civilian and the military (and the others they might presuppose and reinforce, like "ideal" and "material"). As a result, more people, places, stories, and histories are implicated in permanent war preparation than we might tend to imagine. This book's distinct structure, which I discuss for the remainder of the introduction, aims to challenge this virtual separation by focusing on people who make sense of and make do with military waste outside of formal war zones.

This book focuses on people who do not experience the direct consequences of war, people who are not among the official combatants engaged in conflict or the many civilians killed, displaced, and dispossessed as a result. The experiences and struggles of people implicated directly in military violence are deserving of attention, but the acts of production and creative destruction that make such violence possible implicate and impact even more people and places whose stories are rarely told. There are many examples of people in the United States impacted by the permanent war economy, but not by war directly. For instance, consider the numerous base closures that followed the conclusion of the Cold War and the military boomtowns that eventually went into decline after they lost critical defense contracts. In April of 2018, the Pentagon released a report stating that 401 active and Base Realignment and Closure (BRAC) installations had reports of toxic perflourinated compounds being released, 126 of which involved water contamination.[8]

The ethnographic context for two of the chapters, chapter 1 and chapter 5, is the Southern Tier of New York State, a region that has suffered from loss of the defense industry that built up the area in the 1940s and 1950s. The reason I have also focused on other microworlds than this one is to defamiliarize where military remnants are thought to surface and to unsettle expectations about what can be made of them and by whom. Just as war preparation impacts people outside of formal war zones, it also comes into the lives of people outside of formally militarized spaces like testing grounds, factories, laboratories, and bases.

Chapter 1 hews close to such spaces and focuses on a site of military production, a Lockheed Martin facility in Endicott, New York, focusing especially on conceptions of waste that develop within the design and production process. Among other things, the chapter shows how representations of warcraft as waste can shape competitions for DoD contracts as well as weapons testing, research, and development. The people in chapter 2 are more distant from explicitly military spaces, but only slightly. They work at a museum and other businesses that grew alongside a military base outside Tucson, Arizona. Unlike Lockheed employees, who actively seek out military connections, some of the curators and artists involved in remaking and preserving military planes struggle to distance their activities from their militaristic origins. Such distance is not merely aspirational for the entrepreneurs and divers in Key West, Florida, who are the subject of chapter 3. While they are still concerned with clearly militarized objects, such as warships mothballed and scrapped as wrecks or recyclable metal, some are engaged in a more radical rethinking of ships as homes for marine life and a cure for an ailing ocean.

If the second and third chapters involve attempts by civilians to demilitarize what are clearly military objects, the final three chapters involve by-products that few would claim have military origins at all. The first is orbital space debris, the topic of chapter 4. This would appear to be completely distant, symbolically and geographically, from any formal military base or actor. Moreover, space debris is often regarded as a problem for civilian science or private industry, yet I argue it is a by-product inseparable from the militarization of space. This view is supported by the fact that many of the agencies aiming to solve the space debris problem are directly connected to defense, especially the Defense Advanced Research Projects Agency (DARPA). These agencies also tend to share a commitment to *techno-solutionism*, a conviction that technical mastery can solve the problem of space debris, despite the fact that such an ethos created the debris problem in the first place.

There are many ways that the excesses of war preparation become part of lives and communities nowhere close to a military testing ground or base, a museum or wreck. Chapter 5 focuses on the object of guns and, more specifically, the problem of mass shootings with which they are ideologically and practically related. Like orbital space debris, mass shootings are normally discussed apart from the American military altogether. Yet, mass shooters have been made possible by the militarization of the small arms industry, which also has its historical origins in white supremacy and settler colonialism. More broadly, mass shooters can be characterized as the unexpected by-product of a culture of militarism that disseminates prominent narratives about white men regaining honor through violence. In this way, militarized and militaristic storytelling shapes the motivations of would-be murderers, public representations of their acts of violence, and proposals for preventing more deaths in the future. Moreover, by denying alternative ways of framing these events, narratives of guns "in the right hands" or "in the wrong hands" limit how these problems are imagined and helps replicate circuits of violence again and again. As new relationships between the permanent war-readiness and civilian life become visible, so do new projects of demilitarization.[9]

Chapter 6 also complicates the recognized scope of American militarization and militarism, like the previous two, in this case by examining the environmental devastation that imperils the small outlying islands and atolls incorporated as part of US territory. Expanding what counts as "home front," the chapter explores hazards that threaten marine environments, in response to which the United States has deployed a global marine conservation strategy, a strategy that also serves longstanding imperial interests in converting islands to wasteland. In this way, various sites and subjects become newly visible as by-products of a history of a geographically unbounded American empire that stretches back before the Cold War.[10] If the first chapter shows how military wastes can be domesticated and made meaningful by weapons manufacturers, by the final chapter the ocean-in-itself cannot be reduced in such a way, threatening to unmake American empire.

With each chapter, personal relationships to the American military appear more and more distant from explicitly militarized domains, telescoping out to include new problems and places. War manufacturers (chapter 1), businesses alongside military bases (chapter 2), and businessmen using military material (chapter 3) all maintain some literal connection to military microworlds, even though with each successive chapter that connection is more and more indirect. Consequently, in those latter two chapters I describe social actors occasionally trying to demilitarize military products, that is, trying to reuse and represent them in such a way that they have different associations.

Very different is orbital space debris (chapter 4), which is not typically characterized as a symptom of defense objectives and agencies, any more than is space exploration generally. Mass shootings (chapter 5) would seem even harder to relate to the military, as if they were entirely a problem of civil society: gun ownership, vulnerable institutions, or health care provision. In these cases, there is a sense in which various problems are already demilitarized in the interpretive domains of public discourse. In these final two chapters I highlight the widespread influence of militarization and militarism in order to demonstrate how the civilian science of space exploration and the civil rights debate around guns, respectively, are continuous with histories of permanent war preparation. In the last chapter, the very boundaries of the American home front become indistinct from its empire overseas. Most Americans are not aware of the country's historical relationship with its Minor and Outlying Islands, let alone that they have been represented and treated as critical waste over successive phases of American empire (chapter 6). This telescoping structure is meant to deliberately challenge assumptions about the scope of war preparation and its costs, whom it impacts, and what it entails.[11]

In the same way that this book attempts to complicate the meaning of *military* waste by exploring intersections between seemingly distinct military and civilian worlds, it is equally experimental with the idea of military *waste*. Approaching the significance of the American military through its waste may seem like an unusual analytic strategy, yet reference to money and lives wasted is actually a fairly common trope in public discourse around the costs of war. There is a long tradition of characterizing both war and war preparation as wasteful in the United States, and accusations of unnecessary spending and misspent funds have dogged the American war economy (see chapter 1). Waste, in this sense, refers to something lost or misused, as in a waste of money or time.

For many in the field and practice of environmental justice, the idea of military waste would understandably conjure visions of the toxic remnants of war. This is an important dimension of military waste and one that will come up in the chapters that follow. But toxicity is not the only quality associated with waste, at least not the only one that matters to people in a given place and time (see Millar 2018, 32). Following Michael Thompson ([1979] 2017), when objects are discarded as rubbish they do not necessarily lose value, but may acquire a quality of indeterminacy, or what Kathleen Millar calls "plasticity." By this I do not mean that their material qualities are unknowable, but that there is often more than one thing that can be done with them. As a consequence, rubbish can be revalued, sometimes as more valuable, or differently valuable, than it was in its initial use. Thompson's work was an early contribution to what later became known as material culture studies (Appadurai 1986; Miller 1987, 2005, 2010) and investigations of materiality more broadly (Munn 1986; Ingold 2000, 2011; Keane 2003; Latour 2005; Harman 2009; Bennett 2009). But, for Thompson, rubbish is not just one material like any other, but a distinct kind that represents the limit point of valuation, where one group of people stop caring about something and allow it to become something else entirely.

Wasted warcraft are littered throughout the world as rubbish, left behind with little or no commemoration and unclear possibilities for reuse. Characteristic in this regard is the SS *Richard Montgomery*, which crashed into a sandbank on the Thames River while delivering munitions in 1944.[12] It has remained there ever since, but recent plans to build a nearby airport have raised concerns about the entombed explosives. Rather than something to memorialize or mitigate, the *Montgomery* is an unpredictable hazard. Rubbish such as this can be found not just in current and former war zones, but in sites of war preparation. This insight resonates with ethnographic studies of memory politics (Navaro-Yashin 2012; Yoneyama 2016) as well as the archaeology of the contemporary (Buchli 1999; Gustafsson et al. 2017), both of which excavate leftover traces of war and war preparation as productive even in their present absence.

The massive arsenal built for a third world war that never happened met with a very different fate. New treaties, especially the Strategic Arms Reduction Talks (START), the Chemical Weapons Convention (CWC), and the Conventional Forces Europe (CFE), required disarmament of nuclear, chemical, and conventional weapons stockpiles, respectively. The end of the Cold War left behind excess military buildup that had to be sold, abandoned, or disposed of in some way.[13] Much of the research on the impact of war preparation has focused on nuclear weapons research, testing, and economies, and for good reason. Nuclear weapons development represents an extreme case of environmental destruction caused by preparation for an all-out war that never happened and hopefully never will.[14] According to Joseph Masco:

> How individuals engage the nuclear complex puts them in a tactile experience not only with the technology of the bomb but also with the nation-state that controls it, making the interrelationship between the human body and nuclear technologies a powerful site of intersection in which to explore questions of national belonging, justice, and everyday life. (2006, 12)

This is also true of conventional weapons and warcraft, albeit to a different extent. Most obviously, military waste might be evaluated in terms of utility or economic salability. The end of the Cold War also meant that the official arms market was gradually replaced with illegal and quasi-legal trades of excess weapons, which dominate the contemporary global arms trade. The global arms trade reached its height beginning with the 1973 OPEC oil embargo, as Western powers indirectly paid for oil with weapons (Becker 1982; see also chapter 1, this volume). According to official data, the arms trade reached its peak toward the end of the Cold War. However, it is likely that illegal arms trades increased at the end of the Cold War (Wezeman 2014).[15]

Yet selling old weapons is not always so simple. On the one hand, the more powerful and destructive some military objects are (with nuclear weapons the most extreme case), the less easily they can be sold as commodities with ordinary exchange value.[16] Masco (2006) regards military weapons as an unusual commodity for this reason. Marx famously credited the moment of exchange with concealing the conditions of the commodity's production and replacing it with a fetishized image, which is all the buyer and seller usually encounter. Military objects can act as fetishes because they circulate globally as images of power and destruction, whether or not they are exchanged on a market. Understanding military weaponry and warcraft as fetishes highlights the fact that military buildup serves functions beyond their possible "consumption" in warfare. Following Mills (1956), this results in a militarized metaphysics— instead of military equipment being seen as a means to an end (namely peace), "military strength," equated with the cost and size of military budgets and products, becomes fetishized as a valued end in itself.

If military weapons serve as fetishes of national power and security, they are also just objects. They age, wear, and fall into disuse; they also shape and are shaped by places they occupy. As Masco (2006) also documents, the mitigation of aging, disused weapons is a growing concern for the American military. Tracing military waste in this way can highlight the instability of national fetishes. According to Peter Custers, the unproductive inputs and by-products of military production, and the final disposal of obsolescent military products themselves, represent a form of negative exchange value. Insofar as these military wastes need to be managed and mitigated, they require the investment of further money and labor, which may overshadow the (also negative) use value of military products as instruments of physical force and national power. Negative exchange value is no mere abstraction. Sailors of the American and Soviet navies were dumping radioactive waste from nuclear projects into the ocean for over a decade after the conclusion of World War II. American sailors were told that this was harmless and given no special training to eliminate unfamiliar by-products of the nuclear age then emerging. The VA and the Navy did not follow up on the health impacts of this harmful exposure, despite unusual health problems reported by some of the service members.[17]

In Peter Sloterdijk's words, "The twentieth century will be remembered as the period whose decisive idea consisted in targeting not the body of the enemy, but his environment" (2009, 43). If what he says was true of the preceding century, ours might one day be known as a time when proliferating military wastes no longer respect divisions between weapon and target, ally and enemy, when circulating materials, of uncertain value and toxicity, manifest in open-ended ways. Warfare always implicates environments to a certain degree. What makes the era of industrial warfare distinct is the severity and unpredictability of the hazards that litter and contaminate postconflict zones. In chapters 3 and 6 I use the concept of the *Polemocene* (from the Greek word *polemos*, meaning war) to think through the relationship between war preparation and environmental transformation.

Contamination can occur even where no battles transpired, as happened after decades of military exercises on the island of Vieques in Puerto Rico. Though never an official US battleground, Vieques was a strategic base due to its proximity to the Panama Canal and its ability to simulate amphibious warfare in the tropics. Antibase activism ended the US occupation in 2003, but the area ceded by the US military was badly polluted.[18] In addition to heavy metal contamination, devastation from repeated bombing, and the storage and dumping of many other toxicants, one of the most alarming legacies for the people of Vieques is the radiation left over from the use of depleted uranium munitions. The impact of leftover radioactive uranium in bases like Vieques, as well as war zones like Iraq, led the US military to switch to tungsten munitions for a time. This lasted several years before new health studies suggested that this "green alternative" might act as a carcinogen as well. More broadly, the ecotoxicology of explosives has been a concern of NATO and the DoD for decades. Mass-produced materials like TNT are not only hazardous ordnance, but threaten human and nonhuman health as they decay over time. The DoD has identified some ten thousand formerly used defense sites (FUDS) in the United States and its territories, whose assessment and remediation had been conducted by the Army Corps of Engineers as of 1986 as part of the FUDS program (Copp 2018). In many cases, toxic substances were not treated with sufficient care, and billions have been spent on their cleanup.

In other cases, there have been efforts to convert closed defense sites into wilderness areas, also known as M2W conversion. This does not put an end to the problems posed by such sites. As geographer David Havlick puts it, "What M2W conversions may put at risk, then, is not simply the character and budget of national wildlife refuges in the United States, but the broader understanding of what it means to militarize certain places" (2007, 162). As I discuss in chapter 6, military sites can also be transformed into wilderness in order to maintain power and erase historical connections between the United States and certain places it has militarized. That chapter begins by associating contemporary American marine conservation efforts with American settler colonialism and the creation and repurposing of wastes and wastelands. This had its foundation in the systematic dispossession of native lands that were represented as "going to waste," but by the mid-nineteenth century this same logic was necessary as a means of acquiring guano to cure widespread global soil exhaustion. The chapter ultimately traces a parallel between the shift from a dependence on natural to artificial fertilizer and the transition from guano to oil imperialism, identifying the distinct ecological rifts and challenges that arose as a consequence. These metabolic disruptions on land and sea have not only made possible American empire, it is argued, but been exacerbated by it and potentially placed it at risk.

These examples illustrate two key arguments of this book. First, not only war but also war preparation can transform and contaminate spaces and lives. Second, these impacts are not straightforward but manifest slowly, in open-ended and often unpredictable ways.[19] The disuse of military objects can introduce even more open-ended possibilities. This is where, in Michael Thompson's terms, military waste transitions from transient to durable value, as when vessels become sites of creative remembering. For instance, an old military wreck may be reassessed later as a transcendent symbol of the nation-state, like the USS *Arizona*, sunk during the attack on Pearl Harbor in 1941. But this kind of shift in rubbish value is not guaranteed.

Much of this book considers the productive afterlife of military waste, not only economic but artistic, ecological, scientific, and discursive.[20] As already mentioned, waste need not be taken as a lost expenditure or the opposite of productivity, economic or otherwise, but can instead be regarded as a source of creativity (see Navaro-Yashin 2012, 150–1). If the production of nuclear arms represents the ultimate disvalue—an absolute threat to human and nonhuman life—there are far more open-ended forms of military waste revalued and reimagined while they circulate as rubbish. The toxic remnants of industrial war, including leftover explosives and radiation, are more than objects of destruction. Surprisingly, the presence of lingering hazards in such places may be imaginatively integrated into everyday life.[21] I use different theoretical terms to express how social actors productively engage with military waste, from reflexive practice (chapter 1) to affordance (chapter 2), world-making (chapter 3), attunement (chapter 4), transvaluation (chapter 5), and wastelanding (chapter 6). In each case, I highlight how people actively engage with waste-related objects, stories, and sites in creative ways. As with many forms of waste practice, making and unmaking are not clearly opposed, like before and after, but exist, to paraphrase Leah Zani (2019), *in parallel*.[22]

I characterize these as various costs of war preparation, costs that are incurred whether or not wars happen, if a society wishes to be ready for all-out war at all times. These costs I have glossed as "wastes" in order to highlight that they are often unintended or involve excesses, accidents, collateral damage. But they are, in each case, ambiguously related to economic and moral forms of valuation. In some cases, waste comes to mean something like "opportunity cost" in an economic sense; in other cases waste represents the limit of any form of economization, where the regeneration of life itself is placed at risk.[23] Some of the people in these chapters imagined or sought out connections with discarded material remains for profit, artistic enjoyment, or political expression. Some of them avoid contact with military waste, which flashes across their vision like so much unwanted dust from the heavens, getting in the way of what they really want to witness. Some find themselves living out their own or other people's violent militaristic fantasies, trying to fulfill or survive shootings made possible by an overabundance of guns. Some, finally, are trying to imagine relationships with wasted places that have been cast aside, deliberately hidden from reclamation by rightful inhabitants and scrubbed from official American history.

People all over the world are increasingly forced to consider what happens when a global military begins to wear and rot. This might mean recycling old and disused weapons as scrap, discarding them in the ocean, waiting for them to fall from the sky, or mothballing them temporarily until a use can be found for them. Their indeterminacy can be hazardous in many circumstances, but it can also provide opportunities for artists, entrepreneurs, activists, and curators who would make something new out of military discards. In doing so, they contend with both public expectations about how military materials should be treated and the material characteristics of crumbling and unpredictable artifacts. While the revaluation of such materials is therefore constrained, alternative uses of military objects are possible, uses that may challenge representations from popular entertainment, the defense establishment, or the national security state. By exploring relationships with the unintended and unacknowledged by-products of the military, I hope to offer new ways of thinking about the hidden costs of permanent war-readiness which affect the entire world, including forgotten postindustrial towns of the rust belt, distant atolls in the Pacific, and satellites orbiting the planet in space.

METHODOLOGY

With few exceptions, all of the people interviewed for this book are middle-aged or older and white, and all but three are men. This disparity in age, race, and gender reveals important insights into the nature of this research topic and how I chose to approach it.[24] All participants in the 2001–2 and 2015–18 research were sought out through institutions. This included prisons, charity organizations, museums, junkyards, artificial reef-making operations, and a private space technology contractor. For the more recent ethnography, institutions were specifically chosen for their connection to some sense of military waste, and older white men were disproportionately represented in these institutions.

One thing that many of these institutions have in common is a connection to science and technology in some form, so that expertise in or passion for topics related to machine tinkering was common. The charities in the Southern Tier of New York were used as sites to recruit current and retired IBM and Lockheed Martin employees. They were all engineers, and they were attracted to charity organizations that involved tinkering with technology in some form. This was also true of the amateur astronomers (which included some of the same people) who spent a significant amount of their time tinkering with telescopes, computers, and cameras. This is the case with people who work with junk and artificial reefs, as well. Many of the latter came to the industry through diving, which has historically also been a more male-dominated activity, as one of the few women interviewed explains in chapter 3. Even the artists and art critic discussed in chapter 2 engage in a form of artistic practice that often requires some technical facility.[25] The museums, finally, were typically concerned with technology, and in one case military technology. And the two museums that focused on less strictly technical subjects, a diving museum in Florida and an art museum in Wisconsin, account for two of the three women who were interviewed. Technical expertise and interest were therefore common among people recruited to the project, precisely because the institutions with which they were affiliated tended to favor technically mediated relationships with forms of military waste. As evidence has shown, exposure to science, technology, engineering, and mathematical (or STEM) fields has typically been gendered and racialized in the United States, both historically and in the present day.[26]

That being said, race and gender are not fixed categorical types—they are fluid and shaped by everyday and extraordinary actions. As Connell and

Messerschmidt argue, "Masculinity is not a fixed entity embedded in the body or personality traits of individuals. Masculinities are configurations of practice that are accomplished in social action and, therefore, can differ according to the gender relations in a particular setting" (2005, 836). Moreover, "hegemonic masculinities can be constructed that do not correspond closely to the lives of any actual men. Yet these models do, in various ways, express widespread ideals, fantasies, and desires" (2005, 838). The same goes for whiteness (Hartigan 1999). The activities of engaging with and being affected by the wastes of the permanent war economy also involve doing (and undoing) masculinity and whiteness in various ways. Sometimes this means embracing humility and care before things that cannot be controlled, as I argue amateur astronomers tend to do, or choosing to act nonviolently or celebrate antimilitarism in some form through art and technology, as some of my other informants do.

Using waste as a methodological guide, the reach of the military industrial complex expands in unexpected ways. Early on in this research, in an incident I recount at the start of chapter 1, I set out to interview an amateur astronomer and instead was surprised to learn that he had much more to teach me about the curious ways that waste is conceptualized by military manufacturers. This moment of ethnographic surprise led me to look more into the history of the greater Binghamton area and its reliance on defense contracts, from the city's origins to the present day. When I started my affiliation with amateur astronomers, I had intended to learn only about distant and generally demilitarized space junk, but it led me somewhere else, somewhere a lot closer to the functioning of military industry than I ever thought I would get. Similarly, I started this research with the intention of tracking disused and decaying military objects, like ships and planes, to see what had become of the military built to fight World War III after this conflict never came to pass. Instead, I ended up following forms of waste as they traveled from tests of military product quality to art projects and coral reef regeneration, to orbital debris pageants, mass shooting incidents, and atolls covered with seabird guano.[27]

I follow waste in these various directions largely in order to collapse the distance between military and civilian worlds, complicating how these two seemingly distinct "realms" interrelate. War preparation can contribute to background conditions of social life that fade into invisibility even and especially to the degree that we depend on them. As Deborah Cowen (2014) documents, for instance, the logistics of global trade and travel that are now taken for granted were directly shaped by twentieth-century war and war preparation. To take one example, at one time, the shoes people wore all over the United States were unknowingly connected to a factory near Binghamton, New York. At critical times in its history, that factory benefited from wartime and postwar military contracts, without which those civilian shoes would not have been produced, sold, and worn, The industrial ruins left behind bear witness to these past connections. The shoes we wear now are no different. As Cynthia Enloe writes, global trade is often premised on militaristic associations:

> Threaded through virtually every sneaker you own is some relationship to masculinized militaries. Locating factories in South Korea was a good strategic decision in the eyes of those Oregon-headquartered male Nike executives because of the close alliance between male policymakers in Washington and Seoul. It was a relationship—unequal but intimate—based on their shared anticommunism, their shared commitment to waging the Cold War, and their shared participation in an ambitious international military alliance. (2007, 28)

Given the size and scope of US empire, these kinds of connections are unsurprising. But Americans do more than passively consume products that have military origins. It is also important to note how many continue to profit in unexpected ways from the permanent war economy.

The production of shoes is not so different from the production of knowledge. It would be wrong to imagine a divide between my research and writing process and its object, that is, between ethnography and war preparation. Historically and in the present day, these are not opposed endeavors. For as long as there has been a military industrial complex in the United States, ethnographic research has been a part of it. Anthropological practice has been just as complicit in war preparation as has any other science, in some cases even more so, as ethnographic data has served as important information for war planning and counterinsurgency operations. In many cases, key global areas of concern to the US government were investigated with funding from the CIA through dummy organizations, though anthropologists did not necessarily know this at the time. As David Price's (2008, 2011, 2016) extensive research has uncovered, some did know, some suspected. But even those anthropologists who were not funded directly (or might have rejected such funding had they known) could still produce usable intelligence simply by doing what anthropologists do best. This Price calls "dual-purpose" anthropology, since it could both serve academic interests, careers, and agendas and also help inform the US security state and military (cf. Paglen 2009: 8–9). This is not some relic of the Cold War, moreover. To this day, American anthropologists are [mis]taken for CIA agents when they work abroad, which can impact the relationships they form and what they end up knowing and writing about, whether or not it is true (see Borneman and Masco 2015; Verdery 2018). Ethnographic research has recently been treated as war preparation in another sense, specifically by supposedly helping prep potential recruits of counterinsurgency efforts. A good ethnographer with the right linguistic and cultural knowhow became an asset to the US war effort during the short-lived and controversial Human Terrain System (2007–14).[28]

I am no more removed from the legacy of the permanent war economy than my informants. I too am living with its consequences, unknowingly citing or gaining enrichment from anthropological research that was backed with CIA funding or has been useful to war preparation and global securitization. It occurred to at least some of my would-be informants that my research might be valuable to the military as well, in some way neither I nor they could yet imagine. My point is not to attack the value of anthropological research and writing, but to challenge the possible assumption that I am detached from the permanent war economy under investigation in this book. In the very same way that some of the amateur astronomers I met have a bond beyond their passion for astronomy, one that links them to military manufacturing, more than a few of the academics I know have a relationship to war preparation, though it might seem the furthest thing from their everyday lives and personal values. It is not only ideas and methods that are implicated in this system, but the very substance of academic life, which for many means living at a distance from the potential consequences of knowledge production.

Thinking about my position as an academic and how that impacts how and what I research involves a form of what is known as *reflexivity*. Reflexive approaches in social science normally consider subjective "identity" (for instance, my race—white, gender—male, class—upper middle, and so on) as well as personally held beliefs and values that are something of a filter through which researchers perceive and engage with the world. As a white, male, leftist pacifist, I no doubt had different interactions with my informants than if I were, if I perceived myself to be, or if I were perceived by others as a different kind of person. This is also true for Priscilla Bennett, who assisted in some of the research for this book and coauthored two of the chapters. Like me, she was born and raised in the US, but she is a white woman and wife of a US military pilot. All of these factors no doubt have influenced this book. But this kind of reflexive attention to categorical type (race, gender, political identity, etc.) only makes up part of the story. There are also broader power relations that connect any ethnographer to the context they investigate and the people who appear "already there." The apparent divides of ethnographic fieldwork (before and after, the already there and the newly arrived) are not given. As Jennifer Robertson argues, "A major problem with 'writing as a [name the category]' is that the ethnographer's positionality either precedes the fieldwork experience or is deployed after the fact, during the write-up phase, to locate oneself in what might be termed the 'topophilic' academy" (2002, 788). Put differently, certain kinds of positionality are considered more worth talking and writing about than others. Roberston also describes the importance of new experiences in the field, not simply the a priori categories one inhabits, for providing opportunities for reflexivity (790). In a complementary way, it can also be productive to reflect on how one ends up with specific opportunities for new encounters in the first place.

Somehow, I ended up being employed in the vicinity of amateur astronomers with connections to military manufacturing. I did not seek out and find employees of Lockheed Martin through sheer pluck and determination; I stumbled upon them while trying to recruit amateur astronomers, which they also were. This ethnographic serendipity was not a matter of dumb luck, but reveals something about how the permanent war economy can unknowingly thread its way through many people's lives. My employment as a tenure-track professor at Binghamton University, beginning in 2012, was a professional goal I finally attained after years of worrying it would never happen. And for quite some time I imagined that there was nothing further from what I was being paid to do there than what engineers at Lockheed Martin were doing in a neighboring town. On the contrary, I told myself that I was promoting a cosmopolitan respect for human difference that in some small way might make the world more peaceful, rather than more violent. Given how difficult the academic job market can be, I was and still am very grateful to have this opportunity. Until doing research for this book, however, I seldom thought about why I was hired when I was where I was.

For one thing, Binghamton University is also here because of war and its aftermath. It was created in 1950 as Harpur College, primarily to serve returning GIs who had been incentivized to go back to school by the US government's 1944 GI Bill. This required state-sponsored institutions to meet student demand; in much the same way that the war economy had previously required a manufacturing base, there was a need for higher education institutions.[29]

The connections between permanent war preparation and my career do not end there. What I gradually learned was that I was hired, along with many other people, as part of a plan developed by New York and the SUNY system after the financial crisis of 2008.[30] My university hired new faculty over the last decade, admitted new students, and built new facilities with this investment, but it has also redeveloped parts of the greater Binghamton area. Why should places like the tri-city Binghamton area be so attractive as an investment opportunity for Albany, such that it was able to hire people like me to teach the greater number of students now admitted? There are many official reasons: a beneficial ratio of applicants to admitted students, campus infrastructure in need of updating, core areas of expertise (smart energy, pharmaceuticals) and so on. But at least part of what made this possible was all of the dead capital acquired relatively cheaply and renovated into something new. And this capital—the dilapidated buildings becoming university housing or classroom spaces, the old shops becoming trendy cafes (where I wrote much of this book), the labor force offered lower salaries and fewer benefits in the service industry—exists because of the war economy. These still-useful materials and still-employable people were left behind when businesses like IBM abandoned the city and military contracts went elsewhere. And as has happened in many other places, other service industries (hospitals, colleges) and their employees have benefited from this absent presence.

The Binghamton area is not unique, nor is my professional situation. There are many places undergoing similar processes of de- and reindustrialization throughout the United States (Walley 2013) and the world, and many of them have been deeply tied to permanent war preparation and its cycles of investment and divestiture. But that does not change the fact that at least part of the reason I am now here, and why I had the opportunity to meet the people I have for this book, is that military-civilian relationships were here first. And that is why I met members of the military industrial complex when I joined a local astronomy club. I was right to suspect that they knew many things about war manufacturing that I did not. My mistake was misrecognizing the forces that had drawn us to this part of the world in the first place, which made our eventual association much more likely. They had ended up in the Binghamton area to take up those jobs in military manufacturing that still remain; I ended up in Binghamton as part of an effort to regrow the community through its postmilitary dependence on the growing university.

Many more people are implicated in permanent war preparation than we might usually assume. I am, at least indirectly, whether one considers my employment or my research opportunities, both of which owe something to the abandonment and reclamation of a formerly militarized region. I am not relieving companies like IBM and Lockheed Martin of their responsibility, or holding those who benefited from their war profits directly or indirectly equally accountable for their actions. Complicity means being somehow involved in wrongdoing, but makes no necessary distinction between a person's relative level of involvement. It is worth pointing out, first, that warring groups do not always make this distinction. In fact, for military strategists, any harm that comes to those who live near a military manufacturing facility might be considered acceptable if it can bring war to a swifter conclusion or prevent one from starting. It is for this reason that the US Federal Civil Defense Administration (FCDA) considered the people of New York's Southern Tier as likely targets during the Cold War. Two maps were created by the FCDA as part of a simulated nuclear attack exercise that was conducted in 1955. One can plainly see that the Binghamton area is very close to a "Critical Target Area" in the first map and directly under "Other Targets Bombed" in the second map.[31]

The global empire does not respect divides between home front and war front. If any critique of the military is to have any impact, it is imperative to document the ways many lives are implicated in one of the largest and most expensive militaries ever assembled.

CHAPTER 1

Worth the Waste

Waste features prominently in discussions of the US military, offering one way of reckoning with the impact of permanent war preparation, bridging the virtual gap that appears to separate civilians from the costly and destructive military assembled in their name. In a 1968 issue of the *Washington Post*, an article on military procurement reported that "much of the $45 billion spending buys nothing" (quoted in Melman 1970b, 181). Half a century later, it is still routine to read about the Pentagon wasting billions of dollars on unnecessary or overpriced materials. Many accusations of wasteful spending circulated during the startling military buildup of the Reagan years, especially surrounding the Strategic Defense Initiative (aka "Star Wars"). But criticism of these practices also continued afterward (Turse 2008, 83).

Lockheed Martin leads all military manufacturers in profits from arms sales, with over $53 billion in net sales in 2018 alone (Lockheed Martin 2019). It is also the recent beneficiary of some of the largest military contracts ever, contracts that have been heavily criticized by prominent politicians, from across the political spectrum, as enormous wastes of money. These criticisms suggest that military waste is a result of pure greed, that is, the self-interest of politicians, members of the armed services, and corporations. Worse, it is greed that hides behind the perceived need for a strong national defense. While this can explain a lot about what has happened in the United States over the last century, things are more complicated if one examines the functioning of military contracts in practice. Drawing inspiration from the history of critical military studies, this chapter asks to what extent people who work within the defense industry think of and anticipate the problem of waste.

It is important to understand the worlds and lives of people who make the world's weapons, because criticisms of military waste that fail to do so have proven ineffective. In the last ten years there has been an ongoing national debate about controversial government contracts for the F-22 Raptor and F-35 Lightning, incredibly expensive fighter jets whose utility for the War on Terror has been called into question by both politicians and military analysts. Both planes were developed by Lockheed and have cost the Department of Defense (DoD) record amounts (Soar 2017).[1] In part the planes are so costly because their production is distributed throughout congressional districts, and this is what makes it difficult for the likes of Barack Obama or Donald Trump to succeed in eliminating them entirely. During the budget cuts of Obama's first term, the F-22 was criticized as the most expensive fighter jet in the nation's history, costing as much as $350 million dollars per plane yet useless for the new kinds of wars being fought in Iraq and Afghanistan. Moreover, in the month following September 11th, the Bush administration had awarded Lockheed Martin what would amount to an even larger contract for the F-35. The Obama administration did not scrap either program completely, but claimed that the F-35 made the F-22 redundant and capped production of the latter at 187 planes. Given that forty-four states benefited from producing parts for the F-22, however, even this decision was bitterly fought within Congress and required the threat of a presidential veto. Obama was partly successful in placing spending caps on military expenditures, enacted in 2010 as a product of debt ceiling negotiations with House Republicans. More recent politicians have criticized these caps, as have members of the military establishment.[2] Early in his first term, Trump began criticizing the F-35 program as wasteful in public addresses, promising to renegotiate the contract with Lockheed. When the price subsequently went down by $700 million, Trump took credit (despite the fact that this reduction in price had already been arranged).

Obama and Trump are only continuing a tradition in American political discourse about the risks of wastefulness from war spending. Concerns about complicity between the DoD, politicians, and military manufacturers are often traced to former general and president Dwight D. Eisenhower. During his farewell address in 1961, Eisenhower echoed concerns, expressed by C. Wright Mills five years earlier, that an emerging military industrial complex was beginning to dictate foreign and domestic policy and hijack American democracy for its own ends. According to the military industrial complex thesis, a permanent war economy can lead to a mutually beneficial relationship between politicians, the military and industry as a result of each group pursuing its own interests. In effect, what is normally perceived as a public good, defense and security, becomes instead tethered to the abstract law of competition that is meant to characterize the market. Eisenhower sought a way to render legible new forms of power and corruption that threatened American society. Put differently, Eisenhower's reference to the complex was calling for the public to hold the power elite to democratic account. Throughout the Cold War, it was debated whether military buildup could be ultimately converted to civilian use or, as some argued, represented a disruptive and parasitical influence on the economy.[3]

The notion that the American military budget is bloated and inefficiently spent is over a century old. Thorstein Veblen—often credited as the first major critic of conspicuous consumption—defined all militaries as wasteful, not because they are immediately harmful economically, but "because these expenditures directly, in their first incidence, merely withdraw and dissipate wealth and work from the industrial process, and unproductively consume the products of industry" (1904, 90). In 1918, at the conclusion of World War I, Veblen's concerns were realized as congressional investigations accused newly developed airplane manufacturers of being wasteful war profiteers. Lockheed was among those accused.[4]

At the onset of the Cold War, America's contemporary war economy and security apparatus were established. At this time, military lobbyists successfully argued that domestic military industry might stagnate without permanent state investment, which would allow the United States to fall behind its global competitors. As government spending went down in the late '60s, in response to the high cost of the Vietnam War, so did the profits of armaments manufacturers. This hit airplane manufacturers especially hard and, in 1971, Lockheed pleaded for a loan from the government in order to avoid bankruptcy. The Nixon Doctrine was partly a solution to this crisis, encouraging the sale of US arms to allies abroad in order to offset the cost of permanent war preparation (Custers 2007, 327). Not long after Eisenhower's warning, the complex appeared to be beyond the control of politicians and voters, partly because the United States became the world's weapons manufacturer. Even after Trump's criticisms of the company, for example, Lockheed still recorded higher profits than expected in 2017, credited to the sale of F-35s to England

and elsewhere. This also has its origins in the Cold War. From one point of view, military spending is a wasteful use of taxpayer money. In the case of nuclear weapons, Peter Custers argues, the polluting by-products, the wasted money, and the wasteful destructiveness of the weapon itself mean that their production amounts to a net loss of valuable capital, labor, and life, whether or not they are ever used in warfare.[5] From another point of view, what Custers calls the "social waste" of military products helps to productively sustain armament corporations and national economies through the "substitution orders" of arms exports, largely by making use of unequal and disparate exchange with poorer nations (Custers 2007, 381). This more global focus on circuits of capital is what makes Custers's Marxian-inspired critique different from the more statist criticisms of Eisenhower, Obama, and Trump, despite their shared focus on waste.

Though the military industrial complex is most closely associated with Eisenhower, Marxian theorists have been the most consistent critics of this arrangement, beginning with the connection Rosa Luxemburg and Lenin (1917) made between imperialism and capital accumulation.[6] At the start of the Cold War, Paul Baran and Paul Sweezy developed Luxemburg and Veblen's ideas; they argue that state military expenditures are more attractive for manufacturers because, unlike investment in public infrastructure, for example, they require endless innovation and "include a generous margin for a mythical risk factor" (1966, 208). It was easier for industry to make these demands during the Cold War, which involved a shift, in the United States and other militarized democracies, from mass conscription to greater military capitalization, including investment in expensive ships, bases, submarines, bombs, satellites, and aircraft (Holley 1971, 18). According to Baran and Sweezy:

> It is a commonplace that warfare is becoming more and more a matter of science and technology, less and less a matter of masses of men and weapons. Rockets and missiles are replacing bombers and rendering fighter planes largely purposeless; huge fleets of surface vessels are obsolete; massed armies are giving way to highly specialized troops wielding an array of fantastically destructive weapons (1966, 214).

They go on to argue that, with more money spent on outlays for research and development and less for mass production, far fewer people are employed by military spending than once were.[7] Processes like research and development, which will be considered below, would be among the wasted and unrecouped expenditures associated with military production. This is so because a product that is tested and not procured by the defense establishment is a loss of capital investment rather than a source of new capital in the form of profit (Custers 2007, 67–69).

One thing that criticisms from presidents and social critics leave out, however, is that military manufacturers have their own methods of conceptualizing and eliminating waste as part of product design, development, and maintaining customer ties. The people who make the permanent war economy possible live by certain values and typically believe that what they do contributes to the public welfare.[8] Strange and alien as the complex can seem, it requires actual people to make it possible, negotiating contracts, changing designs, testing products, and sometimes maintaining them after they've been sold. Each step along the way can lead to waste: wastes of money, of time, of effort, and of lives.

Waste can be thought of in at least three senses, all of which I consider.[9] First, waste can be associated with wastefulness or profligacy and lead to accusations of moral wrongdoing from others. As we have seen, this way of talking about waste has been common in discussions of the US military over the course of its history. Furthermore, avoiding this kind of waste, or accusing others of it, can be ethical acts that help a person identify as part of a like-minded community: in the case of military manufacturers, this might include being a good engineer or project manager. Second, waste in a more strictly economic sense can be considered as including any externality or by-product of value accumulation, anything unnecessary that results from the creation of something else. This is more closely tied to the Marxian critique of militarization already discussed. In my analysis, this includes places like the tri-city area of the Southern Tier of New York that have suffered from deindustrialization as circuits of capital leave material and human waste in their wake. Finally, waste can be considered more ontologically as the inevitability of entropic change, which means that no form lasts forever and all will eventually cease to be. This last sense of waste tends to be absent from public critiques of the permanent war economy, but it is very evident in conversations with military manufacturers.

I first contacted Simon, a retired resident of Binghamton, New York, because his neighbor told me that he was an avid amateur astronomer and I was interested in orbital space debris (the topic of chapter 4). But when we finally sat down together in his modestly decorated living room, we ended up talking mostly about his career at Lockheed Martin. Within a few minutes, Simon began describing his life as an engineer for the world's leading weapons manufacturer and the difficulty of disposing of military technology. Crouching forward and speaking in his high, nasal voice, he spoke of the Seahawk helicopter, which he had worked on for several years:

> [It] has certain equipment on board that is classified, not top secret, it's classified secret or other classifications. . . . So even if the aircraft is lost in battle, you have to dispose of the pieces, sometimes by bombing the carcass. If it goes down in Afghanistan, you bomb it in Afghanistan. . . . Sometimes it's too hard to destroy, or sometimes it's radioactive, or sometimes it's an emitter.

He went on like that and, much to my surprise, we talked less about astronomy that day than I had expected. Simon was the first person to make clear to me just how much military manufacturers think about the subject of waste in that third sense, that is, about how all products eventually fall into disuse. Even during its initial design, manufacturers are thinking about the end of a product's life. This is an altogether different way of conceiving of waste, as the inevitability of entropic loss rather than the by-product of inessential and self-interested human decisions. And, as I will argue, it is important for casting or avoiding blame for moral wrongdoing, or waste in the first sense.

Military manufacturers like Simon also spoke about wasted time and money, but these were also typically interpreted in a way that not only differed from the military industrial complex critique, but anticipated and deflected such blame. Based on interviews with current and former military industry insiders, I argue that some forms of waste are meant to build relations of trust between military manufacturers and the defense establishment, while others are incorporated into design and testing production processes, as with the Seahawk helicopter. Far from an irresolvable contradiction within circuits of capital, waste is actively managed and imagined within military industries as they endeavor to build enduring customer relations and durable machines. I do not accuse military manufacturers of being wasteful, in the first, moralizing sense, per se; rather, I review the ways in which they knowingly produce or avoid waste while pursuing other ends, including but not limited to private self-interest.

Drawing on interviews conducted with current and former employees of the US DoD and Lockheed Martin, I focus on the *reflexive practices* of military producers themselves, that is, what they know and how they talk about what it is they do. As Collier and Ong characterize it, reflexive practices are "modern practices" that "subject themselves to critical questioning" (2005, 7). Critical questions possess political, technological, and ethical dimensions that test normative assumptions about how things are built. The three sections of this chapter focus on these dimensions in turn. Rather than pure, impersonal greed or corruption, the actions of arms manufacturing insiders appear governed by a variety of personal motives and social values. Rather than conceive of military waste exclusively in terms of money, moreover, they tend to frame waste in terms of engineering practices, which—far from being purely technical—may alternatively depoliticize and de-moralize the waste of the American military, or identify altogether new targets for public scorn.

My goal is not to trivialize the very real dangers that the military industrial complex poses, but rather to make it easier to relate to the permanent war economy, which can otherwise appear governed by impersonal entities (the DoD, Lockheed) and irresistible forces (greed, corruption). Talking about human stories and motivation scales such phenomena down to size and makes the abstract complex a matter of ordinary people struggling for themselves and their communities. The point is not only to make it easier to understand those making a living off of an entrenched system, in this case the permanent war economy, but also to sharpen our ability to critique and rethink that system in response.

IBMers

The Owego Lockheed Martin plant began as an IBM facility, and locals still refer to all those who work or worked there as "IBMers." The plant supplied high-end electronic equipment to the US military since the time of the Second World War. IBM was especially critical in the development of the Cold War continental surveillance system, Semi-Atomic Ground Environment (SAGE), "the single most important computer project of the postwar decade" (Edwards 1997, 75). IBM gained its reputation for computing as a result of its work on SAGE for the Air Force and would continue this relationship with the military for the rest of the twentieth century. The IBM facility in Owego was built as part of a general shift toward high-tech military weaponry. Part of IBM's Federal Systems Division, the Owego plant helped to develop technology for government censuses, satellite programs, and other high-tech equipment. IBM was attracted to the area because of the existing manufacturing base, established by the Endicott-Johnson Shoe Company (known as EJ), which had flourished from its own military contracts, producing boots for infantry until as late as the Vietnam War. EJ is credited with building up the tri-city area, from parks and carousels to residential areas and large factories.[10]

The end of the Cold War meant a radical reduction in military production all over the world, the effects of which are also debated. After military buildup in the 1980s, US defense budgets fell by nearly 30 percent, more than two million service members and civilians lost their jobs, and over a hundred military bases closed. Though military spending increased in the early twenty-first century with the new War on Terror, the impact of spending cuts was felt throughout the country. The results were uneven—just as military buildup impacted different regions in different ways, so too did the radical reduction and restructuring of defense spending that followed the end of the Cold War.[11]

IBM eventually sold off the military division during the post–Cold War spending cuts of the 1990s, leaving the area almost entirely not long after. When EJ and IBM eventually sold off their local capital and shuttered their doors, the local community was devastated, leaving very few still employed in manufacturing. If one goes by voting results, locals tended to believe Hillary Clinton in 2006 when she ran for her New York seat in the US Senate and promised to bring work back to the Southern Tier. They also supported Governor Cuomo when he said the same thing in 2010, and some blamed him when, for example, Restore New York grants from Albany failed to support local initiatives. On the same day that Albany announced it would not support a local bid to develop two casinos, in 2015, the state government also issued a ban on fracking to extract energy from the gas-rich Marcellus Shale, which includes all of New York's Southern Tier region (as well as neighboring Pennsylvania, where the practice is allowed). This was enough for various towns across the Southern Tier to begin talk of seceding from the state to gain the attention of lawmakers (Susman 2015). It is no accident, therefore, that most voters in this area did not support Clinton's presidential run in 2016 or Cuomo's reelection for governor in 2018. When Southern Tier voters changed allegiances and overwhelmingly voted for Trump, unlike New York State as a whole, it was in part because he claimed he would bring back American manufacturing.

On the one hand, these losses, hopes, and disappointments are a familiar part of the gradual process of deindustrialization affecting the whole country and many parts of the world. Christine Walley (2013) points out that this is more aptly characterized as reindustrialization, or accumulation by dispossession, as global markets are used as an excuse to introduce more flexible and profitable arrangements (i.e. reduced wages and benefits) and overall "leaner" workforces. On the other hand, for military manufacturers, the gradual disappearance of military contracts from the area is part of a general geographical shift. The economic effects of permanent war preparation have never been uniform, throughout either the United States or the world. The Cold War ushered in the growth of an American gun belt, stretching from the Pacific and Mountain regions across the South Atlantic and into New England (Markusen et al. 1991). As the gun belt grew, people suffered in those regions historically dependent on manufacturing, including the Midwest, Northeast, and Mid-Atlantic, leaving a rust belt behind.

In an online discussion forum known as City-Data Forum, a thread was created in 2009 titled "is binghamton, ny really that bad . . .?" One person, self-identifying as a lifelong resident, summarized the city's history in this way:

> Once upon a time, the entire Southern Tier was a great place to live and then one by one, the factories and big-businesses moved out. Some of the most important to the area: Endicott-Johnson Shoe Factory closed it's [sic] doors, IBM-Endicott closed their doors; NYSEG downsized and laid-off, Frito-Lay has downsized and laid-off, basically over the years business has declined or moved. Now, Binghamton has a large population of senior citizens and students and an even larger population of people who are "stuck." This area is a vacuum it sucks you in and you can't get out because you never have the available resources.[12]

What is stuck in the tri-city area is not only people, but buildings. Much of the previous gun belt has begun to rust. Urban spelunkers record their journeys into old EJ factories with Go-Pro cameras mounted to their heads, posting them on YouTube or bragging about them on Reddit. Some of this old capital—which might have been maintained through corporate or state investment—is now being scrapped and remade into a pharmacy school by Binghamton University with a grant from the state, and members of the Environmental Studies department giddily imagine how to reuse these materials as "green infrastructure" to create living buildings in situ. An Upstate Revitalization Initiative is providing half a billion dollars over five years, which may finally lead to demolishing and refurbishing properties long thought too cost-prohibitive to restore (Platsky 2016). Meanwhile, at TechWorks, a local museum and hands-on educational workshop, retired and employed IBMers work with local college students tinkering with salvaged products created by local industries, from space-simulators produced for NASA to typewriters, printers, and old IBM computers. The archaeologist who runs TechWorks and her volunteers are trying not just to preserve the area's material history but to show it off and make it sing.

If all this abandoned capital is waste—and I suggest we call it that—it is not just the waste of industry, but of the uneven investment cycles characteristic of the permanent war economy. The sale of the Federal Systems Division, followed by the departure of IBM, led to massive layoffs from which the area has not recovered. The old IBM, people like to say, really cared about its people and the community, but all that unexpectedly changed in the 1990s. Implicitly, that means they blame *the new IBM*, first and foremost, for what has happened since. In 1996, the former IBM facility was purchased by Lockheed Martin, a California-based aeronautics company that was nearly sold off to a scrapyard during the Depression, but was now leading the corporate consolidation of the post–Cold War era, along with the other big military manufacturers. Eddy, a former employee, told me that people who split off from IBM along with the Federal Systems Division managed to survive the layoffs that came later, though no one in the area was completely immune. Consolidation and plant closings furthered this transformation into a more post-Fordist production regime, which American military manufacturers were arguably shielded from during the 1970s and 1980s.[13]

POLITICAL DIMENSIONS: CULTIVATING CUSTOMER TIES

As Walley (2013) argues of industrial Chicago, industry has not entirely disappeared from the Southern Tier. Lockheed is still operating out of the Owego plant. But recent changes have created greater competition among the remaining companies for existing contracts, putting more pressure on military manufacturers to appeal to the client, that is, the DoD. As a result, current employees feel additional scheduling and cost pressures. In some cases, these pressures manifest in the social relationships of client and seller. However, market relations are never purely reducible to economic competition, which is premised on an idealized conception of marketplaces and market behavior.[14] From the point of view of those involved in military contracting, wastes result from trying to please and maintain a good relationship with the customer, not simply as part of the abstract logic of the marketplace. The ultimate meaning of this relationship may still come down to reducing cost (for the client) and growing shareholder value (for Lockheed), but in practice it involves real people communicating with one another to solve problems and come to agreements.

I talked about this with Louis, a retired analyst for the DoD (specifically the Defense Contract Management Agency, or DCMA). I met Louis through the local Kopernik Astronomical Society, where he has volunteered in retirement alongside other current and former DoD and Lockheed workers. Louis explained to me how trying to satisfy the customer could lead to waste in the form of "mission creep":

> It's a fancy term for, you start out and you say "I want this vehicle to do mission one, mission two, mission three. . ." And then, two years later into the development cycle, a new secretary of defense comes along and says, "Oh, guess what: I want you to do X, Y, and Z in addition to one, two, and three." And all the military planners go, "Okay. . ." You know, and then they go back and look at all the other contracts and say, "Well, we're developing this vehicle that can do these things, but we really need to add more capability." Never mind the fact that it doubles the price, and/or increases the delivery schedule by more years.

Louis explained mission creep to me while we sat in the children's section of a Borders bookstore, where he liked to go with his grandchildren sometimes, and the occasional child or toddler wandered in and out of our peripheral vision. He refused to discuss specifics, unsure of what would constitute treason, but he could tell me that mission creep could waste time, money, and effort. Manufacturers might even be aware of this, but be unable to resist the requests of their primary client. Both the manufacturer and the client might invest more than necessary in the development of a product that would never see the light of day, or would be purchased but end up with unnecessary multifunctionality simply because of the caprice of "military planners."

The military spending cuts of the 1990s meant fewer companies but also fewer big-budget projects to go around. Sometimes budgets were cut on ongoing projects. But there are strategies for dealing with this as well. As Louis explained:

> Usually the response to having your budget cut is you tell the contractor, "Well, instead of delivering twenty-five vehicles this year, and fifty the next year, I want you to deliver ten vehicles this year and fifteen vehicles the next year." And then the contractor goes crazy! Or you say "Well, we changed their mind [i.e., the DoD], instead of having capability to do X, Y, Z, let's just do X and Y, forget about Z, and reduce the quantities." Or come back and say "Well, instead of having them ready by 2017, we'll stretch it out to 2019, can you live with that?"

From Louis's perspective as a former agent of the DCMA dedicated to overseeing and monitoring military contracts on behalf of the DoD, Lockheed Martin was not necessarily to blame for any wasted time, money, or resources in the process,

"My personal experience with Lockheed Martin was they're fairly responsible. There are other military contractors that don't necessarily have the best track record." He then paused and added, "Reasonably responsible," perhaps thinking of instances where Lockheed crossed the line into wasteful irresponsibility.[15]

Routine aspects of contract negotiation, like mission creep, are not entirely reducible to ordinary market logic, which pits buyers and sellers with their competing interests against each other. Rather, they are also a product of social relations between people who know each other well. For employees at the DCMA, military industry is not a collection of faceless corporations, but people with whom they share a community. In this community, I have known DCMA and Lockheed employees who continue to socialize and volunteer together after retirement—including at the Kopernik Observatory. They tinker with machines together, teach young people about the value of science and technology together, go camping together, run charity events together, get to know one another's families, health concerns, and passions. Perhaps because of this social intimacy, no one described the relationship between Lockheed and the DCMA as oppositional or combative.

Even so, as representatives of buyer and seller, respectively, there can be disagreements and misunderstandings. As Hugh Gusterson observed of nuclear weapons scientists at Livermore National Laboratory, many work-related stories by weapons designers "involve a sequence of events in which scientists fear that machines will not behave as predicted but, after a period of painful anxiety, learn that humans can predict and control the behavior of technology" (1996, 159). In the stories I heard, people were as much a source of anxiety, and people also needed to be predicted and controlled to have successful outcomes. One current Lockheed engineer described how this could happen in the bidding process for a new contract:

> When we're in the bidding process to get a job. . .we'll go in and. . .we'll do our first estimate of what we think it's gonna take to do this job. And then in our reviews we'll say, "Aww, that's gonna cost too much money, our inside information says the customer only has this amount of money and they won't go over that, so, get it down!" So you get it down. And then when you win the job and you're actually performing the job, you realize that the first number you put out was the real number. That happens an awful lot.

He went on to tell me a story:

> One project I was involved in, we had a supplier who was providing the software, and they went bankrupt in the middle of what we were doing. So there was a lot of

internal hand-wringing: 'What are we gonna do about it? Are we gonna do the work ourselves? Are we gonna farm it out to yet another company?" And I was the one that had to do the analysis of what we were going to do and say, could we do it, and said "Yeah, we could do it," and decision was we would do it, which was the decision I hoped we weren't going to do, because it was a lot of pressure, both schedule and cost. It was unanticipated cost because we had given money to this company and expected fully that they would deliver us a product and now they weren't there, so we were gonna have to do it. And it's something that we had no expertise in at all, so we had to learn fast. And we had to have it done in six months.

When producers bid for projects, they present an initial price for meeting customer demands. When the cost of a project goes up, they risk being blamed by the client or the general public for wasting government dollars or jeopardizing defense needs. Yet, this example shows a simple contingency that can set production back (a supplier who unexpectedly goes bankrupt). If wasted money and time are avoided in this instance, it will come from manufacturers with "no expertise" working hard to deliver on their company's promises. And, if they do not, they may be blamed by others but will not blame themselves. It is a failure to predict the actions of other people that is held responsible, as if they too should behave as reliably as machines.

Simon explained other specific examples where projects could live or die as a result of social relations maintained with the clients, who might disappoint or frustrate producers:

I was also on a couple top-secret projects. . . We were making brand-new aircraft for DARPA. It was called UCAR [unmanned combat armed rotorcraft protocol]. DARPA has their own internal engineers, the customer was the Army, and the Army would have their own staff of engineers. . . We'd show up for a meeting and there'd be DARPA engineers and there'd be generals. . . We were in a four-company contest to make this UCAR.

The UCAR was considered a small project for Lockheed at the time, but still an important contract to get.

We were down-selected from four to three and three to two. So we were at one of these presentations where the generals and colonels and DARPA. . . We were making our presentations, and typically it's death by PowerPoint slide. Over two days, over six hundred PowerPoint slides. So these poor generals and DARPA people, they know what's coming. So during the first presentation, the lead engineer from weapons and fire control in Orlando, Florida, was making his presentation about his wonderful weapons, and a general said, "Well what about that?" And he said, "Be quiet, I'm not done talking yet." He said that to a general! So we walked out of that meeting red. Green is approved, yellow is caution, red is you're gonna fail. So we plied him with beer and cigars all night. "I know I'm right, the general's wrong, he just didn't understand me. . ." You don't talk to a general that way! So right about midnight I called his VP, I said "This guy isn't getting it, can you talk to him?" So he went in the next day and apologized to the general. So we survived that.

And what is the point of the story? For Simon: "The customer is always right." And yet, after all that, "The Army canceled the program eventually because they needed armor for the Humvees. So the ten billion dollars went for armor plating under the Humvees rather than our aircraft, but they're still building robots."

In fact, Simon ended up with two patents for his robotic copter, which he was issued in 2010 and 2011; they are proudly displayed on the wall near the entrance to his house. Which is to say: the design still proved valuable. From a more critical standpoint, this is private enrichment from public investment— Lockheed and its employees benefited from merely being considered for the contract anyhow. Yet, what can be lost from such a critique is that this preference for high-end military manufacturing also can be associated with higher moral ends and public goods. Simon can tell himself he did what he could for his country and for the future of robotics. This is not to divide moral from economic considerations; they are in fact thoroughly interwoven. Some forms of "waste" are related to building relations of trust and dependability, or a moral economy of customer ties between military manufacturers and the defense establishment. While this benefits the company, of course, it is also seen by many as part of satisfying the defense needs of the country. Any designs or efforts sacrificed in the process are worth the waste if the client—in this case, the defense establishment—is satisfied. For the DoD and Lockheed employees I spoke with, blameworthy wastefulness was something that occurred when deliberate moral choices were made to take advantage of the government, acts which they claim not to have witnessed or committed. Being responsible might mean spending time and resources that never materialize into a finished product, but as long as this was not deliberate, done in the interests of maintaining ties with capricious officers and politicians, then contractors did not blame themselves.

TECHNOLOGICAL DIMENSIONS: QUALITY CONTROL AS AN IMMANENT POETICS OF WASTE

The rhetoric of wastefulness is not merely an external critique brought to bear on military industry, but is also immanent to the production process: for those involved in military production, it is waste elimination rather than wanton wasting that is taken to be ideal.

One of the engineers from Lockheed Martin I spoke with, who went by "Bork," had lived his whole life in the Southern Tier. He began as a temporary worker (known in Lockheed as the workforce extension program, or WFE, pronounced "Wiffy"). Soon he was promoted to a permanent employee (though not before suffering cutbacks in benefits, and not without surviving multiple waves of layoffs). For most of his time at Lockheed he has worked on software: "We were putting together a new graphics card and. . .we were using at the time a 3D labs graphics chip. . .for a helicopter. So it would be in the cockpit, drives the panels that the crew are looking at."

Early on in our conversation, the corporate risk of investing in military equipment came up. According to Bork, this graphics chip, one of the first projects he worked on, could only be sold to the US government:

> No one was gonna pay that kinda money for something like that, yeah. The power of the graphics card that you have in your laptop there [gesturing to the interviewer's computer], we work with things that are comparable to that, but, your laptop doesn't have to work at minus forty degrees Celsius or plus fifty degrees Celsius, so part of our value add is testing this hardware at extremes of temperature, extremes of vibration. . .so that there is assurance that it's going to work in all sorts of environments.

In this sense, what Baran and Sweezy (1966) call a "mythical risk factor" is taken for granted within military manufacturing. The benefits of testing are not reducible to economic interest alone, but also include personal and social investment in one's labor. Much like nuclear weapons scientists, "by means of this lived journey from anxiety to confidence, structured by the rhythms of the testing process itself, scientists learn that weapons behave, more or less, predictably, and they learn to associate safety and well-being with the performed proof of technical predictability" (Gusterson 2004, 160). Bork added that very few consumer products require testing at similar industrial temperatures (garage doors in temperate zones, for instance), but that military equipment "is built to be more durable. It's built to be more rugged." He went on:

> Reliability of the equipment is. . .very important, we are still running equipment that was built *twenty years ago* or so, and even those cards that. . .I came in twelve years ago. . .they're *still* in service, still pumping along. I think one of my favorite stories was that. . .a test engineer had accidentally left a. . .blanket on top of one of the mission computers, and the blanket got sucked into the air inlets of the com-

puter. . . Now, the computer's a pretty big box, it has lots of cards in it, and it's got a big fan on the back that *screams*, I mean, the fan is so loud and it eats into your brain, and so he had this blanket on top of it to kind of quiet it down, and he kinda forgot about it, and the blanket got sucked into the inlets and it generated so much heat that the material that got sucked into the inlets actually starting shooting out as flames outside the back of the thing. During this whole process of flames shooting out this computer, it was still running! It was still running its tests and passing! So. . .we absolutely do value making a quality product.

From the perspective of military manufacturers, more money is paid for what they do because they invest additional resources in producing durable, military-grade products—i.e., things that will resist falling into transience and disuse. In fact, many of those I spoke with seemed proud of the fact that military equipment remained usable for generations. It was as if the reliability of products, proved through testing, reaffirmed the reliability of the engineers and managers tasked with designing them. They were proud of what they had done, in other words, precisely because they could see how waste, as inevitable entropic decline, had been anticipated and avoided. Taking satisfaction in one's work often meant defeating waste.[16]

In a way that might seem paradoxical, these discussions of prized durability were never far from examples of failure and obsolescence. Rather than treating durability and transience as opposing qualities, engineers connected them as the product of one's labor and the background conditions against which one struggles, respectively. Insuring quality meant careful attention to every product's slow descent into waste and worthlessness, formally assessed as mean time before failure (MTBF). This required extensive testing, as Simon explained:

> Every single piece of equipment on the helicopter and all of its support equipment is analyzed by logistics to mean time to failure. So we know that of a thousand pieces for five hundred helicopters so many are gonna fail per year, so that's how many you keep in the spare parts inventory. And it's just failure—they're in the ocean, salt water is spraying on them, could be in the Arctic, very adverse circumstances.

The Seahawk helicopter that Simon worked the most on was intended for the Navy for purposes of doing search and rescue. And this could include the open water or downed pilots in Afghanistan, where all components needed to work to guarantee both safety and mission success (and, by extension, the presumed public goods associated with military strength).

> People have been building these parts for fifty years, similar parts. And you do stress tests: for every part it has to go through an air-worthiness test and an

environmental test. Environmental test puts it through cycles of heat and cold and banging around and dropping and being exploded.

This is still about preserving customer ties. According to Simon, the DoD representatives "either witness the tests or see the results." When the Seahawk was in development the Navy sent its own engineers, mostly former pilots: "There would be all these very strong tests. Plus you would have the history of very similar built equipment, and they would all be built to military specification standards. Some of them are very old."

Tests during product design and development also include models for the eventual breakdown of military products. As Simon pointed out, this means:

> Life cycle. . .cost analysis. . .including disposition of all parts and of the military craft itself. . .decommissioned and everything. . . Typically you do a war game and you say how many are to be destroyed in battle, how many are left on the battlefield, after twenty or thirty years of useful life, how many have to be decommissioned, and the costs for that, and the expected disposal and reuse. All that's calculated for every military program. . . Typically you end up using the Army or the Air Force or the Navy [method of life cycle analysis] but you still gotta use your company's, so I'm familiar with Lockheed Martin where they have what they call logistics. . . . Analysis of every part and every military aircraft or ship or whatever and they'll say over the twenty-five-year life you need to have so many spare parts stored in the US, near the battlefield, close to the battlefield, so that they can be taken care of during battle and during battle damage and during normal wear and tear. . .and then they do a disposal cost for each one of those.

In other words, every product's inevitable entropic decline into waste is incorporated into its design and sale to the DoD. Like neurotic subjects who seek out that which fills them with dread, Lockheed personnel keep waste in abeyance and carefully account for it. When accused of being "wasteful" by presidents, Marxists, or anthropologists, this is what industry engineers will be quick to point out. They are not disappointed or dispirited by the descent of even the most durable of products into disuse, as far I could detect, because they spend a great deal of energy imagining such failures and planning for them.

Bork balked at the notion that the production process might be wasteful. For him, as for many engineers, "waste" meant wasted time and effort. They associated it with products that did not work, that failed or broke down, and served no purpose for the customer. This is precisely what they tried to avoid through good customer relations and extensive product testing and design.

The primary goal of production was to reduce such waste, both in the product produced and in the production process itself:

> Whenever something fails, the first person that gets called is the software engineer to explain what the failure is, and why it failed. And I still do that today, I get calls, "We got a failure in the lab, can you explain what this is?"... We've got one group that does all sorts of testing, so that's the diagnostics group, that's the group I'm in. And so, when we're doing these environmental tests, we're the ones that write the tests and then interpret the failures...writing software that tells you why it failed is much more expensive than writing software that tells you, "It failed."

The former is known as mean time before failure (or MTBF) in engineering parlance. Knowing that something failed, that it is not meeting criteria promised to the client, is not enough to ensure that it does not fail again. One must know why, and for this the interviewee offered two options: either they, the software engineers, are called upon to explain why something fails, or a "more expensive" form of software is developed to tell them why. This means that their efforts on behalf of a better product avoid waste in two senses. First, a product that might otherwise turn out to be waste is engineered to last (that is, to function with a more acceptable MTBF). Second, there is a savings implied when an engineer does the work that expensive software might otherwise have to do. The value of the product is saved, and the company—and potentially the client—save money.

The military and manufacturers also employ additional analysis of their products to maximize utility and minimize waste. At the same time, the pursuit of quality could itself be regarded as wasteful if it meant being noncompetitive. IBM had a reputation for perfectionism going back many years. According to Bork:

> IBM had a big stick up its butt for the longest time. They always had this Thomas Watson Calvinist engineering approach. You could even see that in the tail end of the IBM commercial products. Before they got out of their desktop PC. Their equipment was always overdesigned and overbuilt, I mean you could drive a car over them and barely dent it. It was the corporate culture, was one of exacting quality. To a point of not being competitive. If you were getting some knockoff place in Taiwan making cheap PCs, how can you compete with that?

The cost of "overbuilding" products was not just a loss in corporate profit, but could be seen everywhere in the community, where global competition (with Taiwan for instance) is blamed for loss of jobs and local decline more broadly. Sometimes creating a quality product could waste time and resources as manufacturers encountered technical problems. Louis said that the DCMA regularly encountered this phenomenon:

> You can also have technical problems come out in the course of development work. And I've seen where the contractors will come back to the military and say, "You know, we don't have a really good fix for this. We can't do what you want to do. We really need to. . ." what's called rescope, that is, change the scope of requirements: "These things that you've asked us to do, we cannot do. We need to delete them or substitute other things."

"Rescoping" is also known as "requirements turn," since it involves modifying the requirements as one develops a product, which can lead to dramatic scheduling and cost changes. Unlike mission creep, rescoping involves manufacturers having to admit to the client that they need to alter the initial contract. This is the least desirable of all options and can therefore make working conditions and social relations difficult, even "hostile" at the plant. Several of the men I interviewed partly blamed this for a high turnover rate among young engineers.

Finally, some product designs inevitably become obsolete, even before they are supplied to the military, simply because of the nature of contemporary war-readiness. This cannot be explained by decisions or difficulties on the part of either client or manufacturer. It represents, rather, the inescapability of entropic loss as a general principle in the material world. This in theory presents problems to any creator of any product, but is amplified in the context of a permanent war economy that demands continual improvements and updates. Simon first explained this to me:

> Another aspect. . .is that this helicopter is flying with six million lines of code or so, because each box is a computer, the radar is a computer, the torpedo is a computer, the bombs are computers, the sonal buoys are computers, and they all have to work together. And a lot of that equipment is obsolete. When the aircraft first gets accepted by the Navy, the computers on board are usually ten years obsolete.

According to Simon, it is code that goes obsolete the quickest. This would appear to be akin to unplanned obsolescence, assuming producers did not intend for this to happen and that changes in computing are at least somewhat unpredictable. Ironically, creating a product that is already useless waste can occur precisely by attempting to avoid this possibility in pursuit of quality:

> That is because of all this testing, and manufacture. It starts obsolete. When you plan for the aircraft, ship or whatever, you plan for it starting obsolete, and that's

why they have a phase one, a phase two, a phase three of upgrading it. And that's
where you make the money, is in the upgrades. There are classified war games,
computer simulations, that you go through. And you know the computer systems
of your opponents.

Simon depicted military equipment that was obsolete as soon as it was sold, a
perfect illustration of the dynamics of endless innovation that Baran and
Sweezy warned of more than half a century ago. But firms were aware of this:
it meant constantly tending to products after they were sold, endlessly producing them in a creative process that never ends until they are decommissioned,
destroyed, or both. For this reason, good management, for Eddy (an engineer
retired eleven years), meant recognizing that military production is "managing
change," constantly adjusting as products evolve, and as costs and schedules
change along with them. Whether the demand to change emerges through
interactions with people, process, or product, managing it means trying to
avoid waste in its various guises and to preserve value, relationships, and community more broadly.

Faced with change and uncertainty in their work process, the engineers and
accountants I spoke with took pride in their own effort and expertise, first and
foremost. That a project might fail to materialize, might be obsolete upon
release, or might cost more than initially projected were out of their control by
comparison.

ETHICAL DIMENSIONS: RISK AND BLAME

Experiences of responsibility or blameworthiness arise through social interaction, because ordinarily people only think to provide explicit justifications for
what they do when impelled to do so by others (Keane 2016, 78–79). And
distinct social situations can direct and deflect blame as a result. Inside the
microworld of arms manufacturing and military contract procurement, for
instance, one is more likely to be called upon to explain one's work performance in certain ways and not others. As mentioned, in public discussions of
the permanent war economy, blame is normally assigned on the basis of perceived self-interest—politicians want reelection, military personnel want
more power, and corporations want more money. But in military production,
blame is determined internally through product testing and audit.[17] Put differently, testing products is a reflexive practice with greater social implications,
beyond customer ties alone. That is because, in addition to demonstrating

technical reliability that workers may take pleasure in, testing is an ethical activity that offers preemptive defense against blameworthiness, an alibi that allows engineers to manufacture products with a belief that they did the best they could.

Generally speaking, corporations in a neoliberal era use auditing practices to reduce various risks to the durability and reliability of their products by increasing the predictability of their processes, including employee performance (see Shore and Wright 2000, 85). What this means for Lockheed employees is that at various stages in the design of a product they must reflect on product success in specific ways even before they pitch a project to the military. The more important the product, the more that is invested in predicting and preventing (or rather delaying) the product's failure and therefore mitigating any person's sense of accountability. More scrutiny with safety-critical products means more testing of software itself, but not necessarily more environmental testing. Simon explained this to me in detail:

> There's a formal thing called a risk analysis, and you do a twenty-year risk analysis. This is a brand-new aircraft, brand new radios, brand new mechanical, computer brain that's gonna be self-aware. What are going to be the technical challenges? All these things either won't be built, can't be built. . . what's the plan? So you do a formal risk analysis and say, "At this point in time if we don't have this design mature enough, we have to go to plan B or plan C." And this formal risk analysis is approved.

Here, formal risk analyses translate "waste" into a series of tests and procedures that arguably deflect responsibility by distributing the labor involved in creating instruments of violence. Testing and auditing also mean inviting other people into the product assessment process:

> Another thing Lockheed Martin does (and I assume other companies do) is, you present your design to an internal panel of what's called "Wise Old Owls." These are old scientists and engineers that have been through all of it before, and you first do a red team and a black team and they can shut down the Lockheed Martin effort and fire all us engineers if they don't think we're gonna win.

These internal "gatekeepers" monitor and assess projects and can have them thrown out for technical reasons, but Simon did not seem concerned about the human or financial cost, likening it to a form of blind peer review (perhaps because I was his interlocutor, and he was searching for an analogous domain of socially mediated audit).

If internal competition and risk analysis can lay waste to projects, in anticipation of their presentation to the client, this is actually meant to save time and money in the long run. If a project is committed to for twenty years, then even more capital, human and financial, is at stake. But too much process analysis can also be wasteful, from the perspective of Lockheed workers. The new face of manufacturing is not about being productive, Bork told me, but predictive. He said a lot of time and resources are now invested in cultivating reflexive attention to processes. What does this look like in practice? As Bork put it:

> So that you have a set of rules that will always give you an expected result coming out. "I have this much time to develop this, and based on my processes, I know I need this many people, this amount of time and this amount of money, and in the end I'll have what I'm asking for." So it gives you predictability, that's the big thing.

If a process was supposed to take you an hour but actually takes much longer, you want not only to shorten the amount of time it takes, but also to understand why you had it wrong the first time. This means asking not only what happened, but also how one can improve in the future. This is not bad, necessarily, but since new approaches are rarely implemented uniformly or perfectly, it ends up taking even longer to do one's work. It is easy to get cynical about predictive management for this reason:

> You've got the new darling method of development that's making the rounds right now: Agile. This is the latest round of Kool-Aid. Every six or seven years, there's some new paradigm of how to develop software that makes the rounds, and it's gonna be the savior of everything and everybody, and it's gonna make us so much more productive. The DoD has actually asked for more programs to be Agile. And they're the main client, so everyone says "Yes, we're Agile!"

Agile is a project management method that attempts to divide up tasks into small, two- to four-week bursts of activity, or "chunks." Bork is of the opinion that it doesn't actually accomplish anything and is almost a complete waste of time and effort. Agile represents additional auditing that the customer asks for, but according to those I've spoken with, Lockheed is just as capable of chasing the latest pointless craze as the DoD. Even this can come down to customer ties. Sometimes, as Bork joked, the method they end up using might just come down to some salesman who had "a really really good golf game!" Here, Bork can be seen as implicitly blaming the capriciousness of sales and marketing personnel for wasting his time, those who he suggests deliberately engage in leisure activities and pretend it is work.

Adding more time to any process typically gets more expensive, sometimes for the company and not only the customer. If you bid a "firm fixed price" on a contract, for instance, then any additional cost from extra testing is not covered, which means managers get nervous and executives get upset. This can be remedied if the process and product are of high enough quality that they draw the customer back again. But since this is no guarantee, it can create pressures to hurry up and finish things by scheduling deadlines and cost limitations.

In some instances, however, wasted money and time are equated with doing things right and achieving greater public goods—durable products, predictable processes—even if they come at the sacrifice of private profit. If additional testing and risk analysis can waste money and time, some of my informants also associated it with higher moral ends, especially saving lives and the national defense. I should note that none of my informants offered this naturally in our conversations, but only after I asked more probing questions, arguably shifting their familiar way of assessing accountability and blame.[18] But they did have responses. As Bork put it:

> You have lives of your countrymen that are reliant on what you're doing. Just as if you were writing software or doing something with a jet airliner, you've got lives on the line of the people that are up in the air. So, depending on what you're writing the software for, there can be a high degree of scrutiny on what you do. And the levels of testing get extremely expensive to guarantee as much as possible the reliability of that product.

Bork said that the fact that lives depended on safety-critical products was not explicitly discussed often, but generally understood by all those at Lockheed. He added that this might be easy to forget because of a division of labor where they might only be testing a particular widget that goes in another machine. This not only means that more people in more states and more congressional districts have jobs (thereby making the military industrial complex possible); it also means that the product that will be consumed—and its potential destructiveness—is also removed from view. The symbolic distance between war front and home front is bolstered through a literal spatio-temporal difference, one that serves to alienate military manufacturers from the consequences of their actions. Instead, they are consumed with reflexive attention to their work performance.

Bork said that engineers generally knew if some feature was safety-critical (e.g., for engine control), because it changed quality-testing standards during product development:

If you have something that's safety-critical, that word itself implies that people are going to die. So if you're working on a product that's safety-critical, then you're going to have the highest level of scrutiny. If you have something that's mission-critical, you know that if it fails, "Okay, so they didn't drop the bomb on this little village, they have to fly back." So there's less scrutiny. So where you would tend to let something slide is when you'd have some minor annoyance, something that would bother the operator, but that did not affect the operation, then you'd let it go by with agreement from the customer.

What further distances manufacturers from actual service members ("operators") is the customer (the DoD), who stands in between them. The gap between safety-critical and minor annoyance is not absolutely and purely technical, but is at least partly mediated through social negotiation between manufacturer and client. As long at the DoD mediates on their behalf, the people using these weapons and the people they are used on are not the responsibility of the manufacturers. Better said, the potential consumption of weapons in war is not legible within the testing and experimenting that manufacturers perform with products, no matter how extensive, except as abstract operators and targets.

When he was younger, Bork worked with his father's company, which was contracted to do work on military projects by GE. He remembers his father telling him as a young man just out of college, "Remember, whatever you do, somebody's life is depending on what you do." "I always think about that," Bork says. Lockheed engineers I have spoken to are more likely to raise moral concerns when it comes to "safety-critical" products, that is, those that are necessary for the safe deployment and return of service members. The thought of making a mistake with safety-critical implications was deeply unsettling, whereas mission-critical ones ("making sure a bomb is dropped in the right place," as one informant put it) provoked less of an ethical response. Simon did not seem to reflect much about the implications of the UCAR for which he owns patents. He mostly thought of it as a challenge to overcome, like others he had encountered previously in his career:

This was to be a completely robotic helicopter—could think for itself, could arm itself, could fly back to base and rearm without humans, could go out and task and kill without human intervention. . . I was the communications engineer, and I was making a self-aware radio system. Never been done before. If you have a team of four of them flying and they're gonna go around a mountain and fly low. . .they would lose communications as they flew around the mountain, so my self-aware radio would tell my mission planner, "Hey, in five miles we're gonna lose radio communications; fly over the mountain so we can keep radio communications."

For Simon, a UCAR that could task and kill without human intervention was a technical challenge, not a moral or ethical one. Put differently, their reflections upon technical challenges, audits, risk analyses, and tests are where their ethical focus lies. After all, life-and-death decisions are ultimately offloaded to the client. Social relations with distant combatants that one never meets face-to-face are arguably more difficult to maintain than those with customers and coworkers with whom one directly interacts, depends upon, and is accountable to. Here Marxian analyses again provide insight. If classic commodity fetishism obscures the production of a commodity in the moment of exchange, then arguably the market in military products serves to obfuscate their consumption in violence.

WHOSE MILITARY? WHOSE WASTE?

To conclude this chapter, I want to consider a seemingly simple question: who really owns America's enormous arsenal of warcraft? Answering this question can help clarify who benefits from permanent war-readiness and, looking ahead at the next several chapters, what ought to be done with its remains. If it is possible to establish to whom military weapons belong, this might help determine responsibility for what becomes of them when they fall out of use. As this chapter has shown, responsibility is no simple matter.

Let us start with an individual plane or ship. When it is undergoing design and testing, prior to sale, in a sense it is owned by the manufacturer, its team of engineers, accountants, managers and, ultimately, its shareholders. To the extent that it belongs to the manufacturer, the manufacturer can profit from or be blamed for its creation (i.e., if it is overpriced or worth the cost, malfunctions or performs properly, breaks down or is durable, etc.). And yet, if certain designs are not purchased by the DoD, in theory the manufacturer may not be allowed to sell them to other countries or the private sector, although they might not always follow these rules in practice. This is part of the risk taken on by military manufacturers. Therefore, manufacturers do not have total ownership—they cannot do whatever they please with their designs and products.

So, in some sense, even before the DoD's purchase, warcraft belong to the department and, ultimately, the federal government, because they are the ones who can decide whether it can be sold and to whom, just as it was their decision whether it was to be used and on whom. To the extent that it is the DoD's, the DoD also decides whether it is turned to scrap, sold, or loaned for an exhibit.

As I will discuss further in chapters 2 and 3, the military might therefore be blamed when it chooses to scrap what could be considered important historical artifacts or reusable assets. And yet, in theory these government entities are legally and morally bound to work on behalf of the American people, whether or not they always do so in practice. This is why the representatives of the government and military are blamed for making what some consider unnecessary or insufficient purchases. Once again, this is not total ownership—they are accountable to someone else.

One of the more common-sense ideas implied in debates about government spending is that wars and the military exist because of the American people. This can be taken in at least two ways. On the one hand, it is meant to be *for their sake* that national defense exists in the first place—"freedom isn't free," as the familiar adage goes. On the other hand, it is generally thought that the taxes of ordinary Americans finance the military. Many people interviewed for this book characterized old warcraft waste as belonging in some sense to "the American taxpayer" for this reason. Legislation on the disposal of naval ships, for example, asserts that their fate should be decided according to what is best for the taxpayer. If this were true, it would only be appropriate that ordinary citizens reuse and reimagine old warcraft as they see fit, thereby reclaiming what was always already "theirs" to begin with.

And yet, things are not so simple. To begin with, there is not always a clear relationship between the things that the military does and the needs of ordinary Americans. This is common knowledge, even if it sounds like conspiracy theory. Depending on who is in office, a large fraction of Americans will readily claim that an act of war is not really about their concerns, but oil, foreign allies, poll numbers, special interests, and so on. They might not always be right, but they are correct to assume that everything the US military does is not about the needs and interests of the general public.

Moreover, it is not the case that American taxpayers exclusively finance American war-readiness. Taxes have steadily gone down over the last several decades, in countries like the United States, the United Kingdom, and Canada, while public spending—measured against inflation—typically rose.[19] Changes in fiscal and monetary policies, beginning in the late 1970s, essentially transferred the cost of public spending from the ordinary taxpayer to financial elites and ordinary investors all over the world. All of this was deliberate. The Vietnam War was both very unpopular and very expensive. Political elites found two ways to reduce the impact of the costs of war on the voting public: ordinary citizens would no longer be directly conscripted to serve in the military and ordinary taxpayers would no longer exclusively finance it (though they might do so indirectly, through personal investments, retirement funds, or by having their social services sacrificially slashed to "balance the budget"). The massive American budget, including its costly military, is in effect financed through loans from the global financial sector to the government. This includes regular people who invest in government bonds for their retirement, but it also includes sovereign wealth funds from the Middle East and investors from China. What all of this means is that international financial institutions, other countries, and investors who buy bonds are helping finance military capitalization in a way that extends far beyond what could be supported by taxpaying citizens alone.

It makes sense that more of the world would have a stake in financing the American military given the global projects the latter has been engaged in. As David Graeber puts it:

> The essence of U.S. military predominance in the world is, ultimately, the fact that it can, at will, drop bombs, with only a few hours' notice, at absolutely any point on the surface of the planet. No other government has ever had anything remotely like this sort of capability. In fact, a case could well be made that it is this very power that holds the entire world monetary system, organized around the dollar, together. (2011, 365–66)[20]

This ability to mete out destructive violence, anytime, anywhere, instantly, is about more than defending ordinary Americans, in other words. It is also (or, maybe entirely) about keeping the world economy together in its current form, which revolves around the dollar as a default global standard of value. What this means is that, around the world, material goods and whole countries can be appraised in terms of dollars. And if the world economy runs in some sense on the American economy, it is just that much more appealing to invest in.

If Americans have long criticized wasteful military expenditures, what has changed is that contemporary debates tend to focus on whether *particular machines* are necessary, not whether a *permanent war economy* is. In a time of otherwise intense political polarization in US public culture, it is rarely acknowledged that cutting military waste is one issue that can create unity across political parties. But a critique of military expenditure is easily paired with a call for the preservation of the military from the influence of greedy politicians and businesses. In an executive order signed on March 14, President Trump proposed eliminating wasteful spending at the Department of Defense (DoD) and Department of Veterans Affairs (VA), asking that the

Office of Management and Budget involve the public in finding ways to "improve the efficiency, effectiveness, and accountability of that agency." Yet, just two days later Trump asked Congress to approve a $54 billion hike in military spending, a portion of which was meant to pay for the proposed border wall with Mexico. These requests can be reconciled as part of the twin pillars of contemporary American political discourse, which blames the nanny state for misusing public money and insists on an ever-deepening commitment to military Keynesianism.[21]

My point is not to challenge these critiques of wastefulness but, rather, to argue that they do not go far enough. From the point of view of the military manufacturing industry, they already think of themselves as doing a lot to trim waste and improve efficiency. They are motivated, moreover, not only by profit motive (although this is clearly central), but by a variety of commitments to making quality, durable products, to solving problems and fixing errors, to improving ties with the service members and government agents whom they deal with on a regular basis. One could reduce these motivations to economic or class self-interest—as in critiques of the military industrial complex— except that does not explain why these men continue to associate with one another doing volunteer and charity work after they have ostensibly retired. It does not explain why they devote their time to technical problem-solving at the local observatory or maker-spaces, except that they enjoy it. One could add that they enjoy not only the technical labor itself, but the social microworld that it entails and its familiar ethic of responsibility. One engineer, Eddy, claims that retirees like volunteering for these charities because the work resembles what their job used to entail. Eddy is even "managed" at a maker-space and living museum, TechWorks, by the same man who once managed him during his time at Lockheed!

However waste is understood, based on the experiences of military manufacturers, that waste arises from military production whether or not weapons are ever finished, whether or not they are ever purchased, whether or not they ever leave the factory floor. Most people typically do not see unfinished, unsold, or unusable warcraft. It is far more common to encounter warcraft when they are deployed in military operations, before they can be used or after they have fallen out of use. This arguably reflects a deliberate defense strategy: commissioned and active warcraft are icons of military strength, meant to frighten potential enemies, comfort allies, and attract buyers on the international arms market. They serve this purpose better by looking new and capable, not ineffective, incomplete, old, and worn. But waste is part of military industry whether every dollar is accounted for or not. The GAO will continue to point out where money was misspent and funds wasted. And Trump, like Obama, now promises to eliminate waste. But accuse military manufacturers of being wasteful, and they can easily document in painstaking detail exactly how much more they have thought about waste than one can imagine—perhaps even too much in some cases, where quality controls and risk analyses run rampant and slow work down, wasting money and time. Another strategy might connect the work of Lockheed Martin or other manufacturers to destruction around the world, but this can also be easily justified in terms of familiar public goods, such as national security, especially when civilians and military manufacturers are distanced from the "consumption" of military products in war.

A different approach is to argue that America's massive military is not only poorly financed and organized, but has *never been necessary* at all, not now and not during the Cold War. For most of the twentieth century, the United States possessed far more nuclear weapons than the Soviet Union, but justified the necessity of amassing this excessive arsenal by claiming the very opposite (Masco 2014, 127). American military historian Paul A.C. Koistinen applies this same criticism to conventional weaponry: "In its ongoing quest for higher-performing aircraft, missiles, ships, tanks, and the like, America competed with itself, not with either its enemies or its allies" (2012, 168). While it is important to criticize policymakers and businesses for egregious expenditures, it is also important to note that even if this money were used with maximum efficiency, the US military would likely remain the biggest in the world and the nation's greatest expense, no matter how efficiently the Pentagon spends "its" money.

One final problem with the idea of the military industrial complex is that it can conjure images of military, political, and economic elites working behind the scenes, in darkened halls of power, as if they were completely detached from ordinary people and communities.[22] As if *we* have to compel *them* to act if we want to change how things are, with the implication that "we" have no real agency. For the remainder of this book, I focus more on how military waste can be made productive in the hands and imaginations of civilians.

CHAPTER 2

Flight or Fight

COAUTHORED WITH PRISCILLA BENNETT

The permanent war economy of the United States has produced the world's most powerful and destructive airborne fleet. According to the CIA, the United States has over thirteen thousand military aircraft in operation today, while its nearest competitors, Russia and China, have about half as many combined. But planes do not remain combat-ready indefinitely. In this chapter, I follow military aircraft as they are transformed through reuse, preservation, and memorialization, each of which involves tensions over what can be done with them and what they mean.[1] In some cases, people attempt to rethink planes beyond their application in war, or to demilitarize them. In each case, the possible affordances of planes, as material objects, complicate the view that they are nothing but tools of violence or propaganda to justify permanent war-readiness.

Whatever the tactical benefit of having a permanent supply of destructive aircraft, the enormity of the American fleet creates no shortage of logistical problems. The United States needs more space to keep and store planes, spare parts, tools, and repair staff. No object remains the same over time without constant attention. This effectively means that aircraft are perpetually re-created as they are fixed, improved, updated, and cared for. As discussed in the previous chapter, this is a key part of how materials are designed, tested, and retrofitted by military manufacturers like Lockheed Martin, even after they are sold.

When planes outlive their usefulness, they usually go to the Davis-Monthan Air Force Base outside Tucson in Arizona. Davis-Monthan is one of the largest areas in the US Air Combat Command. Due to its size, the dry desert climate (which helps avoid corrosion), and depopulated surroundings, it became the base of operations for the Military Aircraft Storage and Disposition Center (MASDC). This became the 309th Aerospace Maintenance and Regeneration Center (AMARC), popularly known as "the Boneyard." According to Michael Thompson ([1979] 2017), it is precisely when things are intentionally forgotten and ignored—when they become set aside as what he calls "rubbish"—that they are capable of the most radical shifts in meaning and worth. On a tour of the Boneyard, a visitor is just as likely to spot a coyote as a person wandering amid the many, many planes. It is easy to imagine the Boneyard as a kind of dystopian wasteland, and many filmmakers have chosen it as a location for precisely this reason, including for the Transformers and Terminator franchises.

In theory, rubbish potential is amplified in situations where seemingly durable items, like planes, are initially forgotten, only to be resurrected in new forms. Central to my argument in this chapter is the idea, common in studies of materiality and familiar to anyone engaged in repair or reuse, that things like war planes are never just weapons, even for the armed services—they are also material objects. When Priscilla Bennett went to the National Naval Aviation Museum in Pensacola, a volunteer docent reprimanded her for touching the rivets on an airplane wing (even though visitors are explicitly invited to touch). He compared it to the skin of Bennett's grandmother, arguing that one should not be too rough with something so aged and fragile.

Like a living thing, planes possess qualities that require care and attention but also offer affordances, or alternative and open-ended opportunities. An affordance can be understood to usher from materials themselves (Ingold 2000) or more from ethical attunement to their semiotic potential (Keane 2016). Regardless, the key aspect of an affordance is that interactions with things in the world are not decided in advance and can lead one in new and unexpected directions: "The idea of affordance usefully draws us away from treating material forms as wholly transparent" (Keane 2016, 30).[2] This sense of affordance fits well with the literature on repair and reuse. Every act of repair is simultaneously an act of discovery and a learning process. The role of the unknown endemic to repair leads to various tensions: between design and repurposing (Houston et al. 2017), between stability and breakdown more generally (Graham and Thrift 2007), or as part of distributed expertise associated with "enacting the object" through "regimes of maintenance" (Denis and

Pontille 2017; Houston 2017). In this sense, an exploration of exceptional moments of repair exposes the underlying politics of remaking. Connecting these ideas, what Thompson considers rubbish arguably offers exceptional affordances for new uses, while also exposing political and moral tensions associated with remaking and enacting objects.

I combine these literatures to explore the re-creation of aircraft around the Boneyard, especially the tensions evoked by nonstandard uses of military craft. Airplane rubbish can be examined in at least two ways. One is exemplified by the Boneyard. As an active part of a permanent, global, and airborne military, the Boneyard is also a locally circumscribed place that releases materials over time into the hands of civilians in the surrounding area—by donating them to the collection of museums or scrapyards, for instance. This chapter begins by examining what becomes of rubbish planes, how they are assessed, remade, and displayed, and to what ends. I argue that reusing planes around the Boneyard tends to involve a tension between their technically and aesthetically valued capacity for flight and their ability to serve as signs of military history and national identity. Based on interviews with civilians working and tinkering around the Boneyard (some retired service members, some not), I find that repurposing these artifacts can involve struggles over their historical and ideological relevance.

The Pima Air and Space Museum, which has developed around the repairscape of the Boneyard, exemplifies this tension between fight and flight. Museums are intriguing institutions because they are not monolithic, but lie at the intersection of a variety of interests, publics, and values.[3] The different actors involved in museums may not all agree on what specific exhibits to display and how, what kinds of crowds should be sought after and appealed to, and which outside parties to partner with to accomplish these goals. And the clash and commingling of these different positions are evident in the semiotic labor of display. Presented with the display of any object, one can ask how it is meant to resemble other forms it is more or less similar to, how it is meant to point to its history of relations with other contexts and entities, how it is meant to represent more general values and shared understandings. As Terrence Deacon (2012) argues, furthermore, different ways of signifying often work together as we think, thereby forming a semiotic scaffold between the first thought and the next. In this way, deeper symbolic meanings can be propped up by the more direct associations our minds tend to make. Direct associations include materially perceptible qualities that underlie interpretation of a more conventional sort, including forms of patriotic reverence or war memorialization. When a restored plane points to historical relations or resembles an acknowledged prototype, these associations become part of the semiotic grounds of a struggle that is at once about what is present and what is absent, about the material and the immaterial.[4] In the case of Pima, according to its director, there is a competing focus between displaying planes for military commemoration and displaying them as tokens of aeronautic history. In other words, it is not necessary that the restoration and exhibition of a flying machine glorify warfare and war preparation—other ways of interpreting planes are possible and always have been.

At the same time, this distinction between the Boneyard and its civilian surroundings threatens to reaffirm a divide between militarization and militarism, or between the material project of war (at bases and in battles, in the hands of pilots) and its cultural and ideological reckoning (at museums and in public storytelling about warriors and warfare, in the hands of civilians). In order to challenge this categorical separation between war's conduct and its representation, I also consider how reusing and aesthetically decorating planes has been part of competing interpretations and uses of them since their earliest involvement in warfare. Here I draw inspiration from Deleuze and Guattari's conceptual distinction between states and nomadic war machines, respectively, where the latter tend toward an anarchic aesthetics of singular decoration (1987, 395–403), meaning weapons are affordances that suggest open-ended uses that go beyond their designated state function (Adkins 2015, 203–10). The war machine and the state have become mutually dependent over the course of history, yet the "exteriority" of the former (its "capture" by the latter) is evident in tensions around the use and reuse of planes. The "minor art" (Deleuze and Guattari 1987, 401) of weapon decoration that I highlight is the frequently observed practice of nose art, where squadrons and pilots decorate their planes with iconography irreducible to mass-produced warfare and the interests of the state, which has inspired other artists affiliated with the Pima.

VARIETIES OF REUSE

What does it mean for something to be repaired or restored? This question helps to address the distinction between what goes on in the Boneyard and what goes on at Pima and related enterprises surrounding the base. Minimally, repair means that there is something broken that is being returned to a previous state of usefulness or wholeness. That previous state, which the damaged thing differs from, can be thought of as a prototype, an idea of what the thing was meant to be, or once was and could be again. A brand-new plane is not broken and in need of repair, but neither is one that has been broken down into metal scrap—the former is too close to the prototype to seem broken and the other is too far gone to be acknowledged as reparable. In its most basic sense, "Repair restores degrees of past capacity for present and future use," in Lara Houston's words (2017, 51). A broken thing is fixed to the extent that it more closely resembles this ideal type in the mind of the repairer, in the diagrams and instructions they refer to, according to aesthetic or functional standards they apply and so on. In practice, there can be extreme differences in degrees of repair in relation to the prototype. For example, with the new F-35, all of the components are so expensive that if a maintainer drops a tool on the wing and dings it, it has to be reported as a Class C mishap. By contrast, on an F-5 or F-18, if some component gets bent and can be pounded out it is not even reportable.

Rather than a place where disused machines are permanently dumped, the Boneyard is the open-air garage of the US military, where machines from the Air Force and all other branches are set aside, tinkered with, stripped for parts, and occasionally scrapped. These decisions ultimately depend on how the material qualities of planes are assessed and creatively manipulated. Paraphrasing Stephen Graham and Nigel Thrift, the repair and maintenance that goes on in the Boneyard is not incidental, rather it is part of what we might call the "engine room" (2007, 19) of permanent war-readiness. With low humidity, little rainfall, and high altitude, the site is ideal for preventing rust and corrosion. Of course, in the Arizona sun, paint peals and interiors steadily deteriorate, but this still has the desired effect of limiting the range of "different rhythms and durations of breakdown and repair action" (Houston 2017, 55). Consequently, more than four thousand aircraft are stored in these conditions and cared for, making the Boneyard the largest aircraft storage facility in the world, which is only appropriate for the largest airborne military in world history. Visitors to the Boneyard can take bus tours around the base, after showing an ID and getting past the gate attendant. And as one learns on the bus tour, they have the necessary tools for every aircraft present, in case they are put back into production. This is ultimately a cost-saving measure, allowing them to supply repaired and retooled planes on behalf of other bases and global military operations. The Boneyard is thus a repair-scape, meaning that this site and the people who work there are engaged in an ongoing process of *differentiating* objects, or determining the fates of their various material components in an open-ended fashion. This means saving some things, extending their usability for the time being, as well as routinely dismissing and disposing of other things.[5]

When done intensively, differentiation at a repair facility can beget all new forms of differentiation. Put differently, sorting and re-sorting objects can allow new qualities and new concerns to come to the fore. Shortly after World War II concluded, as a permanent war economy was being established, one notable entrepreneur in Tucson began acquiring surplus planes from the General Services Administration and melting them down. At the time, smelters were benefiting from the high price of aluminum. But sometime in the early 1950s, that operation also began restoring and collecting planes for display and sale. That business eventually became Aircraft Restoration and Marketing (ARM). ARM still exists today beside the Boneyard, with decades of accumulated knowledge related to repairing and rebuilding various aircraft. A number of other operations grew around the Boneyard, involved in experimental and virtual reuses of the landscape, whether to store objects or simulate interactions. Heading toward Phoenix, as you approach the county line, there is another site that stores commercial airplanes and airliner components. Out there in the desert Federal Law Enforcement agents train with tribal police, practicing maneuvers with cars. To the north is where scientists set up the Biosphere II initiative; after its conclusion, some recall an art display took its place: Native American "tribal masks" made from the distinct casings and flanges of nuclear weapons.

While many disused planes were ultimately scrapped for raw material, the military also practiced some preservation. Near the Boneyard, on the west side of the airport, there are still two wooden hangars left from World War II, which also used to serve as a bomb shelter during the Cold War. That the Air Force also began to preserve planes nearby is not surprising since preservation and restoration are arguably just more exaggerated forms of repair, involving further acts of differentiation. If all repair refers to some aspirational state, restoration suggests more careful standards regarding how this is to be accomplished. According to Elizabeth Spelman, "In its service to the past and the preexistent we find reasons to distinguish repairing something from creating it or replacing it, and in the conservative commitment of repair to continuity we note its difference from destruction" (2003, 126). With restoration, there is some sense that continuity itself is valuable, almost as an end in itself, an aesthetic quality quite apart from the ideal prototype associated with repair. Saying "this is a restored mansion" says as much about the virtues of restoration, of respect for aesthetic standards of design and construction for instance, as it does about the building itself. Unlike a repaired thing, however, when something is described as "restored," this does not necessarily mean it can be used as it once was.

Some of the Pima museums planes are reclaimed by others and fly again. This is because museum objects are not deprived of use value or authenticity, but somehow saved and redeemed from a rubbish state.[6] When staff at the Pima museum "restore" a plane for display, this does not necessarily mean that it is capable of flight, however, only that *it looks like it did when it could fly*. This is what ultimately divides the Boneyard from neighboring preservation and restoration operations. According to a brief, unpublished history written by James, director of collections and aircraft restoration at Pima:

> The concept for the Pima Air & Space Museum began in 1966 during the celebration of the 25th Anniversary of the creation of the United States Air Force. Earlier the commanders of Davis-Monthan Air Force Base and...MASDC...recognized that the historic World War II and 1950s era aircraft stored on the base were rapidly disappearing into smelters and that the flames were consuming not just metal, but the aviation heritage of the country. On their own initiative base officials began to set aside examples of the many types of aircraft stored in MASDC's yards. These planes were placed along the base's fence line so that the public could see them through the fence.

Unlike formal restoration, as done by (some) museums, repair and maintenance are common and critical elements of our material environments.[7] The choice between repairing and restoring is not absolute, moreover, but is a matter of practical decision-making as actors engage with materials at hand, with different categories of utility at issue, and with different sets of skills and resources at their disposal. There are, in fact, operations in between restoration and repair, more similar to ARM—salvaging, scraping, and making things capable of flight—and others more similar to the Pima—preserving, restoring, and displaying objects.

The Cold War introduced world-picturing and world-destroying planes and satellites circling overhead, which were a source of both dread and fascination.[8] By the 1960s, people would reportedly line up along the Air Force fence to see what had been saved. In other words, this act of preservation became a public display of the sheer variety of aircraft that had been employed by the growing American empire. Inspired in part by the public reaction, the base commander of the Boneyard worked with local veterans to create the nongovernmental Pima Air Museum (named after the county whose land they ultimately rent). They also began to acquire additional aircraft from abroad, including the last Consolidated B-24 Liberator in the world, donated by the Republic of India in 1969. The museum opened officially in 1976, and was initially hard to distinguish from the surrounding Boneyard, to which it was also indebted for its collection. As James describes it,

> In the beginning the museum was little more than a fenced in field with airplanes parked on it and a small, white, trailer to serve as ticket booth and administrative office. By early the next year further small improvements to the museum's infrastructure were put in place. The museum acquired several surplus storage buildings and erected a small, open-sided shelter for aircraft undergoing restoration in 1978. The dedicated staff and volunteers made the best of the primitive conditions and slowly the museum's aircraft began to be reassembled, repaired, and repainted. In the early years the museum could be easily mistaken for a part of MASDC, or one of the numerous scrap yards in the area.

By the 1980s, the museum grew to include several hangars, a gift shop, and more professional museum displays. In 1982, the Tucson museum community approached the Air Force about preserving missile silos that were being retired along with the Titan II ICBM system. According to James, these silos too were part of "aviation history." Even so, as a relic of the Cold War, it required international cooperation to verify that this was, in fact, no longer a useful and repaired artifact, but a useless and restored one,[9] complicating varieties of reuse as they apply to military waste:

> After much negotiation both within the U.S. government and with the Soviet Union it was agreed that one silo would be preserved for use as a museum...and after Soviet satellites were given time to verify that both the silo and the missile that would go in it had been rendered harmless, work began to set up a visitor center at the formerly highly guarded site.

The Titan Missile Museum eventually opened in 1986, "offering a rare look, both above and below ground, at the top-secret world of a nuclear missile silo." James credits the addition of the silo with the beginning of a new direction for Pima, because "the original museum and foundation names no longer represented the true scope of the institution." Pima stopped being primarily a military aircraft museum in the 1990s, when it was officially rebranded with a general aeronautics focus, "from balloons to outer space," as James puts it. In 1992 the museum's name officially changed to the Pima Air & Space Museum and the foundation became the Arizona Aerospace Foundation. In 1999, Pima opened a new space gallery, to further this larger aerospace focus (although James bemoaned the fact that it has not been sufficiently updated since that time).

If Pima began due to the proximity of the base, today only half of its collections come from the military. And it is primarily military museums they now work with to get these planes, located in Dayton or Quantico, not the Boneyard directly. The other half are not lent but purchased from private sellers and businesses who have no more use for a plane but do not want to see it scrapped. Beyond the museum's origins, as a by-product of the Boneyard, the reason for this has to do with the greater availability and variety of military aircraft when compared with commercial planes or spacecraft. Like other local businesses and organizations, Pima is indebted to the permanent war economy's abundant expenditure of objects, in this case conveniently concentrated in one location.[10] Yet, what it does with airplanes is quite variable. Today, the museum is no longer in the hands of military officers or veterans, although it may engage with either depending on the exhibit in question.

A contrasting example is the 390th Memorial Museum, which is a separate entity from Pima, but is located on the same property. The director, Wally, is a retired Air Force pilot, and sees the primary focus of the museum as the memorialization of the 390th Bomb Group and the equipment and people who supported their efforts during World War II and Korea. The displays in this museum did discuss missions, specifically with B-17 and photographs of bomber crews. According to Bennett's field notes:

> A docent in the Memorial Museum had only been working there for six weeks. He explained that his uncle was a pilot in WWII who was killed in action and his dad was also in the military, a tank commander who was wounded in Korea, so he's always "been in it."

One of the volunteer docents at this museum comes from an "Air Force family." Like many children in military families, Chuck grew up all over—primarily in Dayton, Jakarta, and Colorado Springs—but he eventually ended up in Tucson in 1978. He used to be able to see the tails of C-141 Starlifters at the Boneyard in the distance when he was lifeguarding as an adolescent. He thought they looked like whale fins. Those planes were eventually all recycled, but Pima got one. He remembers that, after his father retired, he worked for

Western International Aviation, which acquires and refurbishes military planes from the Boneyard to resell. "I remember one time, they repaired a plane, got it flying, took it to France for someone there...and then another specific time they got a C-54, which is a four-engine cargo plane, running again and they took that up to Alaska for the fishing industry, for the canning industry so they could run stuff back and forth." Like his father, when Chuck was finished with his military service, he also became involved in the restoration of military aircraft, along with the commemoration of service members.

As I will discuss below, at Pima these twin pursuits are in tension with one another. In Chuck's case, he has worked both as a docent at the museum and as a model builder. In 2010, he cofounded the Sonoran Desert Model Builders (SDMB) club, a chapter of the International Plastic Modeling Society (IPMS) and the second one in the Tucson area. Some of the other modelers have military backgrounds; some are artists, carpenters, or work in electronics. They build all kinds of things—scenes from movies like *Jaws*, boats, commercial aircraft—but they do a lot of work at and around Pima and the 390th Memorial Museum, as well as with contemporary and retired military pilots. Along with the IPMS, the mode builders donated boxes of models and supplies to Iraq for model-building clubs in the armed services to use during their downtime. And one of those service members eventually joined the SDMB.

In 2014 the SDMB completed a project on World War II spotter planes that drew the attention of the board members of the memorial museum. In 2015, they began a project completing a model of the airfield in England used by the 390th. Fourteen by eight feet, the Station 153 Parham Field Diorama shows not only planes flying but the infrastructure that kept them flying. In this way, the model of the airfield reflects the repair-scape that surrounds and supplies the museum. This includes, in Chuck's words, "individual squadrons, where they stayed...maintenance squadrons...where the women stayed. It represents the whole thing, so it's not just about flying planes, it's about keeping planes flying, all the supplies involved, all the people involved." The finished model, we were told, would include a baseball game, dogs, people on bicycles, and letters reflecting on life on and around the airfield at the time.

Wally, Chuck, and the other volunteers see the diorama as a way of situating military machines within a place and a time, as well as a specific war. Wally explicitly said that this conflicted with the emphasis of Pima. As someone actively seeking out militarized human connections, Chuck has been collecting models of A-10 Thunderbolt II's in his spare time, thinking that they could be used in a future project painting them, perhaps with young people. Such an event might draw Martha McSally, Republican US senator from Arizona, who flew the A-10 when she was an Air Force colonel, or the female commander of the local base, both of whom came to Pima when they launched their latest exhibit on women in flight. Wally also trained people on the A-10 during his service, so Chuck realizes there is a lot of potential for this old plane to inspire interest and excitement among commemorators, like himself.

Flight or Fight

Attempts to demilitarize the museum and foundation are not done in name only, but involve making available different ways of interpreting planes on display. Put differently, it means taking a weapon out of circulation, restoring it, and displaying it in such a way that visitors can come to appreciate alternative ideas about military objects. According to James, the way that artifacts are displayed at Pima is fairly uniform, whether or not they were used in the military, in space, or for commercial purposes. This is despite routine feedback from visitors that indicate something else is expected or desired. As he put it, "In general, the public expects the military stuff to be displayed in a more commemorative tone than the nonmilitary aircraft on display. They expect us to be a little more worshipful of people who were using these things in the war."

James was typically this open and direct in conversation. Like many of the people interviewed for this book, James characterized himself as both insider and outsider. Many people came to the area as military personnel or as children of them. Others settled in the Southwest after growing up elsewhere in the country, but became drawn to the area around the Boneyard in one way or another. James received a master of arts degree in public history from New Mexico State University, and working at the museum was his first job out of college. He describes himself as always having been enthusiastic about aviation and aeronautics, though not wealthy enough to fly. Besides, he said, taking apart planes and finding out that commercial airliners are held together by four to six two-inch bolts, and nothing more, can put one off of flying entirely. When asked, James was quick to voice criticism of military spending, in line with the focus of chapter 1:

> Obviously we need to have a military. I personally think our military wastes an awful lot of money on things that they don't necessarily need to be spending money on. Everything wears out and gets to that point in its life, so it wasn't necessarily a

waste of money to buy those things at the time, although it kind of seems like it when you see four thousand of them just sitting in the desert. It's more a matter of how they decide to spend money, [and] the complete dysfunction in the way the Pentagon budget is set and spent is really disheartening.

James has no military background, though around half of his volunteers and a significant number of visitors do. If there are many who expect that the museum's staff will be dedicated to commemorating the military, loan agreements with the government state that any borrowed planes should be preserved, as James put it, "in a manner that does not produce a detriment to the image of the military." But this stipulation allows for a wide interpretation. And this is evident in the way they restore planes and arrange their exhibits. According to James, "We've tried to move away from [military commemoration], but it's a fact of how this is done. The cultural attitude of 'the greatest generation'. . .is very ingrained, and with the events of the last fifteen years, the attitude toward veterans, anyway, has become much more respectful, perhaps overly respectful in some cases." In effect, there is a tension within the museum between two competing approaches: one, more about war and those who fight wars, and the other a more technical history of flight itself. James expanded on this at some length:

> Probably our greatest competing focus is between technological history presentation and military commemoration. . . We try to stay to the technological history side, rather than the commemoration side. There are other organizations that do commemoration and do it better than we could, so that's not our primary focus. But a lot of people think, "Well, because you have military stuff you must be a veterans' worship organization." And we recognize the veterans, we respect what they've done, but. . .our primary focus is the technological development of aviation from balloons to outer space.

The expectation of commemoration is not just about patriotic ideas of respect for service members. Arguably, any act of reuse means reckoning not only with the pieces and materials an object is made of but also the lives they shaped and were shaped by, and the stories people tell about them, big and small. Like all reusers, the staff at ARM, Pima, and other surrounding enterprises can choose whether or not to attend to what James refers to as "the human connection" in practice, and to what extent. Because the objects they are reusing and remaking are associated with the military, their decisions and designs can have profound implications.

Let us say that you come across a military aircraft. You might reasonably wonder what branch of the military made use of it, which specific squadrons and individuals flew it, what battles it was used in, if any, and whether they were lost or won, whether anyone was killed or saved through its use, and so on. If you have insider knowledge, you might know to look at the fin flash or the squadron tail art to retrieve some of this information.[11] All of these characteristics are part of its history of use and may be detected by searching for features that resemble, indicate, and/or symbolize these historical connections in particular ways. The surface of a plane might reveal traces of past skirmishes or theaters of operation. This was mentioned in an interview with Carlo McCormick, an art critic who helped curate the Boneyard Project (about which more will be said below). When you are reusing old planes and come across bullet holes, you are particularly struck by what he called the "historical resonance" of the object. This is another way of saying that what is absent stands out as much as what is present before you. In fact, what is absent stands out *precisely because* of what is before you: symbols denoting a military vehicle and bullet holes indicating that a battle once took place. For Carlo, the presence of these signs only amplifies what is not there, the "resonance" of a history that happened and is now over, including the actual sweating bodies and fearful voices of the plane's former crew.[12] Such present absences can be ignored, in theory, if instead you want a plane to fly again, let alone drop bombs or fire bullets. In this case, you would need to know something about aeronautics, something about its design and makeup, and something about what it has been through. To begin, you would explore the object as best you could for signs that it can still perform as desired. You would also want to store them in such a way that they could be easily found for repair and reuse.

At the Boneyard, like any scrapyard, items are differentiated according to type, with fighters and bombers grouped together. Insofar as these types can be readily interpreted as resembling one another, their resemblance affords ease of storage and access for the repair crew. There are other divisions of the space of the Boneyard that facilitate its actions as a repair-scape. One section, known as "celebrity row," is for those planes that could potentially return to service. In a different section they store those planes that are being stripped for parts or dismantled, which will never return to service. Even if Boneyard mechanics are unable to make a plane fly again or are uninterested in doing so, it still must be kept in a state such that its parts can be harvested as needed. Everything that comes in gets washed on what is known as "the wash rack," which every base has. Even those items in storage that may be disposed of are routinely washed, sometimes three or four times a year, at the wash rack,

though if items come in large enough numbers, this can prove difficult to manage, as happened with a group of C-130 Hercules, which were delivered
recently and went unwashed. Planes at the Boneyard are further draped with
plastic sheeting over the windows, nose, engine, and/or propellers, to protect
the plane and its valuable components from the elements. The only nonmilitary plane at the Boneyard in the summer of 2015 was a commercial Boeing
707 that was acquired in order to strip its engines and put them into a KC-135.
In general, there are about twice as many engines as aircraft on site, since the
engines wear down faster than the planes themselves. That way, an engine is
sitting waiting while another is in use, which helps maintain the engines over
time.[13]

Unlike repairers, restorers will rely on some shared, yet arbitrary, understanding of what counts as "continuity" with a past, idealized state. This decision is arbitrary because making an object look like it did five minutes or five
weeks ago might accurately depict a past state, and yet not count as "restoration." Evidence of repair is seeing something work as it once did; evidence of
restoration would be seeing something that seems like it once did. If this is
about iconicity—about relations of resemblance between an ideal state and a
current state—this resemblance is mediated by a specific, shared idea of what
a restored plane is supposed to look like. That depends on conventions maintained by airplane museums and held by visitors. The important point is that
if you only want a plane to *seem like it did* when it flew, you interpret its qualities differently and end up with a potentially very different object—the simulation of a plane rather than an actual flying machine. Items at the Pima are
cleaned up, painted, and, when possible, labeled with the markings they had
when they were still in use.

Specializing in restoration, rather than repair, means developing different
practical relations with artifacts. According to James, "Primarily their main
requirement is that we keep them in a clean and presentable condition. The
loan agreements say something to the effect of 'in a manner that does not produce a detriment to the image of the military.' Basically their main requirement
is that we keep them looking good, as much as possible." Keeping planes "looking good" is an open-ended request, and certainly has nothing to do with keeping them in a flyable condition. Yet, paradoxical though it may seem, making a
plane look good can serve to represent *flyability*, or flight in the abstract, better
than a raggedy-looking plane that can *actually fly*. This is so whether or not the
restored plane itself is or has ever been flyable and, therefore, represents a ten-

sion between flight as a real potential of a machine and flight as a virtual or symbolic idea that is held by museum visitors and that calls to mind particular forms and configurations rather than others.

The tension between actual and virtual flight is managed through restoration and repair, but can also be left in suspension. Any aircraft on loan could theoretically leave again and even be returned to flight, but that is not Pima's concern. When they do need a plane restored to flyable condition, they typically use outside expertise. At the time of the interview with James, they had two planes being returned to flyable condition in Australia. Here restoration means not only making something seem capable of flight, but making it actually able to fly. While this is not necessary for Pima's purposes, as a museum focused on display, some of the planes they have on loan may eventually leave and be returned to flight.[14] Yet, a plane can be repaired so that it might again fly, but appear nothing like a "restoration" of some original condition (because it makes conspicuous use of contemporary components or paint, for instance). The conditions that must be satisfied for something to count as a restored museum artifact or a repaired plane can be, and often are, very different depending on the circumstances.[15]

If a plane is being reassembled to be used as a target for a gunnery range, the requirements are different than if it needs to be set aside to be harvested for future parts or sent to be put on display in a museum. Restoration practices are fairly uniform in the latter case. "Metal is metal," as James puts it. One big exception to a uniform treatment of aircraft is that planes located outside typically have their windows painted blue in order to prevent the sun from degrading plexiglass and interiors (uncovered, the insides of planes could reach temperatures of 180 degrees Fahrenheit; covered, they typically do not get hotter than 140 degrees). Moreover, some of the space-related objects can be more sensitive and deteriorate rapidly due to the materials used in their construction. This is the case with space suits, for instance, which Pima used to display.

At museum exhibits, artifacts are displayed with additional information to assist the observer in interpreting the object symbolically and iconically as a token example of a particular story they want to tell. During tours of the Boneyard, narrators explain the background of different planes, including their use in various wars and military operations.[16] When it comes to the Vought F4-U-4 Corsair on display at the Pima, by contrast, there are other things to refer the visitor to than military campaigns. In place of narration, the curator has arranged collateral information to help the visitor interpret the plane in various ways. First, there is a conventional set of technical specifications, specifically, figures and pictures that can be interpreted as icons of the plane (or the plane of them) insofar as they bear a resemblance to one another. Next, there is a symbolic narrative provided that places the plane in a larger historical account of flight (describing the speed records it broke among American fighter planes at the time) and, finally, war (explaining very briefly both the branch of the military that made use of it—the US marines—and its use in World War II and the Korean War). As James says,

> The story of the people who did that and used them is important, but we're not here to memorialize or commemorate their achievements or wars and so forth. There is some of that, you can't just present this stuff with an object with no human connection. The human connection is there obviously.

In theory, that "human connection" would include the private owner and not just the marines involved. It requires a decision on the part of the person arranging a display to highlight one, the other, or both. For the U-4, there is no additional information on or about the plane itself to index or point people toward these past relationships.

What draws the eye, far more readily than the black and white photo or the monochromatic schematic on the placard, is the more colorful image related to the animated Pixar film *Planes* (2013). This is part of an additional "scavenger hunt" activity that the museum provides, primarily intended for children, which encourages visitors to find the planes throughout the museum that match characters from that film. The scavenger hunt is an explicit attempt to make the museum more appealing for children and families. But children also must be assisted in forming connections between museum objects and meanings. By placing this particular *Planes* poster next to the Corsair, visitors are encouraged to form an iconic interpretation seeking out resemblances between cartoon and plane (perhaps inspired by the animator's intention). Establishing these resemblances encourages visitors to further relate the real stories of the type of plane, in general, and this plane, in particular, to a fictitious and anthropomorphic tale of talking machines. Regardless of what visitors make of these connections, the elements of the museum display work together to provide an interpretive scaffold for more imaginative thinking about the place of the plane beyond American conflict alone, bringing the U-4 into the realm of aviation history and animated fiction. Once again, a repaired plane with no polish, no story, no collateral semiotic associations might function as a flying machine without appealing to the imaginations of visitors as virtually flyable.

One of the anthropologists who conducted research for this book, and a coauthor of this chapter and the next, is Priscilla Bennett. She toured the Pima museum and the Boneyard for the first time with an American fighter pilot in civilian clothing (who would eventually become her husband). In her notes on the trip she remarked that "he could identify almost every plane and missile in the museum, and the mechanics behind jet engines, etc."[17] When speaking with docents and volunteers at Pima, they would often bring up their familial ties to aviation. They would take interest when they learned that Bennett's companion was an aviator and ask him questions. For Bennett, having this connection to the military, and aviation specifically, gave her access to stories—a further "human connection"—that she would not have heard otherwise. Bennett's pilot companion did not conflate a collection of military warcraft for a collection about the military, per se. As she wrote in her notes:

> He didn't perceive the museum to be military centered; rather he believed the military is intrinsic to the history of aviation. Other employees in the museum shared similar perspectives, saying you can't have an aviation museum without a focus on the military.

James and his curator are ultimately responsible for the content and tone of displays and, to them, military planes are just planes. But it also means that planes are not *just* planes; they are *planes!* That is, they are exciting artifacts that represent human ingenuity and the history of movement through the air and beyond the Earth altogether. Under James's directorship, the museum is interested in embedding military aircraft within a larger story, rather than one group's "tiny little bit of it." And for some this larger story of flight is as compelling as that of war and the nation-state, especially for those many foreign visitors to the museum.

A Machine to End All Wars

It can be difficult, in a world irrevocably shaped by aerial bombardment, to reimagine planes apart from the possibility of violence. This is the case not only with actual warplanes, but with civilian flights, which are continually militarized through a growing security state apparatus. The terrorist attack orchestrated by Al Qaeda in 2001 made even ordinary commercial flights seem like tools of mass destruction. Arguably, commercial air travel is one of the primary ways that many Americans are encouraged to imagine even the humblest of objects—shoes, belts, laptops, shampoo, beverages—as weaponized devices, and fellow passengers as potential terrorists once airborne.

But there are alternative histories, or *understories*, of flight.[18] These exist in parallel to and in tension with conventional military history. Many of the earliest appraisals of the plane considered this new machine as something more than a mere weapon of war.[19] As historian Robert Wohl writes, from nearly the moment of its invention the airplane "created a sense of power and pride and endless possibility—and in the minds of some less given to optimism about the increasing mechanization of life, it gave rise to anxiety and a sense of encroaching doom" (Wohl 1994, 260).[20] In the United States, the airplane was initially greeted with reverence, which Joseph Corn characterizes as a *winged gospel*:

> Like the Christian gospels, the gospel of aviation held out a glorious promise, that of a great new day in human affairs once airplanes brought about a true air age. Lindbergh offered one version of this gospel, prophesying a future in which air travel would be commonplace and large transport planes shuttle from city to city, unhampered by the weather. Other enthusiasts voiced even grander prophecies, looking to aircraft as a means of achieving perfection on earth or even immortality. (1983, 27)

Flight was not only appreciated as a technical achievement apart from the possibility of violence. According to some, it represented a potential end to war itself:

> Yet another widely anticipated change in attitude would have the result of curbing violence and bringing about the end of war. Airplanes, prophets thought, would usher in an era of perpetual peace, deterring aggressors and even eliminating the conditions that cause war. . . . Only "fools" would dare fight when armies employed flying machines. (Corn 1983, 37)

This mindset was very different from European anxieties expressed around the same time, most famously represented in H. G. Wells's 1908 story *The War in the Air*, which depicted a world vulnerable to attack from air raids.[21]

The more utopian American prediction was premised on the widely held belief that airplanes could be cheaply made and would soon be available to all, as had happened with the bicycle.[22] Eventually even very small countries would be able to cheaply manufacture their own air force and deter stronger countries from attacking, it was thought. It may be that a failure to recognize the military value of planes led to the United States lagging behind its allies and enemies in air defense during World War I. Mexico, which remained neutral during the global conflict, spent more than three times the United States on aerial appropriations, most likely out of fear of a possible invasion from the north. The Wright brothers immediately saw the military application of their popular invention, but they were promptly turned down by the US government before war broke out and had to turn to Europe for potential buyers.[23] After the war, congressional investigations accused airplane manufacturers of being wasteful war profiteers: "The World War I aircraft program represented America's first taste of the seemingly inherent wastefulness and uncontrollable costs of military aircraft production, and it left a bad aftertaste for a long time" (Vander Meulen 1991, 39).[24]

Even after World War I broke out, some ardently claimed that airplanes would soon bring an end to war by reducing the geographic barriers that had for so long isolated the world's peoples from each other. Despite attempting to sell the airplane he coinvented to warring nations, Orville Wright believed it "made war so terrible" that no country "will again care to start a war" (quoted in Bilstein 2003, 19). Some went so far as to propose that by 1970 a new super-human race would evolve. Dubbed "Alti-man," they would dwell permanently in the heavens above the lesser, ground-dwelling peoples.[25]

Such "airmindedness," as some called it, was easier to adopt during the inter-war period if one was white. In 1921, incendiaries were dropped from private planes to help destroy a prosperous black neighborhood in Tulsa, Oklahoma. This was done after African American obstruction of an attempted lynch mob, which was followed by widespread white rioting (Snider 2003). For white America, optimistic visions of flight would not be challenged until decades later. "Assimilating news from Pearl Harbor, Midway, London, Dresden, Okinawa, and eventually Hiroshima and Nagasaki, Americans inevitably came to think of the airplane first and foremost as a weapon, as an instrument capable of unprecedented destruction and horror" (Corn 1983, 65). The greatest war in history ended after just two bombs proved capable of incinerating hundreds of thousands of men, women, and children in a single instant, bringing a powerful empire to its knees. And, in a nuclear age, it is assumed, states can no longer take years to develop competitive weapons, least of all aircraft and missile defense.

This was not an inevitable conclusion, but gained traction due to pressure from corporate lobbying groups.[26] Fear of a threatening airborne enemy was marshaled from 1955 to 1957, when politicians, industrialists, and military officers conspired to convince the American people that the country was vulnerable to Soviet attack due to an alleged "bomber gap."[27] While visions of one-sided aerial warfare also helped, in some cases, to turn public opinion against war, the perceived militarization of flight has endured. Where celebrations and commemorations of flight continue today, they are generally associated with symbols and stories of the nation, its service members, allies, and enemies.

A century that began with optimism about an airborne world was instead punctuated by two airborne attacks separated by sixty years, Pearl Harbor and September 11th, both of which ushered in distinct periods of American global dominance premised on permanent war-readiness and aerial supremacy in particular. Most American visitors to the Pima will likely have images of terror by means of aerial attack firmly implanted in their minds. And those who flew to get to Tucson will have had a very recent experience of being made to feel that even civilian flights can be instruments of death and destruction. Regardless of their personal beliefs, this experience of flight is part of what visitors to Pima bring with them. To some extent, Pima's directors and curators have to anticipate such preconceived notions in order to make their displays comprehensible and engaging.

Yet something might happen to those visitors when they see the Boneyard. The sheer volume and variety of planes that permanent war-readiness has brought into being and turned to rubbish in the Boneyard might suggest new possibilities.

On the one hand, as we have seen, this draws people who see the mass wasting of planes as a way to reckon with the broader history of flight. The Boneyard is not just a military junkyard; in James's words, it is also a "pilgrimage site for airplane people," who come from all over the world for the unique spectacle of so many planes in one place. This includes organizations like Worldwide Aircraft Recovery, based in Nebraska, that work with Pima and ARM trying to save rare aircraft from being lost to history. Pima takes planes of all kinds and embeds them within a global history of flying machines. It is as if there is a surplus beyond or underneath their military significance. This can be brought to the surface through displays and curation that emphasize the technical and practical aspects of flying. This may rely on stories and experiences from veterans and service members, but it recasts them within a different frame. In effect, one can draw out practices that coexisted with the military apparatus, yet fall outside of the official state semiotics of force and destruction.

But that is not all the Boneyard makes possible. Seeing so many planes grounded and preserved also supports anyone who would like to imagine them as works of art. If repainting and displaying planes in a restorative manner is one way to deal with them, another is to draw on alternative capacities or affordances of the plane as a material object. Planes can fly, and planes can project and drop things from great heights. But planes are also heavy. Planes are curvy in some places and flat in others. They have interiors different from their exteriors. Beyond only thinking about planes as either weapons or flying devices, what else can such objects do? What thoughts can they provoke other than military record, wars fought, or people killed? Or can they be re-presented to change how those are interpreted?

THE BONEYARD PROJECT

In 2010, Arizona gallery owner Eric Firestone, who had been spending time in scrapyards, came up with the idea of the Boneyard Project, which developed in collaboration with ARM and Pima. One of his closest collaborators was Carlo McCormick, an art critic who would curate the collection. Unlike James or Eric, Carlo explicitly describes himself as antiwar, saying that his ideas about the US military were formed more by his brothers resisting the draft to go to Vietnam than his father and father-in-law who served in World War II. According to Carlo, Eric was visiting scrapyards and thinking, "Well Jesus, all this stuff out here with this remarkable history." Eric came out of a tradition of "pickers" in the art community of the American West: "people who would go to thrift stores and find mid-century modern clothes when it was out of style," in Carlo's words. "A lot of the great stuff was getting picked at that time: 'We're building a really fancy restaurant in this five-star hotel, wouldn't that fuselage look fantastic if we made it a souvenir?'" Eric's initial interest in the materials coming from the Boneyard was not about nostalgia or kitsch, however. According to Carlo, "[Eric] has a good eye and a good sensibility for old things that people don't really recognize or value." He noticed that there were hundreds of nose cones lying around scrapyards surrounding the base. In the past they would have been recycled as scrap along with the rest of the plane, but manufactures started building nose cones from fiberglass by World War II. The idea came to him that both the nose cones and entire planes could be repurposed as canvases for street artists.

Eric procured four planes from the ARM and two from Pima, at approximately $10,000 apiece. With Carlo's help, he arranged for a variety of street artists from Arizona, Brazil, and Germany to come to Arizona to paint. Some locals referred to them derisively as "taggers," Terry from ARM explained, because they use spray paint to decorate planes and nose cones as they might the side of a building. But many of the artists were celebrated and internationally renowned. For a year, the Pima hosted an aircraft exhibit and a nosecone exhibit, presenting the results of the project. James described this as essentially marketing for Eric's gallery, since they were advertised for purchase.

If Pima could be said to have demilitarized its artifacts—by withdrawing them from military use as well as reframing their interpretation as tokens of aeronautic history—then the Boneyard Project seems to reimagine the plane entirely as a static canvas, rather than an object in motion. Put differently, it means establishing continuity between the reused object and understories of art, some of which subsist within the military itself.

Nose Cone Art: The Plane as a Canvas

In Deleuze and Guattari's *A Thousand Plateaus* (1987), "the war machine" is one of many rhizomatic figures that they use to rethink the origins and the limits of the state. Better said, they develop the obverse of Pierre Clastres's (1974) claim that the state exists as a threatening possibility even among nonstate societies, arguing that nomadic anarchism is also ever-present as a threatening force immanent to state societies. The reason for this is that states have, in a sense, captured and domesticated the revolutionary potential of collective violence in order to effectively wage war, all while struggling to maintain hierarchical control.

One way that Deleuze and Guattari develop this idea is by contrasting how states regiment "tools" at their disposal with how the nomadic war machine relates to "weapons." Like arguably all the figures in their book, these are playful ideal types rather than literal persons and things, and I take them as such. At the same time, the idea of the immanence of the anarchic war machine within the state's orderly military, a radical exteriority lurking within, is a useful counterpart to the idea of demilitarized affordances immanent within planes as material objects. They explain the divide between tool and weapon partly by suggesting that there is a nomadic tendency to decorate weapons with jewelry, a singular act that reflects and enacts the singular and emergent unity, or assemblage, of weapon and warrior. Importantly, this is an assemblage beyond the direct control of state-organized violence. Nose cone art, I submit, is helpful to think about as a "minor art" in Deleuze and Guattari's sense, subsisting within the state's official military.[28]

As they began to undertake the Boneyard Project, Eric and Carlo knew that there was a parallel history of flying machines as a canvas for artistic display. In nose art, the fuselage of the aircraft is painted with images and words. Carlo says he has "always been a fan" of nose art, even as a teenager when he became interested in tattoo art and folk art more broadly. He likened nose art to artistic drawings on skateboards, both of which represent "iconographies that developed around utility" or functional commodities.

It is difficult to find discussions of nose art outside of books for and by enthusiasts. The tendency for cultural historians, on the contrary, has been to focus on depictions of and from planes in the air, rather than depictions on them, best seen when they are grounded. The plane was perhaps too dynamic as an object of movement, the aesthetics of flight too beguiling, to be contemplated as a resting surface. Avant-garde cuba-futurist and suprematist painters and poets were inspired by the transcendence of flight, especially the feelings of awe and horror with which this new form of locomotion was associated. Planes have been considered art objects in and of themselves, which especially manifested in the spread of streamlined, smooth, and frictionless surfaces in the period leading up to World War II. For these manufacturers, artists, and historians, it might have seemed anachronistic to treat the plane itself as a canvas, not least because this tends to challenge the ideal of an object perpetually floating above.[29]

What art *on planes* highlights instead is the object in process, the object unsettled in what it is. In this sense, the plane as canvas challenges the tendency to fixate on the plane as a stable form; rather, it is a bundle of affordances. Some nose art enthusiasts have suggested that the practice may have begun as an answer to the sculptures and paintings historically placed on the bow of boats, or the standardized markings of Roman chariots. What is known is that it was found as early as World War I and then became very common in World War II. The most well-known figure was that of pin-up girls for calendars and advertising, but nose art also featured prominent cartoon characters, graffiti, and cultural references.

Befitting nomadic decoration, nose art was officially disallowed in the service but existed for years among both airmen and airwomen. Many nose artists were sign painters, which also might explain their drawing from popular use of pinup girls in advertising of the 1940s. As Velasco writes:

> Anyone able to draw, sketch or paint was sought after to apply a design on one's aircraft. The fortunate few artists with talent were in most cases compensated for their services. There were exceptions where the artists [sic] modesty would not

prevail and would do the work for free. This also led to nose art not being signed, forever unknowingly identifying who its creator was. (2004, 20)

Taking photos of nose art was also forbidden by the military, in order to maintain secrecy about plane design, so some artists would paint in cover of night, snap photos in secret, and develop them when back home. The painter of the renowned Memphis Belle bomber, for example, popularized designs that others later imitated. The method was consistent. "The paints used. . .were usually house paint or whatever the military had lying around. He would drain off the oil that accumulated at the top and replace it with linseed oil which worked best for slowing down the drying process in the high heat" (Velasco 2004, 28). And all of this would take half a day or even longer. They were paid in cash or in trading whiskey.

No matter the focus of the art, it clearly deviates from the standardization of national roundels depicting nationality. Wood (1999) and Velasco (2004) therefore relate the rise of nose art to the shift from professional soldiers to conscripted citizens less worried about career advancement. Wood argues that generals and admirals who made rules that govern official markings on aircraft, to make them officially recognizable or camouflaged, "have never accepted the need for 'nose art.' Usually, it is merely tolerated rather than approved" (Wood 1999, 12).[30]

For Carlo, nose art was attractive as an expressive form for precisely this reason. It was a way to reveal the "voice of the civilian" otherwise lost in the regimented and hierarchical chain of command characteristic of military life. "This was a way people resisted the uniformity," he told me. Even if the icons they chose were in their own ways "hegemonic" insofar as they could reinforce masculinist, racist, or nationalist tropes, they represented some attempt to assert individuality, "to find difference within the one mass." Images of pinup models, cartoon figures, and fearsome animals are clearly part of masculine ideologies imbricated with American militarism. And yet, Carlo is not wrong. In theory at least, painting and admiring them involves skills and affects that are formally distinct from the practice of warfare. Beyond their involvement in war, Carlo claims that these iconographies were reproduced beyond airfields, in pop culture, circulating on T-shirts, comic books, and elsewhere in the interstices of consumer culture.

Eric's point of entry into the Boneyard Project had more to do with the tradition of American street art. Eric suggests that the Boneyard Project is a continuation of the many other ways that artists have engaged with forms of modern transportation, from subway and train cars to automobiles. For him, this was connected to the general sense, found both in the military and in everyday civilian life as well, "of things that were so impersonal becoming personalized in creating identity." Nose art was part of that, but in another sense "that was the antithesis of what we used for inspiration for the project." In other words, artists for the Boneyard Project were not asked to mimic or be inspired by nose art. The object, instead, was to imagine the entire plane as a canvas and not just its nose or tail. The object was to paint it entirely as one would a subway car in 1960s or '70s New York City, painting in the dark of night, worrying about Mayor Ed Koch's crackdown on "graffiti" and the police with their dogs. "It is about resistance, it's about having your voice not just heard but seen."

And yet, as Carlo argues, nose art was such a form of resistance. Like some historians of nose art, he suggests it should be considered a form of potentially radical repurposing, an act of creative destruction that playfully subverts military standardization and hierarchy. Moreover, nose cone art arguably subverts the reduction of all aircraft to nothing more than military tools, offering an alternative understory of planes as art objects. It is as if the very surface of the plane bears witness to the nonmilitaristic that subsists alongside the militaristic, the minor art of the exterior war machine captured by the state, a surface trace of that constitutive difference.

Decoration or Desecration?

Unlike the experimental first planes, mass-produced military aircraft are built to conform to a standard of reproducible sameness.[31] For plane mechanics and restorers, the singular form of a specific plane under their care is at issue. They presume a stable or consistent object at their peril. That is what makes the material engagements of a repairer or restorer emergent and open-ended and what makes any observed quality a potential affordance for reuse.

For artists, similarly, the plane's surface is an opportunity to express a singular vision. That might lead one to wonder whether this lent the Boneyard Project an air of mischief, as if they had permission to graffiti a national memorial. Carlo said that some "military buffs" viewed the Boneyard Project as a form of "desecration," a word that Eric also used. The use of a religious concept is telling. By talking about the "desecration" of military objects, they suggest that something held sacred has been violated or spoiled, thereby emphasizing how strongly some visitors feel about their transformation of military vessels. At the same time, expressions like this (or James's earlier reference to the Boneyard as a "pilgrimage site" for plane enthusiasts) could also be seen as attempts to exaggerate what the planes mean to others, and thereby highlight the gap that separates the more secular or sober values of the speaker from those of people referred to. In so doing, Eric and Carlo amplify the tension that divides their own more playful use of planes from what others expect or demand.

Using reported speech, Carlo characterized the familiar and familial tone of the typical objection: "I flew one of these planes," "My brother died in one of those planes," etc. But he is clear that this kind of response was not what any of the artists intended. None of the artists were looking to offend, make an explicit political statement, or attack military machinery per se. The only thing that they refused to do was to treat old military planes with reverence, "which," Carlo insists, "is not the same thing as irreverence," though some people do not see the difference. As James said, "There were some comments from people about disrespecting history because, you know, these are ex-military aircraft, oh, well they should be painted in tribute." Eric said that he's learned to always expect some resistance from "right-wing types" who saw the Boneyard Project as a form of "desecration." He also said that the form of street art itself might have encouraged those kinds of interpretations, but he's not sure, and some people were convinced of the value of the initiative when they saw how beautiful the planes were and how much notoriety the project received as a result. Indeed, all three men claim that such opposition was relatively minor, with the vast majority recognizing the Boneyard Project as a genuine artistic endeavor. Terry, from ARM, said that he didn't encounter any opposition, when asked. At the same time, all could not help being aware of the reverence that surrounds military artifacts in the United States, which provided the broader cultural backdrop for the work they did together. The range of reactions is evident whenever one peruses comments sections of internet stories on the Boneyard Project, for instance.

This reimagining of the plane as art object was arguably in line with Pima's demilitarizing and historicizing focus. Specifically, this fits with the overall tendency for Pima to emphasize the technological evolution of flight, rather than privilege the involvement of planes in warfare and war preparation. An object already demilitarized, or perhaps desacralized, is arguably more readily transformed into an artist's canvas. The artists invited to participate in the Boneyard Project were reportedly pleased with the relative freedom they had to achieve their visions, though many insisted on working at night, in more familiar and comfortable conditions. The planes were located in the desert, about two miles away from the Pima, and Carlo said that artists learned to go early in the morning and come back in the early evening to avoid the heat. Terry, from ARM, had thought the reason they worked in the dark had more to do with the conditions that "taggers" were more used to. As a canvas, the planes were a much different surface, much too small for normal mural work, but also with more dimension and mobile. Even so, they needed occasional help from ARM moving the craft around. ARM also sold them a refurbished flight attendant's cart that had been used in commercial flights to serve drinks for the opening. Terry says ARM made $50 and that Eric took the idea and made $5,000 apiece selling them during showings.

Carlo said that the scale of the objects presented a challenge for many of the artists, who worked in groups and approached the project with different strategies, "The scale is what people don't really get. These things are fucking huge. The canvas is huge, not Sistine Chapel scale, but huge. It took a year to paint one plane." Some did not finish to their satisfaction, because of the difficulty of the work conditions, the scope of the project, or a combination of both. Kenny Sharp and Faile planned their designs in their entirety on a computer in advance, executing, in Carlo's words, "with military precision." Bass went into neighborhood bodegas in the Tucson area to look for inspiration from the community, reclaiming the plane with alternative iconographies.

Carlo did not think the younger artists caught on as quickly as the older ones. Most of the other artists had little experience with planes. Some focused mostly on the cockpit; others painted detached nosecones for a separate exhibit. He was aware of only one artist recruited, Futura, who had a military background, serving in the Navy (1974–78), only later becoming a celebrated street artist. Futura's approach to the plane was clearly very different from the others because he used dazzle camouflage. As historically practiced within the military, dazzle camouflage decorates planes in such a way that they are rendered invisible in flight. This is decoration for the sake of better function as a tool, an art object that is more perfectly rendered the more it literally disappears as a form. There is more than a little irony in using dazzle camouflage on a plane that is immobile and, therefore, perpetually appearing as if ready to disappear.

The Boneyard Project is generally considered by those involved to have been a success. Close to two thousand people came on opening night, a massive

FIGURE 1. *Naughty Angels*, by Faile. Photo by Priscilla Bennett 2015.

FIGURE 2. *Phoenix of Metal*, by Nunca. Photo by Priscilla Bennett 2015.

crowd for Pima; people from the art world, especially from Phoenix, came for the first time to see well-known street artists from abroad. Eric and Carlo so enjoyed what came of the project, nearly a decade ago, that they have been working since 2013 to get a similar endeavor going in Washington, DC.

Terry, for his part, thought that ARM got much more attention when celebrity Robbie Maddison used its planes to do death-defying stunts on his motorcycle. Even so, the overall effect of the Boneyard Project is extraordinary, in part because, in museums and in popular media, planes often appear like an exemplary commodity: a reproducible form of a distinct prototype, replaceable with any other of its kind. Some of the museum staff with military backgrounds agree. Chuck is particularly fond of the work by Nunca, which decorated the plane as if it were a bird, with beautiful feathers. Carlo, as an art critic, relates the results of the Boneyard Project to the long tradition in Western art of depictions of flight, all of those painters who "did Icarus in some form," and argues that many of the planes were painted to make them seem things of myth, transcending their material form and former purpose. Artists, he said, are "the last alchemists on the planet. . .turning shit into gold" by taking "abject materiality and making something magic." If there is something mischievous here, therefore, he would insist it is all the more serious for it. As I explain in the final section, such creative and artistic reuse might represent the future of Pima, ARM, and the Boneyard.

EVAPORATING HISTORY

There is a way in which the very existence of the Boneyard is itself a display of American power, of arcane semiotics at play. The sheer variety and number of planes stored there are remarkable to behold and indicate the existence of a powerful agent to have made it possible.[32] At the very least, one is aware that the infrastructural base exists to design and produce all of these objects and then amass them here. Upon further inspection, one sees relatively new planes there as well, from the A-4 to the F-16, some of which foreign militaries would gladly acquire. At the Boneyard they may be repurposed as mere drones, with no other purpose than to be shot down for training exercises, as if the Air Force has such an abundance of the latest, state-of-the-art warcraft that perfectly good planes can be used for target practice. Another message this sends is that these excess planes are for the DoD to do with as it sees fit.

Let's go back to something said by Simon, the retired engineer from Lockheed Martin whom I introduced in the previous chapter:

> And you can imagine, say, the Seahawk helicopter…has certain equipment on board that is classified, not top secret, it's classified secret or other classifications—and I wrote the NSA protocol for that, so I kind of know how all that stuff is taken care of. So even if the aircraft is lost in battle, you have to dispose of the pieces, sometimes by bombing the carcass. If it goes down in Afghanistan, you bomb it in Afghanistan… Sometimes it's too hard to destroy, or sometimes it's radioactive, or sometimes it's an emitter.

The influence of state securitization on the politics of recovering disused items has generally received less attention in the literature on repair and maintenance. With exceptional objects, it may not be permissible for just anyone to remake something that has fallen into disuse and disrepair. For priceless works of art, only a select few may be seen to possess the necessary skills to actively preserve them. In other cases, for reasons personal, economic, religious, or political, it may be that disposal is meant to be a permanent state of affairs, not a temporary stage before someone else's reuse.

The reused planes I have considered in this chapter are exceptional objects, but they are not classified like components of the Seahawk helicopter. Even so, James says that the military wastes fewer planes today:

> In the '50s or '60s, an aircraft could stay in service for five or six years and then be gone, that's it. And they had spent billions of dollars and built hundreds and hundreds of them, and they'd use them for four or five years and then they'd throw them away. Now an airplane can be in service—one airframe can be in service for twenty years before it's retired. And a type can be in service for forty, fifty, or sixty years before it's retired. So to some extent they're getting better, they are getting more out of each airplane. In the '50s, the technology was changing so quickly that basically by the time an airplane came off the assembly line it was obsolete.

Planes are now kept in operation twice or three times as long, according to James and others. However, token planes are rarely given away now. In the last fifteen years, in particular, James said that they are almost always scrapped into "dime-sized bits" or dealt to foreign buyers. James explained this as a result of government paranoia about the wrong thing ending up in foreign hands. For instance, one of the local yards around the Boneyard recently closed down, in part for selling ejection seats to China that they were not supposed to.

Consequently, most of what operations like ARM have is from the 1990s. This has meant that Pima deals less with ARM than it once did, since its stock is not being replenished like before. Things are getting worse for private restorers and scrappers. Terry, the head of ARM, is convinced that the plane acquisition business will soon vanish entirely, with the government less inclined to sell to private collectors or museums. In an ironic twist, instead of making warcraft become something else, increasingly operations around the Boneyard are helping to stage imaginary and simulated scenes of violence and destruction using military waste.

Terry is a lifelong reuser of metallic objects. His first memories of planes and of metallic reuse involve his father, a marine, who would fly in for brief visits on a DC-10, bearing gifts for the children in the form of Budweiser cans turned inside out and transformed into Japanese toys. Years later, Terry would delight in seeing what else could be done by manipulating metal for entertainment. The first film ARM helped with was *Harley Davidson and the Marlboro Man* (1991), and Terry got to meet Mickey Rourke and Don Johnson. They went on to help with *Con Air* (1997) and the *Expendables* franchise, as well as a soft-porn film that was shot inside one of the planes. They also provided parts for the simulated shuttle crash in the film *Armageddon* (1998), which came from seven different planes. On occasion, film studies classes come out to see where films were shot, or ex-generals with whom Terry remains in contact will come by when they are shooting scenes for movies or commercials. ARM also provides simulation scenarios for the local police department, fire department, and bomb squad, who use old planes to stage and rehearse for various emergencies. The FAA have used them to blow up aircraft, to see what different explosives can do, which cannot be done on the actual base.

It is not only civilian organizations and industries that seek out ARM for their simulacra. Terry explained that the Air Force has not always provided realistic settings for the emergency parajumpers (PJs) to use for practice. ARM provides them with planes to simulate cutting people out of for rescue, which they normally have limited opportunities to do. Although PJs are Air Force Special Forces, according to Terry they are not always allowed to do this at the Boneyard, even though they have plenty of space and planes to spare.[33] When the Boneyard is asked to aid in activities like this, the directors routinely refer people to ARM and other private organizations. From Terry's perspective, ARM provides an essential function.

We can do a lot of things that they can't do because they're military. [Laughs] When they bring a plane over...I call it "Patton's army" because they come over with a couple...vehicles...trucks and ten or fifteen guys. Now, when we do it we send one vehicle and two people. And we can do it that way because we're not restricted.... It's a lot less expensive. Because we can have one guy that can do what ten techs do. Each tech has a certain thing that they can only do. One of our guys can do it all because we're not under their rules.

The semiotic work that Pima, ARM, and other surrounding facilities provide helps distinguish it from the official base, but also belies absolute separation between military and civilian realms. For every plane that is restored as a technological artifact or rendered into an art object, others live on assisting in or simulating scenes of emergency for service members. Some are sold back to the public sector to be used in fire-fighting operations in the West. Planes that may never fly again can still be useful. ARM now makes most of its money from the virtual potential of restored planes. Partly this is because airplane aluminum is no longer very pure, so it is not as profitable to scrap as it is to restore. When Chuck was a kid, long before the Pima hired people like him to guide visitors, the Boneyard would auction off components to the public on site. That eventually turned into an army surplus store, and now a lot of that business is conducted online through third parties. Even if things were more like they used to be, newer planes are made up primarily of new composite materials, like plastics, which cannot be scrapped and restored by junk dealers in the same way.

There are other ways in which the Boneyard as civilian simulation and as actual site are interconnected. On online forums and in person, it is common for people to point out the resemblance between the Boneyard Project and a fictional art project depicted over a decade earlier in Don DeLillo's *Underworld* (1997). None of the people involved in the actual project claim to have read the book or heard of it until it was brought to their attention by others who noticed the similarity. But the comparison is worth discussing, since it brings out how the base and surrounding operations relate and differ, foreshadowing some of the concerns of the next chapter. As John Beck puts it, "*Underworld* is a reflection on what is left after the Cold War and what is to be done with its remains" (2009, 234). When DeLillo introduces the reader to fictional artist Klara Sax, the former lover of the main character Nick, she has been undertaking an art project in the Arizona desert to paint hundreds of old B-52 bombers. Called *Long Tall Sally*, after nose art on the planes depicting a popular pinup girl, "the discarded B-52's, signify the Cold War, and the brink of the world's destruction" (Martucci 2007, 127). But there are clear differences with the Boneyard Project. *Long Tall Sally* represents a longing for the past that serves as "the engine driving the narrative backward in time, retreating from a future that seems to hold no allure" (Schaub 2011, 72).[34] Eric and Carlo do not regard what their artists produced as artifacts of melancholic nostalgia but as forms of joyful expression. Carlo said he finds nostalgia, in general, to be "toxic." James tends to agree that the art objects of the Boneyard Project evoke an alternative sensibility. One particularly flamboyantly painted plane—almost bearing a resemblance to a character from Pixar's film—is used as the banner image for the children's section of the Pima website. Chuck was also taken with the Boneyard Project and hoped to mimic its success to recruit more young people to get interested in model-building. He was hoping to use three-dimensional printers throughout the Tucson community to make planes that young people could paint however they wished, as did the street artists.

What the fictional Klara shares with Eric and Carlo is that, unlike the official Air Force, or for that matter futurists, Dadaists, and pop artists, they repurpose military planes as a canvas.[35] The similarities do not end there. For Beck, *Underworld* reimagines the museum as "the site of a defiant refusal of matter to expertise and also as evidence of the ways in which the interpretation of objects is capable of active and unexpected mutation and transvaluation" (2009, 235; see also chapter 5, this volume). According to Gleason, "For Klara and DeLillo" (and, I would add, for Eric and Carlo) "art is an assertion of freedom, a way in which humanity can reject and survive an American culture whose mass-market capitalism and weapons of mass destruction threaten individualism and human life" (2002, 140).[36] In this respect, at least, the Boneyard Project represents a radical counterpoint to either commemorations or evaporations of military waste.

Many critics have described *Long Tall Sally* as a form of recycling, when it is more accurate to say that Klara Sax, like Eric Firestone, is preventing recycling from occurring. Similarly, as Evans persuasively argues, "Klara. . .is emphatic that one of the prime motivations of her desert project is to *prevent* the recycling of the decommissioned warplanes, their disassembly and reprocessing for other purposes" (2006, 122; italics in original). One of the first things that Eric says to people who condemn the Boneyard Project is, "It's either this or they become Budweiser cans." Terry agrees (though he saw as a child the affordances offered even by beer cans). He sees the scrapping of planes as a waste of taxpayer money. What is worse, Terry and James agree that recycling these planes means losing history. Yet neither seems to believe that holding on to that history means preserving these machines exactly as they were, as if frozen in amber. Sometimes it is only by changing things that you can hold on to histories, or discover all-new ones.

CHAPTER 3

Sunk Cost

COAUTHORED WITH PRISCILLA BENNETT

The origins of America's permanent war economy can be traced at least as far back as the contentious Naval Act of 1794. This was a seminal moment in the "Barbary Wars" of the early Republic.[1] In the absence of a formal navy, American merchant vessels had been encouraged to become privateers during the Revolutionary War, which meant engaging in very lucrative piracy in the British Atlantic. After the Revolution, the Mediterranean was one of the only trade destinations available to American merchants, many of whom continued to present themselves as agents of the British Empire, usually with forged documents, to avoid paying tribute. This set the stage for public alarm in the United States when Algerian corsairs began to raid American ships and capture sailors for ransom.[2] The Act of 1794 established what would become a permanent navy for the first time for the fledgling government, including six warships and provisions for sailors, all to protect American commercial interests in the Mediterranean.

Three elements of this historical episode are worth noting for the purposes of this book and this chapter. First, there was considerable disagreement about this decision between Federalists, who wanted to protect commerce, and Republicans, who worried that a navy would be expensive and antagonize Europeans, especially the British.[3] In other words, spending on war preparation has been contentious from the nation's very beginning. In response, the corsair fleet was misrepresented as enormous and invincible by some American elites, thereby justifying the need for a navy. This is reminiscent of the fraudulent claim that there was a "bomber gap" between American and Soviet forces a century and a half later, which was used to justify investment in missiles and long-distance aerial bombardment. Finally, one clause of the Act called for the cessation of the navy's construction if Algiers and the US agreed to peace. But by the time this had happened, two years later, the French Revolution and subsequent wars further complicated maritime trade with European partners and was used by Federalists to justify completing the navy anyhow. Once people invest in war preparation, it seems to take on a momentum all its own.

The US Navy eventually became one of the most powerful in the world, helping establish colonies and favorable trade relations in the Caribbean, South America, the Pacific, Southeast Asia and East Asia during the nineteenth century. Eventually, this global reach would provide infrastructure for the hundreds of bases the US has overseas today. Supplied, defended, and maintained by means of ships, these bases have created an empire that has supplanted, and in some ways exceeded, those that came before.[4]

According to the CIA, the US Navy alone has 430 ships in service and on reserve. This presents problems that the airborne fleet does not. Ships are typically much bigger than planes and cannot be as easily disassembled and reassembled for convenient transportation. Ships must be docked somewhere, and historically, docks have been places of commercial activity. When they begin to wear, American ships become the responsibility of the Maritime Administration (MARAD). Since 1949, MARAD has decided whether to scrap, sink, or "mothball" old ships as part of the Naval Defense Reserve Fleet (NDRF). This Ghost Fleet, as it is known, consists of the Ready Reserve Force and the Non-Ready Reserve Force. The latter ships do not meet standards for readiness and are docked in three sites to await disposal: the James River in Virginia, Beaumont in Texas, and Suisun Bay in California. NDRF ships awaiting disposal can generate tension between military and civilian interests that planes stored in the middle of the desert do not. Between 2000 and 2003, at least nine spills resulted from the Ghost Fleet docked on the James River, the worst of which came from the USS Donner, which released one thousand gallons of oil in August of 2000 alone (Puthucherril 2010, 48). Suisun Bay became especially controversial over the last decade, when environmental activists produced evidence that the reserve fleet was leaking toxic pollutants into the bay, not far from where civilians lived and worked. After a protracted legal battle, the US government decided to remove and scrap the remaining ships, a process that was still ongoing as of the writing of this book.

Mothballed vessels are ships set aside, disused in reserve; like other forms of military waste, they can be reimagined in many ways. In this chapter, I focus on just one reused warcraft from the Ghost Fleet: the USNS *Vandenberg*, an eleven-thousand-ton transport ship that served in the Navy and Air Force off and on from 1963 to 1984. After it left the service, the ship was still used for various films, including the movie *Virus* (1999), starring Jamie Lee Curtis. After being mothballed, the *Vandenberg* was eventually scuttled off the coast of Key West, Florida, in 2009 to create an artificial coral reef. As with planes from the Boneyard, this ship has been made to matter in various ways by various actors, but its practical transformation is also a way of reimagining how US military products *ought to be used*.

Maritime history is as much about the threat of wreckage as the promise of voyage. In the eighteenth and nineteenth centuries, well before the invention of the submarine, loss of life at sea was at least as common as fatal car accidents are today.[5] As such, the shipwreck "represented a rupture in...networks of trade, knowledge, fantasy, and power. It not only threatened and disrupted the smooth working of the infrastructures which underwrote western culture but also exposed the more disturbing aspects of modernity and its hidden costs and consequences" (Thompson 2014, 17). Due to the commercial attractiveness of shipwrecks, heavily trafficked waterways have historically offered opportunities, not only for piracy, but for all manner of human and nonhuman scavenging. As massive cities sprang up during the Industrial Revolution, extensive networks of rivers and sewers attracted informal salvagers of various kinds who would skim and dive for lost or discarded valuables.[6] Shipwrecks may not be as common as they once were, but sunken ships remain a source of interest and intrigue. Divers still come from all over to seek hidden treasures off the coast of Florida.

On August 19, 2017, news circulated that wreckage of the USS *Indianapolis* had been recovered by a team funded by Microsoft cofounder and billionaire Paul Allen. At midday Allen tweeted, with accompanying pictures, "We've located wreckage of USS Indianapolis in Philippine Sea at 5500m below the sea." Within hours there were thousands of retweets and likes. Shipwrecks can be considered a form of watery ruin. As Tim Edensor writes, ruins "motivate us to celebrate the mysteries, heterogeneous sensations, and surprising associations of the past in the present and encourage a wanton speculation towards objects and places" (2005, 845). Some historic shipwrecks remain a source of public fascination decades later, including the *Indianapolis*, *Titanic*, and *Queen Anne's Revenge* (the ship of the infamous English pirate Blackbeard).

Ruins are not only sites that possess symbolic value, however, but ones that generate open-ended possibilities. Compared to the repair-scape of the Boneyard area, discussed in the previous chapter, the sunken ships around the Florida Keys are better thought of as a *ruin-scape*. Following Edensor, Marta Jecu (2015, 64) describes ruin-scapes as places where remembering and forgetting are ordered and not only through human intervention. Based on her autoethnography of divers who explore underwater shipwrecks, Stephanie Merchant directly compares shipwrecks with ruins: "Objects and beings found at wrecks are so situationally transgressive that their competing material signification (in the form of decay, biological takeover and their potential to evoke intertextual memories) has a noteworthy influence on the embodied practices and performances being played out by those who visit the site" (2014, 119). From this perspective, carefully ordered places might contain abundant waste and yet not be haunted in the same way as neglected ruins. However, it would be wrong to oppose repair-scapes and ruin-scapes as if they were absolutely distinct. Irreparable wrecks can be similarly productive as sites of repurposing, and ruins can be highly ordered in their own way. This is one of the primary insights in Anna Tsing's (2015) wide-ranging account of mushrooms pickers and mycologists, who typically find opportunities to gather in landscapes that have been laid to ruin by capitalist accumulation. I argue that ruin-scapes are not simply places in decline, but places of imaginative possibility, what Tsing characterizes as mutual projects of world-making.[7]

One of the most celebrated American war ruins is the USS *Arizona*, a battleship that sank during the surprise Japanese attack on Pearl Harbor in 1941. The remains of the ship were only partially salvaged, and the bulk of it was left in the water along the Honolulu coast. A museum was built over the top of the wreckage to commemorate the American lives lost, and it remains one of the most popular memorials of the attack. The *Arizona* is meant to demonstrate the misfortune that befalls a nation unprepared for war and, to the extent that the wreck inspires people to fixate upon this possibility, the fallen ship justifies a nation permanently prepared for war (Delgado 1992, 77). In popular American narratives, the military attack on Pearl Harbor and the terrorist attacks of September 11th share this semiotic duality: they stand for the risks of being unprepared for enemy attack, and both arguably promote military buildup during peacetime as a solution.

But even the most celebrated of military ruins are capable of generating other sociomaterial effects and affects that threaten to disturb politically dom-

inant stories. The dust that was released when the World Trade Center col-
lapsed was also a source of harmful pollution that begat successful social activism, though success was only realized through a bitterly contested struggle
(Lioy 2009). Similarly, the USS *Arizona* is not only one of the most high-
profile military wrecks in the world; it is also slowly leaking oil into Hawaii's
marine environment, which has not diminished its allure as a war monument.
Given that Ground Zero and the USS *Arizona* are lasting memorials to the
most famous attacks in American history, it can be difficult to reimagine them
as pollutants.

Like the USS *Arizona*, disused military objects are not stable, but leak and
crumble as they age, which may create new concerns that exceed familiar
nationalist memorials and narratives. Unlike the *Arizona*, ordinary military
wastes can be interpreted and reused in a wider variety of ways. As potential
affordances and risks, they generate more debate regarding the future of a
decaying military apparatus and the possible worlds that emerge in its wake.

KEY WRECKS

Key West residents—or "Conchs," as they are known—live much of their lives
in, on, and under the water.[8] This has been true at least since the first indigenous groups began island-hopping across the Caribbean, followed centuries
later by Europeans who found the Straits of Florida a convenient way to
return with what they had taken from the West Indies. If it is the water that
brings many people to Florida, it was the ruins of war machines that initially
put the state on the map. It was Florida's coral reefs, and more specifically the
shipwrecks they caused, that made Key West Florida's largest city as late as
1876, the nation's first centennial.[9]

Only miles from the shores of Key West, the Florida reef is the only living
coral barrier reef in the United States, measuring nearly 360 miles in length.
Blackbeard and other infamous pirates used the Keys as a base of operations,
which initially attracted the relatively new American Navy (ostensibly created
to combat piracy in the Mediterranean) to occupy Key West. Once Caribbean
pirates were rooted out, Conchs continued to exploit the many shipwrecks
that littered the ruin-scape, many from the Spanish fleet. Before lighthouses
were built in the early nineteenth century, shipwrecks were very common and
the primary source of revenue. The salvage economy was so important that,
two decades before Florida was even a state, the United States required that all

wreckage be brought to the US mainland, rather than Spanish territories, before it could be sold off. Even once lighthouses were created (which, some claim, Conchs resisted), inexperienced sailors would still routinely wreck their ships around the Keys. The Spanish consul complained of "substantial" losses of materials and men as late as the 1850s.[10]

Still today, stories of treasure-hunters, pirates, and famous wrecks continue to circulate among members of the diving community. Many Conchs seem aware that their city's history has its origins in maritime predation and celebrate this fact. In the spring of 2017, coauthor Priscilla Bennett went to a local dive bar in Key West and was surprised that the theme of Trivia Night was wrecks: "They asked questions ranging from the name of the John Wayne movie about wrecking (*Reap the Wild Wind*), the technological advancement that ended the wrecking era (the lighthouse), to important wrecking figures like John Geiger, among several others."

In 1977, Florida archaeologists discovered eight wrecks from the 1733 *Fleet*, one of many ill-fated convoys to Spain (Smith 1988, 96–103), and within a decade, the most valuable shipwreck ever found was discovered. Based on the historical research of Eugene Lyon, twenty-five miles west of Key West salvagers found remains of the *Nuestra Señora de Atocha*—a long-sought-after Spanish galleon—350 years after it sank along with its abundant treasure (Smith 1988, 92–94). For Conchs, the *Atocha* was not just a sunken and valuable piece of history; it was personified in the legend of Mel Fisher, the treasure hunter who discovered it, originally a chicken farmer from the Midwest. Mel and his wife started the first scuba diving shop in the world when they moved to Key West and then spent nearly thirty years looking for the *Atocha*. After the famous discovery, Key West became a prime tourist destination. But for years, some say, the recovered coins and bars from the *Atocha* continued to circulate alongside tourist dollars as an alternative currency.[11] According to Joe Weatherby, who will be introduced shortly, Mel was known to walk around Key West carrying millions in gold and silver in his pockets, wearing a crown, buying people rum and cokes and taking pictures. He died in 1998, but the Maritime Heritage Museum in Key West bears his name.

The same year that the 1733 *Fleet* was found, Jimmy Buffet's breakthrough hit "Margaritaville" described tourists descending on Key West in waves. With a growing population and tourist industry, naturally existing coral reefs began to suffer, as did biodiversity in the Keys in general. In the 1960s and '70s, Conchs were encouraged by the municipal government to dump trash in the water, especially tires, in order to generate artificial reefs to supplement those in decline. This proved unsuccessful and is remembered by many locals as a foolish mistake. Among other things, tires are unstable and roll around the ocean floor, disturbing and killing coral in the process. Artificial reefing clearly had an inauspicious beginning. So, despite the history of wrecks of the Spanish Empire and their importance to Key West, the idea of sinking war vessels to restore the coral coastline was not automatically appealing. It would take some convincing.

Joe Weatherby is exactly the sort of person whom you can imagine sinking an old naval ship off the coast of the Florida Keys. Charismatic and passionate, he claims to have "drunk the Kool-Aid" concerning artificial reefing. Joe won't take full responsibility for getting the *Vandenberg* "on the bottom." That took a lot of people, resources, technical expertise, and support, including a network of friends and specialists he refers to as "real committed zealots." But it is Joe who has become the prominent voice of artificial reefing and sinking the *Vandenberg* in the area. Joe was part of a company called Reefmakers leading up to the deployment of the *Vandenberg*. More recently, he has branched off on his own. Artificial Reefs International, his new company, has since helped turn the USS *Mohawk* and the HMCS *Annapolis*, American and Canadian military vessels respectively, into artificial reefs.

Joe does not refer to himself as a Conch, because he was not born there. Joe came to the Keys on spring break from New Jersey and then stayed, "Once you get the sand in your shoes, it's very difficult to get it out." He clearly loves the city and knows a great deal about it, from local history and nightlife to the success of the high school baseball team (also known as "the Conchs"). But his love of diving was the primary reason he resettled: "The diving thing. . . I mean, from the minute I started, it was over. It was very clear to me that I wanted to do this for the rest of my life, to be involved with this. . . And so there was a bit of an epiphany to it." When Joe's mother passed away and left him some money a few years ago, he chose to buy a house, knowing the alternative would be that he would probably spend it all on diving. Eventually, Joe transitioned from diving as a passionate hobby to working in the diving business and arranging tours of old wrecks.[12] The 1733 *Fleet* and *Atocha* were found just as Joe came to settle in Key West, and the possibility of discovering old wrecks had reenlivened the century-old art of salvaging in the Florida Keys. His biggest early success came from a ship he found in secret: "We found a big old ship out there one day. It was an artificial reef and we kept it secret for a while." Joe had a small dive business with a few boats and a shop and "made a lot of money" by enticing divers to come with them to see the secret, undiscovered wreck. It did not last long after the town government and other businesses caught wind of the operation. After losing exclusive access to what he'd found, Joe moved away for a time. When he returned to Key West, he would learn to work with the city and make projects as public as possible. He would also focus only on making wrecks, not stumbling across them.

By 1990, the Florida Keys National Marine Sanctuary was established, in large part to protect the fragile coral reef. Joe first got involved in artificial reefing in the 1980s, joining a development project that surrounded a large shipwreck. Joe took responsibility for the Lower Keys, working on the Adolphus Busch, a cargo ship, and the Ocean Freeze, a refrigerated freighter, both deployed as artificial reefs in 1998; as well as the Spiegel Grove, a Navy vessel deployed in 2002. The last ship was to be the *Vandenberg*: "I took it on, some of the other business opportunities fell away and I was left with this determination that we were gonna sink this ship." Drawing on his varied experiences on and under the water as well as contacts he had accumulated, Joe was actively involved in raising money, recruiting volunteers, working with the media, and with politicians in Tallahassee and Capitol Hill. Overall, turning the *Vandenberg* into a reef was a thirteen-year, $8.5 million project. The sinking of the *Vandenberg* finally took place in May of 2009 (coincidentally, the same year the Navy began to close the mothballed reserve fleet in Suison Bay).

The Secret Squirrels

Repurposing ships as reefs is very different from restoring them in a museum display. Ships sunk to the bottom of the ocean are not meant to much resemble what they looked like in the service. If this process of transformation begins with planning and fund-raising, it does not end once the ship is deployed. It may become an ecological resource on its own, but to be a profitable and usable asset, drawing upon but exceeding the former military value of the ship, takes additional work. For Joe, this meant thinking through the *Vandenberg*'s relationship to military history and fostering new relationships with veterans and military organizations in the present. Joe and his team, in effect, had to rehistoricize the *Vandenberg* to promote the significance of the reef. "There was no story. We did that story: it was rotting in the river and no one gave a crap."

To assist him, Joe enlisted the support of a group of friends and specialists he refers to as the "Secret Squirrels." Explaining the origin of this name, he

said, "We blow a whistle only squirrels can hear. . . If they can, they show up."
With the support of the Secret Squirrels, a group of divers celebrate Memorial
Day every year by raising an underwater flag on the *Vandenberg*'s mast, mostly
with veterans. On another occasion, they received press for hoisting the largest
American flag on the *Vandenberg* to commemorate 9/11. In 2014, the Secret
Squirrels helped host an underwater race to raise money and publicity for the
Wounded Warriors project—a charity dedicated to wounded veterans. Much
like ARM, discussed in the last chapter, Joe's group also facilitated the use of
the *Vandenberg* by the Navy's Military Sealift Command—responsible for the
DoD's transportation needs—so that they could run simulated exercises. Fifteen or twenty years ago he met the head of Navy diving and salvaging operations, based in Panama City, where the Navy trains its divers. They shared
beers and drank with Joe's crew and, several years later, that man became head
of Sealift Command. "I feel like I helped the Navy," Joe says, "because they're
doing tasks on deep shipwrecks. . . Then they come in to Key West and go to
the Green Parrot every night, and my buddy owns the Parrot!" What the
Vandenberg affords the Navy is a useful place to conduct simulated exercises in
close proximity to the fun and relaxation for which Key West is celebrated.

At times Joe sounds like an environmentalist, at other times a venture capitalist, but he is engaged in reimagining warcraft in both senses, as once remar-
ketized and renaturalized. And this is made possible, he says, due to the allure
of shipwrecks in general and military wrecks in particular. "There's an aesthetic
piece. . .especially with ships. Only because ships have been part of the underwater landscape since the time of. . .right up to the hunter-gatherers, it goes
back to the dawn of civilized man, really, the dawn of trade and exploration."
Echoing Lockheed Martin employees from the first chapter and museum
curators from the second, Joe says that military ships are especially preferable
because they are better made and last much longer than merchant ships. This
is not simply about what military ships mean to people, but the way Joe
describes it, that romance is a product of the material durability of the vessels,
what they were made of and what they were made to do. They last, and this is
also what makes them better for coral reefs than shopping carts or tires:

> The military ships were often, not always, the ones that made history, because they
> were better made, better financed and better crewed, which I think is often the case
> now. A merchant ship, when it's done, it's done. What happens with the military
> ships is they are often obsolete with the systems on board than they are worn out
> physically. A merchant ship, she's ready to sink.

Some of the ships have two generations of the same family that have served on them who want to dive and see it. But Joe says that most Americans have "a feeling" for American military ships, and it is hard not to agree: "These are the ways that America defends our coast; these are the ways to project American power overseas."

David U. is an underwater filmmaker who has worked with Joe on the *Vandenberg* and *Mohawk* projects. Younger than Joe, David U. comes from a military family and served first in the Army, then in the Navy as an engineer on a nuclear submarine during the first Gulf War. But he was interested in ships for aesthetic reasons before he joined the service. He remembers as a child sketching sailing ships that he saw in the Gulf of Mexico, pictures that still hang on the wall of his parents' house. David U. liked how informal working on nuclear propulsion was in the Navy, how he didn't have to shave and barely saluted officers. People had volunteered to work there and it was like working on a spaceship, he said, where they were responsible for generating their own water and air. He also saw signs of obsolescence. His sub was built before he was born. He recalled the teenagers and twenty-somethings on board worrying about working with components far older than themselves. After he retired, the sub was recycled, while the nuclear core was buried in Arizona. It didn't matter that it cost a billion dollars to make and that it cost another million just to train individuals like him to work on it. Once patrols cease, the ship vanishes. According to David U., ships like the *Vandenberg* are described as being on *eternal patrol*: "it's kind of symbolic," he said, "you'll never get scrapped, you'll never die." David U. likes the idea of turning military ships or oil derricks into artificial reefs, which he has now worked on filming for almost a decade. He likens it to washing and reusing Ziploc bags, a practice his coworker and wife got him into.

The *Vandenberg* is not an official veterans' memorial, but David U. heard that some veterans managed to attach personal items of theirs to the ship before it was sunk, creating an enduring connection that meant something to them. Joe and his team interviewed veterans and made them part of the project, including his partner's grandfather. But the veterans also took some convincing. Joe described one representative encounter with a group of veteran sailors:

> Well, it starts out like this: "Well, we can't save the ship as a museum. Well, I guess we're gonna have to scrap it."
>
> "Hi, I'm Joe Weatherby, I'm going to sink it."

"Wait a minute, you're going to sink my ship? No way!" You know, *Vandenberg* was like this: "No way, not on my watch! We're sailors, we don't let ships sink!"

I said, "I tell you what," to the World War II vets, "here's the choice: we can either turn the ship into a world-class educational and environmental research asset and *the* best fishing and diving destination in the world, or we can tow it to Asia and cut it up like her sister ship and they can make Toyotas out of it."

These guys fought the Japanese. They say, "Sink that son of a bitch!" and they give me a \$135... That's what happened at one of the things. It's an eight-and-a-half-million-dollar project, I got all these ninety-year-old guys with cigars looking at me like, "You're taking the money!"

This change in narrative was used in order to preserve the *Vandenberg*, not through museum display but through sinking. At that moment, Joe was not trying to get money, but to convince people to accept the project and not change the public narrative he had worked so hard to construct. To counter their concerns, he reached across space and time, referring to the ship's global past and future and to racialized divides between self and other, ally and enemy. With their help, they crafted a story that reimagined the *Vandenberg* into something to honor as "a frontline Cold Warrior."

Translating the military significance of an artificial reef is also accomplished by instructors and dive guides who bring people to see sunken vessels. This was made clear by another diver who has explored the *Vandenberg*, Lisa. Lisa has a more complicated relationship with the military then does David U. She grew up in Florida diving with her family and then tried to be a diver in the Navy, in 1978, but was told women were not allowed to dive. She ended up taking scuba lessons separately to become an instructor. The class was taught by former Navy Seals, and Lisa was the only woman in a class of twenty, which she says was largely representative of the gender demographics of diving at the time, though not anymore. All the skills are gender-neutral, she says, especially with the user-friendly equipment now available and the practices of use that exist outside of the military. She moved to the Keys for the water clarity and warmth. There are also more artificial reefs for divers, whereas those in the Gulf are primarily for fishing. As an instructor who takes people to see many reefs, Lisa knows to emphasize the uniqueness of a wreck before the divers get off the boat so they know what to look for and how to interpret what they find. Not all divers need such instruction. Lisa has also worked with "military people and their families" who want to see the ships. But anyone who dives on sunken military ships gets the experience of its being "memorialized," she says.

While there is a romance to shipwrecks in general, Joe says that military ships are especially preferable because they are better made and last much longer than merchant ships (echoing statements from Lockheed Martin employees from the first chapter and museum curators from the second). But Joe does not design weapons, and he does not curate or decorate artifacts. He is primarily a storyteller and quite a successful one, likely due in part to the media experience he received working for the BBC in Japan for a few years. Whether he is appealing to veterans, to divers, to politicians or ecologists, Joe's goal is to mobilize support to transform military waste in a way that he argues is both novel and vital. Depending on his audience, the goals of artificial reefing shift. But, he might argue, that is precisely why it is so worthwhile: if one can choose the afterlife of an object of American naval power, why not have it salvage the economy of the Key, salvage "Mother Nature's" flawed and fragile coral ecosystem? Why not give divers a new and interesting location to dive, veterans a new and interesting place to preserve the memory of their service? But these various appeals have also led to conflicts, not only with Conchs, but with people who have other designs on the future of retired war vessels.

VANDENBERG VALUES

The military story of the *Vandenberg* has been "married," in Joe's words, to a wider environmental one about the declining oceans. This is more than aesthetic or symbolic demilitarization, in other words, but a reworlding or world-making—terms used by Mei Zhan (2009, 2011) and Anna Tsing (2015), respectively, to refer to processes of practical action that transform and connect humans and nonhumans, as well as people and places, in open-ended ways. By giving the Vandenberg over to an emergent organism—the coral reef—the ship is transformed into a dwelling for overlapping and intersecting forms of nonhuman life.[13] Recognizing nonhuman relationships and projects coexisting with human designs means acknowledging that the transformation of one ship in the Florida Keys can reverberate across the ocean in unexpected ways. However, reworlding a sunken ship in this way, as an ecological resource, also invites unwanted comparison with other global projects and planetary causes.

Habitat, not Trash

The ecological story of the *Vandenberg* is a more challenging one to tell due to the historical relationship between artificial reefing and the US military. During the Reagan administration, the American fleet was expanded to some six hundred vessels. At the conclusion of the Cold War, this fleet suddenly seemed unnecessary, and Congress passed a new act requiring that MARAD speed up the process of scrapping the "non-ready" ships of the Ghost Fleet. In the two decades since, the number of ships was reduced by over 25 percent.

Since the 1980s, the primary means of doing so was to export ships to be broken up abroad, usually where it could be done cheaply.[14] However, after the Cold War there were also growing concerns around the world about wealthy countries exporting hazardous waste to poorer places and people. Just a few years later, the 1999 deadline Congress gave to MARAD had to be extended to 2006, when it became difficult to continue exporting NDRF ships abroad. Concern about toxic exports became formalized with the Basel Convention agreements of the early to mid-'90s, which forbade the transfer of hazardous waste from OECD to non-OECD countries.[15]

What Basel does not do is prevent OECD countries from exporting hazardous materials to one another. So, responding to the growing global discourse around ship-breaking, the EPA and MARAD tried to export thirteen ships from the James River to Teesside in the United Kingdom. This also failed after successful opposition from the Sierra Club and another NGO representing the Basel Convention, known as the Basel Action Network (BAN). After Basel, BAN's efforts have tried to identify "greenwashed" businesses that disguise polluting practices as recycling, among them ship-breaking and ship disposal at sea. It was on this basis that they accused MARAD and EPA of environmental wrongdoing. However, as documented elsewhere (Alexander and Reno 2012), global markets in recycling are tenacious. According to environmental scholar Tony George Puthucherril (2010, 50), the primary result of the struggle between US government agencies and environmental NGOs was to create a robust domestic ship-dismantling operation, primarily centered near Brownsville, Texas.

But there was yet another loophole that MARAD could use to avoid violating Basel and other environmental regulations. Since the Liberty Ship Act was passed in 1974, the government has donated NDRF vessels for use in the creation of artificial reefs. The SINKEX program sank naval ships off the East and West coasts for years. It was only in the twenty-first century that artificial reefing became a civilian enterprise. The SINKEX program represents an unwanted comparison to the efforts of Joe Weatherby. As a result of this government program, BAN released a 2011 report titled "Dishonorable

Disposal." The primary target for the 2011 report was the SINKEX program of the US Navy, which has used old ships for target practice for many years, causing hundreds to leak toxic materials at the bottom of the ocean. The same year that the report was published, BAN joined the Sierra Club in a lawsuit against the EPA, in an effort to force the agency to forbid the practice, but dropped the suit in 2013 due to lack of funds. The US government has repeatedly claimed that the Navy satisfies regulatory requirements but that it is also exempt from national and international environmental regulations regardless. By association, Joe's activities have come under fire from BAN and other groups.

For decades the *Vandenberg* was docked on the James River and, like its fellow reservists in Suisun Bay, it was slowly falling apart. For this reason, BAN is not alone in representing the ship as a potential pollutant, or mere "trash." This tendency to label the ship "trash" frustrates Joe, since it suggests that people do not understand the real value of what he, the city, and his associates have accomplished. For artificial reefing to gain wider acceptance, people like Joe need to clarify what makes it different from mere dumping. Joe partly does this through language. He uses the verbs *clean* and *deploy* (not *dump* or *sink*) to describe what they do to make reefs:

> I see very clearly the benefits of properly cleaned and deployed artificial reefs. Not as a panacea for the problems in the ocean, but more like selective augmenting of what's going on. I don't agree with trashing the ocean. We're focused on certain kinds of artificial reefs. . . We really like ex-military ships, because of the history and because of the love of people who served on them. . . I'm not a guy who wants to ring the coastline with old ships, or, "Well, what should we do with these old cars? Let's put them in the ocean."

"Deploying" the *Vandenberg*, according to Joe, meant stripping it of toxic components and carefully placing explosives so that it would sink in the right way and end up resting in a stable position on the ocean floor. This careful use of language to avoid misconceptions is common for industries that specialize in reusing, recycling, and disposing of materials in Euro-America and beyond. One such misconception is the idea that what they do is necessarily dirty and polluting. To counter this, Joe presents a narrative about growing environmental awareness. "We know a lot now we didn't know then. Back in the day I used to shoot a lot of Goliath Grouper" (a fish native to the Keys that is now listed as critically endangered). Making a suggestive analogy, Joe compares his new understanding of which species of fish need protecting with his improved technique for artificial reefing. This comparison is a suggestive one, since thoughtful reefing is precisely meant to help fish to thrive.

Sinking the *Vandenberg* cannot preserve the ship as it once was, but only display its slow decay and regrowth into a habitat. As one coral reef expert explained to me, "As a reef, metal ships will probably not last longer than a hundred, two hundred years… If you look at World War II in the South Pacific where a lot of metal materials were put in shallow, high temperature tropical areas and it's sometimes hard to pick out what those structures were." Eventually there will be no recognizable ship to hoist flags onto. Taking a ship out of its normal context of use, below the surface of the water, also means giving it over to nonhuman beings and forces. Joe recognizes this, using it to counter the argument that they are merely putting trash into the ocean: "What we're doing is providing substrate for animals to grow and live in." There is no question in Joe's mind that the Vandenberg was not only a success, but a turning point for artificial reefing in general, a clear windfall for the community and for the restoration of the coral reef:

> This reef bottom is far more productive, economically and biologically, than the natural reef. I'm not downing the natural reef. I'm not against that in any form. But I think that, you know, a million years ago when Mother Nature decided to put a reef somewhere, she picked the perfect spot as she always has. But in the last fifty years with a bazillion people moving down here, you know, and all the attendant activity, whether it's snorkeling, fishing, or your car leaking oil and it running through the storm drains, all these things have impact. And the perfect place for a reef… I mean the coral still grows on the artificial reefs: *Vandenberg* has eleven kinds of coral and three different kinds of endangered coral, threatened corals.

Because the *Vandenberg* is 150 feet deep, larger fish can be found where the ship was deployed. For Joe, "Mother Nature" provides a model for reef construction.

If the US government is willing to turn a blind eye to the environmental consequences of SINKEX and other military ventures, this is partly because the world-making project it is involved in is seen as too important to be imperiled by environmental regulations. Joe counters these claims by emphasizing how clean and careful his company's deployment of artificial reefs is by comparison. He also accuses BAN of being "wolves in NGOs' clothing" who work on behalf of the scrapping industry. In addition to contesting Joe's environmental claims, BAN alleges that it would be more cost-effective to scrap the ships domestically rather than let them go to waste on the ocean floor. Both claims frustrate Joe. To date there is no evidence that the *Vandenberg* is a source of pollution, though this is admittedly a hard thing to definitively prove or disprove.

Asset, not Commodity

The military origins of the *Vandenberg*, Joe argues, are also worth considering when making decisions about its fate. It has been estimated that a billion dollars of taxpayer money has gone into building, refurbishing, and maintaining the *Vandenberg* during its life. "Recycling the steel" not only eliminates the historical artifact, Joe claims, but also does nothing to address the surplus value of the ship, which can never be recovered, only made more meaningful in new ways. In effect, disposal and scrapping of ships is part of a broader story of decline, where once-great vessels have outlasted any value and are only worthwhile as raw material. Joe's alternative story is not purely a triumphalist one; rather, like Tsing's mushroom pickers, he is engaged in reworlding ships through dynamic and interdependent interactions with nonhuman species.

Joe points out that there is nothing new about artificial reefing to promote fishing or as part of military strategy. But there are many ways of creating reefs:

> You can say, "You're dumping your trash in my ocean." But. . .the UN will tell you, depending on whose figures you believe, there's anywhere between three and five million ships on the bottom of the ocean. Not even a measurable number of one percent of those were cleaned. . . Some were spontaneously deployed by leaky bottoms or wartime or hurricanes or some type of catastrophe. But ships purposefully cleaned and deployed as artificial reefs. . .are the most biologically productive parts of the ocean bottom.

Familiarity with the millennia-old practice can lead to another common misconception—that it is relatively simple. If you do not put time and effort into preparing the vessel for deployment, "you're going to end up with a bathtub that breaks up the first time the wind blows." The alternative to these simplifications is to see the *Vandenberg* in terms of long-term economic development. Artificial reefs are very good at aggregating fish for killing, Joe says, but they also become hatcheries. Joe references the famous *Atocha* wreck, which even after the salvaging of a billion dollars' worth of silver and gold and other artifacts still remains a great place to find fish, "but for artificial reefing we're typically not putting down ships for short-term concentration of fish." Joe tends to compare ecological and economic productivity, for instance the economic transformation of Atlantic City that shaped his childhood home and the long-term impact of artificial reefing that has defined the last several decades of his life in Key West.

Thought of in these terms, the *Vandenberg* is an investment that compares favorably to similar city projects, like parking garages and sports stadiums, which are expensive to build, maintain, and insure. In keeping with recent literature on capitalism and the environment, it might seem tempting to describe the *Vandenberg*–coral fish hatchery relationship as a process of commodification or as a form of biocapital (see Helmreich 2008). These ideas have been used in particular to think through emergent economic and environment assemblages in recent decades, but they also run the risk of fetishizing novelty and misrecognizing the origins of value as arising from the environment itself (as Joe, on occasion implies).[16] I will instead describe the *Vandenberg* as a product of familiar social relations of assetification and rentiership.

First, strictly speaking, whether ships are left on reserve, sunk by the Navy, or turned into an artificial reef by Joe, they are not *commodities* because they are not exchangeable in a market of other commodities. They are better thought of as assets, which means property that could be worth something irrespective of being compared with something else. Assets can be anything that does not fit the definition of a normally circulating commodity that is bought and sold. The *Vandenberg*, whether sunk or not, is primarily valued for what it might earn without changing hands, something enjoyed by a diver, something photographed or filmed by artists. Only when it is scrapped for raw material does the ship become converted into something that can be easily quantified and compared with others of its kind, that is, the commodity of scrap metal.

Though the *Vandenberg* is an asset, it is not one that Joe and the Secret Squirrels exclusively own, though they were entrusted with shaping the wreck's value through deployment. Put differently, their efforts making and caring for the wreck could be understood as social practices of rentiership. The common Marxian insight is that rents are not accrued in the same way as capital. They depend on social practices to transform "land"—meaning any socially constructed asset, material or immaterial—into something legally owned by some rather than others, for which landowners are paid some fraction of the surplus value arising from the production process.[17] Ruins are not normally discussed in relation to rents, but a theory of rentiership can help elucidate how ruins become sites of value transfer and recovery. This can explain, further, why an entrepreneur might think to create a ruin in the first place.

"Thinking it through," for Joe, means not sinking a ship at the lowest possible cost and therefore treating it like mere waste, but taking it seriously as an environmental and economic asset. "Thinking it through" means finding the exact right location. The right location ensures the ship will stay stable and not move and disturb the coral; it has the right currents, is navigable, and can be accessed for diving and fishing, because it is relatively close to shore. In the beginning, he and his team had presented the *Vandenberg* as a way of taking pressure off of the natural reef, drawing more divers away from it and aiding in conservation. Their initial models counted on ten thousand divers the first year, but thirty-four showed up instead. Joe argues that the *Vandenberg* is the equivalent of an underwater park, increasing the economic revenue of the whole Keys by 10 to 15 percent. His numbers are derived from overall impact on tourism, or "heads and beds." According to Joe:

> In the Keys you would see that 71 percent of the people who come here interact with the water. Seventy percent of all the revenue that comes off the water comes from natural reefs, and 30 percent comes from artificial reefs. But when you measure that by a thousandth of one percent of the available bottom, you can see that this reef bottom is far more productive, economically and biologically, than the natural reef.

Assessing its impact on tourism, a sunken vessel becomes part of the surplus value of the land around it to the benefit of rentiers. Thinking in terms of rent can untangle the many kinds of ownership at issue in military vessels, particularly ships. An old ship on reserve belongs, in a sense, to the sailors who once dwelled aboard it, as well as the commanders they obeyed, the nation they served, and ultimately the people they swore to defend and whose taxes financed their activities. As such, each of these actors and entities are evoked when an old ship is broken down and scrapped or deliberately sunk. A theory of rentiership encourages us to ask who benefits from this transfer in ownership and to whom value accrues as part of the ongoing productivity of ruins.

Joe's group had to purchase the *Vandenberg* in order to take possession of it. But early on this relationship of ownership was complicated by the process of prepping it for deployment. As it was being cleaned by another company, copper was stripped from the ship for sale, the assumption being that this would go toward the cost of the process. In other words, the *Vandenberg* was an asset in two senses: it could be mined as an asset for useful commodities as it was being converted into a sinkable asset for divers and fishers. Some of the materials salvaged were stolen, however, and never officially recorded. As a result, the company said they would not release the asset from dockage since they had not profited as anticipated. This held up the transfer of the ship back to Joe for another year. As Joe puts it, "There was some odd politics at the end because we came up short. We dealt with some unscrupulous people and I had some things to learn. My education ended up costing the taxpayer some money." This is one of the reasons that the cost of deploying the *Vandenberg* doubled from the original estimate.

What distinguishes people who would scrap a ship and those who would preserve it as a ruin is how rentiers—whether the docking company or the reefing one—seek to benefit from access to the asset. The Secret Squirrels continue to engage with the *Vandenberg* through a variety of activities which are subtle forms of value management. For instance, they need to perform occasional maintenance, keeping things chained down or replacing mooring balls so the ship stays in one place. There is a sense in which they are still responsible for it, and yet Joe and his associates do not have exclusive access to dive there (as they will for future wrecks, like the *Mohawk*). This is very different from scrapping the ship for its value in metal (or "evaporating" it, as scrapyards around the Arizona Boneyard would say). Like all the restorers, curators, and docents who relate to planes around the Boneyard in the last chapter, Joe and his allies prefer some form of preservation to evaporation of the asset, because they all can accrue "rents" from providing access to others. There was meant to be an exhibit associated with the *Vandenberg*, possibly at the Shipwreck Museum, but money ran out. Preservation comes in many forms, however, as does restoration.

Preservation does not always mean remaining the same over time, but can involve salvaging.[18] Joe knows divers and how they engage with historical artifacts. If he scraps the brass door handles of a military ship before deployment, for example, he will make only five dollars per handle. But there are ways to profit from salvaging:

> They're not supposed to, but the divers will steal that stuff. They steal it, they go home to Michigan, they shine it up, they mount it on wood and they take it to their dive bars, say:
> "Look at this hatch!"
> "Where'd you get that?"

"I got that at the *Vandenberg.*"
"Are there any more?"
"Yea, there's plenty!"
So ten of them come down and they spend thirty grand—that's what you sold
that hatch for. . . I know what they do, and I leave the cheese in the trap for them to
do it!

Joe admits that that is a long series of steps, and people need help making those long-term connections. Once again, Joe's imagined dialogue is part of a bigger story, that of diving culture and the culture of salvaging wrecks he learned amid the ruin-scape of the Keys. That ruin is not merely aesthetic or environmental, it is an invented economic asset; put differently, it does not produce new value, in the Marxian sense, but absorbs surplus value by attracting people to spend time and money in the Keys, which primarily benefits those who own or manage property.

Competitive Coral Reef Restoration

A different criticism of the Vandenberg Project comes from those engaged in comparable world-making projects, that is, others attempting to restore coral reefs.[19] One prominent coral reef expert, whom I will call Vaughn, works at the Mote Marine initiative, an educational and research organization based in the upper Keys. A biologist with a PhD in botany and plant physiology from Rutgers, Vaughn originally worked for the marine industry, producing coral for aquariums, among other things. More recently he has moved into coral restoration, which he describes as the result of an epiphany after he met one of the descendants of Jacques Cousteau, a childhood hero. He realized that he was growing coral artificially to sell to people so they would stop taking it from the oceans, but that he ought to be growing coral to replant and replenish the ocean instead. This shift in direction put him at odds with Joe, though they share a mutual respect for one another. For one thing, it is hard to get money to restore coral reefs, and Joe, by his own admission, raised a lot for the purpose. In fact, the project went over budget and became quite controversial. Joe only received the money from the city after a legal settlement was reached. According to Vaughn, "This was at the same time that I struggled and was happy to find a ten-thousand-dollar grant to be planting live corals out there, which *we know* will grow. And what ten million dollars would have done was more than ever was put into reef restoration in the state of Florida for the past hundred years."[20]

Joe agrees that Mote Marine has an impressive record growing coral experimentally to survive in more stressful conditions, which are increasingly becoming the norm for the ocean. He originally got in touch with Vaughn to see if Mote Marine would be willing to pay to plant coral on the *Vandenberg*, and the group declined. Vaughn agrees that a reef can get jump-started by sunken vessels, but warns that "some of the metals and some of the paints are not conducive to coral," and that it can take longer to grow the coral as a result. At Vaughn's lab, they are working from the opposite direction, trying to learn what best facilitates coral growth. With a new NSF grant, they are also trying to make strands that survive in more acidic, warmer waters, to improve their resilience against global climate change. If one is truly interested in ecological restoration, Vaughn insists, then starting with the organism makes the most sense. Joe counters that a smaller restoration operation does not attract the same range of species, since they only serve animals on the very bottom. As evidence, he pointed out that a whale shark was spotted by the *Vandenberg* in 2014. This is a rare sight at the Keys, and according to Joe, a mobile reef in its own right, trailing a panoply of symbiotic organisms within its massive wake. Vaughn hopes that Joe might still have a Cousteauian revelation like his own.

Joe serves on the Sanctuary Advisory Council, where conservation is often discussed. "Environmental altruism is valid and worthy" he agreed, but "it's also difficult and it doesn't really raise a lot of money all the time. Heads and beds, that raises money." According to him, the *Vandenberg* pays for itself, but merely replanting the coral would not. Joe holds the opinion that "if it's all about conservation, then we shouldn't be spending twenty million dollars a year convincing people to come down here and go fishing and go diving. So I think that there's a balance there... I think the truth is somewhere in the middle."

Vaughn is not the only one who thinks that the money spent sinking the *Vandenberg* would have been better used elsewhere. Some claimed that that money should have gone to doing a better job treating the city's wastewater, but Joe claims this would cost nearly forty times more and, as is his usual refrain, not bring in additional revenue. The difference between their projects arguably comes down to what story of success over precarity is preferred— which approach more persuasively saves the oceans and the Keys from the ruins of overdevelopment. Is the true measure of worthwhile efforts profits gained, whale sharks spotted, divers marveled, or humbler efforts to carefully encourage coral to survive the future? Their divide also reflects Joe's reliance on the beneficence and wastefulness of the US military.

Debates around the *Vandenberg* provoke us to examine the relationship between military waste and ruination and world-making. Sinking naval ships to create artificial coral reefs does not solve war or climate change, but does provoke us to think of them together. The most common way to refer to the latter crisis is as the Anthropocene, designating a new geological epoch of environmental transformation caused by people. One of the problems with this term, as normally applied, is that it makes climate change both too particular and too general. Too particular because it makes it seem as if human transformation of the world is relegated to the industrial era and, therefore, only a few hundred years old. But it is also too general because it makes it seem as if all of humanity—*Anthropos*, humankind itself—is equally to blame for this transformation (Tsing 2015, 19). For these reasons, Jason Moore (2017) proposes a new term, the Capitalocene, which offers greater historical breadth and focus. It is not all humanity that is responsible for climate change, but nor is it only the industrial fossil fuel era. Donna Haraway (2016) suggests even more timescales, including Chthulucene and Plantationcene. One way to think about the global empire and global environmental catastrophe together is to think in terms of an additional era of the Polemocene. From *polemos*, meaning war, this would characterize the actual environmental transformations ushered in by a global empire and its troubling, toxic, and uncanny remnants.

Compared to conventional coral restoration, artificial reefing draws on the surplus of military warcraft by harnessing untapped capacities of the objects themselves to serve as artistic canvases, artifacts for public consumption, a home for new life. To put it somewhat poetically, in a way neither man would, Vaughn is not trying to use a symptom of global American capitalism (an old warship) to heal the disease of the Polemocene, but Joe is. In other words, artificial reefing ties war preparation and environmental devastation together, prompting us to consider how they were never really separate in the first place.

DAMAGE TO A DAMAGING MACHINE

The tensions surrounding ownership and use of military waste opens up opportunities to explore what they can mean and, perhaps more importantly, what they can do for us and the world. At the end of the Cold War, President George H. W. Bush and British Prime Minister Margaret Thatcher both spoke of a "peace dividend" representing the transfer of industrial capacity and capital investment from military to civilian sectors. The actual results were predictably mixed, but the promise of a peace dividend invokes the start of Marx's circuit of capital. One is invited to imagine the pure possibility of all the liquid money (M) that would have been realized and trapped in a very limited form of military capital (C), and instead awaits investment in any number of possible civilian ventures. What the theory of the peace dividend leaves out is what becomes of all the capital that has already been realized, those sunk costs whose value appears settled.

Different transformations await military products as they are traded on the international arms market, scrapped for raw material, or repurposed for new ends. No matter how formidable they may have been once, the day will come when even the most expensive and impressive warcraft are worth more in storage, on the scrap heap, or sunk on the bottom of the ocean than they are in battle. According to Custers (2007), this means that the negative exchange value of military products—their useless utility as forces of destruction—are outstripped by the risks they pose as embodiment of negative use value, what it costs to manage and mitigate their potential toxicity as they break down. The threat of negative exchange value thus haunts any attempt to translate dead capital into liquid money.[21] This is what makes Joe Weatherby's approach different. Sinking ships does not simplify acquired assets but allows them to go on "eternal patrol" as a ruin-scape. They may be aestheticized or remilitarized by others, but they remain as an archive. As such they might still provoke reflection on why such excess exists and for what reason it was created in the first place. If evaporated into cash, they cannot.

In a sense, those who seek to scrap are recommending commodification rather than assetification. They want for ships to become something that is easily exchanged on a global market, anonymous and impersonal material that seems to transcend the risks of contaminating environments. But, as Tsing (2015, 28) argues, contamination can be thought of differently, as singular and unrepeatable encounters across fields of difference, where new and unexpected world-making projects can emerge. This includes possibilities of open-ended and unpredictable interactions between divers, artists, and animals of the new reef. The problem of military waste has not been solved or worsened, and neither has the ocean been simply healed or damaged. But, like mushroom picking, these interactions reveal imaginative possibilities beyond this pernicious binary. Whatever else the benefits of scrapping include, these are possibilities it forecloses.

At the same time, from one perspective, any repurposed excess exists to supplement the permanent war economy, a sacrifice to keep it going: no matter how creatively they are reused, arguably, their expenditure underwrites the production of newer weapons. As Kenneth MacLeish writes, "To cast any unwanted excesses of war's violence as second order, peripheral, or 'collateral' to its 'necessary violence' is not only to misunderstand war but also to conspire in a confusion of its means and ends" (2013, 10). It would be a mistake to cast the disposal of military waste as a second-order problem when compared to the more spectacular work of mass destruction. And yet, it would be an equivalent mistake to reduce the actions of civilians actively dismantling and reusing American military waste to the interests of the military establishment. In many ways, this is a false dichotomy. As Judith Butler puts it, rebelling or causing trouble is often caught up in its own reprimand:

> Dismantling forms of oppression. . .involves a certain way of destroying what has been built badly, built in ways that are consequential in the damage they cause. So to damage a damaging machine in the name of less damage, is that possible? And can we distinguish between affirmative ways of "taking apart" the machinery that causes injury and the destructive modes of injury itself? I think we have to continue the labour of making that distinction. (Quoted in Ahmed 2016, 484)

Those who seek to reuse and repurpose military waste for various ends negotiate and trouble distinctions as well, not only between worth and worthlessness—as in ordinary rubbish recycling—but also past relations of global violence, both actual and virtual, and future relations of open-ended material and semiotic becoming. They do so in direct contact with fragments and representatives of the military, rather than from a morally safe distance.

Paul Virilio seems more optimistic than Butler about the necessity of destroying what he calls "modes of destruction" from within: "I believe that within this perversion of human knowledge by the war-machine, hides its opposite. Thus there is work to be done within the machine itself" (1997, 107). If the military no longer costs ordinary Americans as much as it once did and no longer belongs to them either, its leftover warcraft may appear like only so much alien, dead capital. It is perhaps obvious that the stakes of military waste are amplified in comparison with other forms of discard. What I have argued

SUNK COST • 107

is that engaging with military waste need not reaffirm the nationalist ideology that fetishizes instruments and agents of war, as in war tourism for example. It can represent a way of perverting perverted knowledge or troubling troubled histories, of pursuing world-making projects that both derive from and unsettle the permanent war economy.

CHAPTER 4

The Wrong Stuff

As I write this, in the atmosphere miles above me, hundreds of millions of tiny artificial particles and larger fragments are circling the planet, mostly undetected, moving as fast as speeding bullets. This is orbital space debris—artificial objects and materials launched into orbit that no longer serve a purpose—and it has been accumulating in the sixty years since the Soviet Union sent *Sputnik* into space and transformed the stakes of the Cold War.

In this chapter, I review various attempts to witness and revalue space debris, which expose the historical and ongoing militarization of outer space. At first glance, space debris would seem very different from the other objects discussed in this book. On the one hand, they are not as clearly linked to the military and permanent war preparation, because this connection has been actively foreclosed from public awareness by the US security state. Every space mission creates some debris, and many space missions had covert and classified goals that were not disclosed until later, and some never were. One famous example is the cover story used to account for the U2 incident in 1960. Shot down while conducting covert surveillance of suspected Russian ICBM development from Soviet airspace, the U2 spy plane was initially characterized as a NASA weather vessel. However, two days after the cover story was released, a photo was wired to the US government of Khrushchev holding aerial photographs the U2 had taken, proving the NASA story was a lie.[1]

If one problem with examining space debris as military waste is a history of secrecy, another concerns the undetectability immanent to space debris as a material object. It is one thing to write with authority about orbital space debris. It is quite another to *bear witness* to space debris, as one can other forms of American military waste. "To *witness*," Michael Taussig writes, "as opposed to *see*, is to be implicated in a process of judgement. . .such that the mere act of seeing tilts the cosmos and deranges the eyeball" (2011, 71). Yet, with this most cosmic of wastes, witnessing is hard to come by. I cannot swear that I have seen orbital space debris (in orbit, that is) and haven't met many who can. Amateur astronomers sometimes think they have seen space debris, but do not know for certain if they ever will again or if they'll even know when they do. And, more importantly, they probably will not care if they do.

If this book is about finding people who bear witness to military waste, who not only see it but become invested in this act of perception, then in that sense at least this chapter is premised on a failure. Those I spent the most time with—amateur astronomers and a ham radio operator in the Southern Tier of New York—were not already interested or invested in space debris. I did not trace a preexisting network linking nonhumans with humans (Latour 2005). I did not locate a public affected by an act of contamination, slow violence, or environmental injustice (Marres 2012). That is to say, with few exceptions, I did not succeed in finding a group for whom this object matters and using their interest to direct my own. Instead, I found a problematic object and tried to recruit people who *might* care to do so.

One reason space debris is not very interesting for the people I got to know is that anything so labeled is uninteresting almost by definition. Space debris is perhaps the truest expression of what Mary Douglas (1966) meant when she labeled dirt, "matter out of place." Almost anything can be considered space debris if it was launched into orbit and people think it should not be there anymore. It may refer to satellites that have aged and become obsolete or can no longer be contacted or controlled from the ground, thus rendering them useless. Space debris also consists of materials of varying size and substance that were purposely released or jettisoned by vessels and satellites to facilitate their ascent or as part of their ongoing maintenance. But whether something counts as space debris depends on who is making this judgment and how. Part of the reason that amateur astronomers might not care about space debris is that anything they do care about may no longer be recognized as debris.

Consider NASA's *Cassini* probe, which entered Saturn's atmosphere after completing its twenty-year mission on September 15, 2017. I began hearing about *Cassini's* final descent weeks earlier from the members of the Kopernik Astronomical Society (KAS). *Cassini* was being discarded, but it was difficult to find anyone characterizing it as debris. In early September, KAS members were still sharing their best photographs of the solar eclipse that had captivated the country in August. But soon they began posting links on the group's public Facebook page related to *Cassini*'s last mission:

> September 14:
> #Live #Coverage: NASA Monitors #Cassini's #Dive Into #Saturn Friday morning, NASA & #JPL will monitor the Cassini #Spacecraft as it ends its #mission by diving into the #clouds of Saturn. #NASATV and NASA & JPL #Internet #web-sites will provide live #steaming coverage as #scientists #monitor Cassini's "#GrandFinale," as well as #news#conferences before (Thursday afternoon) & after (Friday morning) the #event.
> September 16:
> A fantastic overview of the Cassini Mission, including it's [sic] very last image. Such an amazing mission just to tease our wonder a little bit.#FarewellCassini Explore More!
> September 20:
> NOVA: Death Dive to Saturn

These posts provided hashtags and links one could use to learn about *Cassini*'s final mission, witness live broadcasts, and honor the lost spacecraft. *Cassini* was singled out for so much praise by astronomy enthusiasts for good reason. Many knew it had been responsible for some of the best pictures of the solar system ever captured. As a writer for a science and technology website put it:

> While many uncrewed spacecraft have done an incredible job of revealing our solar neighborhood to us, honestly, none did it better than NASA's Cassini probe. After exploring Saturn for 13 years, on September 15th at 4:55am PDT, the probe will plunge itself into the planet's atmosphere, becoming one with the very object of its fascination. (Paoletta 2017)

As in many examples that appeared around this time, on- and offline, this writer treats *Cassini* like a person. It is as if the probe itself were intentionally doing the "exploring," plunging "itself," and intentionally merging with "the very object of its fascination." Such eulogistic prose could be found among many techno-science and astronomy feeds and sites at the time. Consequently, what otherwise might have been seen as just an expensive, floating camera became instead a subject of interest akin to Saturn itself.

But objects never mean just one thing, even within the same community of practitioners.[2] From another point of view, the disposal of *Cassini* on Saturn was more like an act of cosmic littering disguised as a funeral. One small but vocal group of *Cassini*-truthers claimed that there was another, more nefarious purpose behind the destruction of the probe. NASA was, they claimed, trying to accomplish its decade-old goal of creating another sun by detonating a nuclear payload on Saturn. Known as "Project Lucifer," such a claim had been made before in relation to other space missions. But for every so-called conspiracy theory, there are even more people who delight in debunking and deconstructing them. A decade before *Cassini*'s final dive, an author for the online publication *Universe Today* had already set about deconstructing Project Lucifer's assertions (see O'Neill 2008). It is worth noting, however, that claims and counterclaims such as these, much like narratives of UFO sightings and abductions, are about more than what "really happened." They are more centrally concerned with whether or not hidden powers are operating in the shadows, just beneath awareness. If they exist, such powers are only visible in momentary glimpses and if one looks carefully enough to see the pattern.[3]

Whether *Cassini* is seen as a mournful loss or a frightening conspiracy, it is still not quite "debris" since it has greater purpose than something merely drifting, colliding, orbiting. In other words, whether something counts as debris depends on how astronomical observers (and conspiracists) think about and act towards the things that populate outer space. More than just claims to debunk, conspiracy theories like Project Lucifer raise ethical and political questions surrounding what is otherwise accepted as relatively innocent and harmless civilian science. More to the point, they point toward forgotten and troublesome understories associated with the exploration and exploitation of outer space. It is not so strange to suspect that NASA is concealing the true motivations behind its projects, as it has done in the past and as its less-well-known sister agency, the National Reconnaissance Office (NRO), has done for the entirety of its existence. Fantasies of hidden nuclear reactions on Saturn are not just conspiratorial paranoia, therefore, but manifestations of a general mistrust around state secrets concerning the militarization of space, which did not end with the Cold War. This chapter explores space debris as open-ended rubbish (Thompson [1979] 2017) and as an object of militarized fantasies, past and present. The example of *Cassini* is telling because it represents a situation where what might otherwise be thought of as mere space debris is instead revalued as a sign of discovery and scientific achievement or, alternately, of conspiratorial, cosmic destruction.

The intentional generation of space debris becomes more apparent by linking it with the historical and ongoing militarization of space. My argument is not that the US military is directly responsible for all space debris (a claim that would be difficult to definitively prove in any case). That being said, antisatellite weapons testing has by all accounts made the problem of space debris worse; furthermore, defense agencies have been at the forefront of studying and proposing solutions to space debris.[4] In this chapter, I link *both* the historical and ongoing creation of space debris, as a problem, *and* current proposals to solve it to a common source: a tendency to imagine expert knowledge and technical practice as a form of mastery, despite the fact that they lead to new and unanticipated accidents and risks. Here I draw from the Aristotelian argument of Paul Virilio (2007, 5) that the accident reveals the substance. In other words, the invention of any substance is equally the invention of any of its accidental manifestations. The shipwreck is the invention of the ship (see chapter 3) just as the Chernobyl meltdown is the invention of the nuclear power station. So, too, space debris is the invention of the Cold War space race, an invention distinctly different from the way planets ordinarily shed and reabsorb materials.

Clearly, orbital space debris is very different from things like planes, ships, and guns. Yet, it is productive to think of all forms of military waste not only as different kinds of things, but as associated with different microworlds of action connected with permanent war preparation. For this reason all of these forms, as rubbish, have elements of indeterminacy associated with them, which lead to disputes about their social and material potential. After all, what is difficult to represent clearly can be even more disturbing to imagine, since this usually makes it harder to control and predict.[5] Is space debris polluted and polluting or valuable and meaningful? Is it raw material for a radical new vision or heritage that should be preserved? When objects are simultaneously rare and abundant like space debris, hard to relate to, yet ubiquitous in orbital environments, these questions pose even greater challenges.

Acknowledging the militaristic origins of space debris does not make it more accessible or amenable to reuse and rethinking by civilians. As I will explain, even astronomers might only encounter space debris fleetingly, and only for a brief moment as it quickly vanishes out of sight. In some ways, this makes space debris both less visible and more threatening than the other forms of military waste I discuss in this book. When it comes to astronomical phenomena, seeing is believing. But believing is also seeing, insofar as imagined evidence of aliens or government conspiracy involves prior and ongoing *attunement* toward that which lies concealed beyond familiar experience and official explanation. The idea of cultivating ethical attunement of the senses, especially to *listen* for signs of otherworldly beings and designs, has been discussed for religious subjects (Luhrmann and Morgain 2012; Hirschkind 2015; Zani 2019). I extend this to include visual attunement of lay astronomers. Astronomical attunement can involve searches for alien life, but it can also be more modest in its scope, associated with wise use of and participation in the Earth's orbital environment. I was unsuccessful finding many people who already cared about space debris, but getting to know them I came to see their practices of attunement as an alternative to the dominant strategies to address space debris. Unlike the attunement of amateurs, space agencies represent space debris as a problem to address through *techno-solutionism*. This is a way of valuing the technical fix as an end in itself, and it is deeply connected to the militarization of space and the problem of space debris.

THE COLOR OUT OF SPACE

Space debris comes in the form of subsidiary materials intentionally or inadvertently discarded after helping satellites escape Earth's gravity, as well as the satellites themselves. Some of these objects are broken down by interactions with other bits of debris and physical processes while in orbit, but may continue orbiting the Earth all the same. There are good records of the over six thousand satellites that have been launched since 1957. But they can be difficult to locate and identify from the ground all the same. Depending on the altitude, lost and disused satellites and their accompanying materials either circle the planet at low Earth orbit (LEO), medium Earth orbit (MEO), or geostationary orbit (GEO), and this also affects their relative velocity, with objects further away moving more slowly. The ISS is located about 250 miles above the surface of the Earth in LEO and moves about 17,500 miles per hour, whereas satellites in GEO are located about a hundred times further above the Earth and travel at less than half that velocity. The difference is that disused space junk has lost attitude control, meaning that its orientation becomes more haphazard as it tumbles through space.[6]

As different forms of space debris move, sometimes at tens of thousands of miles per hour, they occasionally collide with one another and splinter into additional, smaller fragments. There are an estimated half a million pieces today, a fraction of which can be tracked by space agencies like NASA. Using the publicized data from the DoD's Space Surveillance Network, there have been numerous models generated to display the problem of space debris as it has accumulated over time.

One of the problems with depicting space debris accurately has to do with the conditions of orbital environments. In time-lapse videos, one can visualize the Earth as if it were sloughing off dandruff—hundreds of thousands of tiny flecks that encircle it at various distances. This metaphor is actually more appropriate than it might seem. Like an animal's scalp, the Earth routinely sheds materials that continue to orbit it or are jettisoned into the universe. As part of this metabolic process orbital environments "self-clean," meaning that various planetary forces allow materials to leave and rejoin the surface, as well as capture that which other planetary bodies have jettisoned. In a certain sense, for something to be called "orbital space debris" depends entirely on human beings deciding something is no longer valuable, useful, or notable. Yet, what becomes of space debris depends on the power of the Earth itself.[7] After all, debris is not something that troubles planets, but defines them. According to Lisa Messeri, the prevailing definition of a planet is an object that is "large enough to have either captured or expelled the debris to other orbits" (2016, 8). If not for Earth's gravitational force, bending spacetime as it does, it would not require so much expenditure to escape its orbit, nor would so much material fall back to Earth or remain in orbit after the fact. As Lisa Ruth Rand notes, "the geophysical world of outer space" is "a historical actor of equivalent importance to astronauts, engineers, governments, and publics" (2016, 13). The planet's metabolic relationship to debris is not simply a threat to life, but may help spread it across the cosmos.[8]

Anthropogenic space debris mixes with the naturally occurring debris of orbital environments to generate new risks and possibilities. Unlike functional satellites, which can be manipulated and brought more or less in sync with the designs of those on the ground, the alternative spatial and temporal rhythms of space debris represent a distinct risk to other things (and persons) in orbit. As such, they also represent a potential barrier to further human exploration and exploitation of space. To begin with, space debris is potentially dangerous to spacecraft. Space debris is partly assessed by treating returning spacecraft in a way they were never intended, as a "hypervelocity impact capture medium" as they are dented more by artificial objects than natural meteorites (Bernhard, Christiansen, and Kessler 1997). The impetus for tracking and modeling space debris thus comes from the temporal possibilities it threatens. This includes a hypothetical feedback process whereby objects continually collide and spread out, converting Earth orbits, especially in LEO, into a hazardous environment filled with tiny fragments. Space debris would then circle eternally overhead like a cloud of bullets awaiting a target, trapping us in fear on the surface. This was used to produce a new element of space horror in the recent science fiction film *Gravity* (2013), where space debris played a key role and was depicted as a monstrous threat—like a swarm of abiotic locusts—that cycled the Earth with an alien regularity. In this film, without warning debris hurtles into view to annihilate spacecraft or slaughter hapless astronauts.[9] Whether this sort of possibility is a likely scenario or not, it reflects anxiety about the unexpected and emergent spacetime of materials orbiting the Earth. The time they threaten is not only the immediate present but future plans, which are increasingly incorporated into fantasies of space travel.

At least one of the astronomers I spoke with considered space debris a broader environmental problem. One of the older staff members at the Kopernik Observatory was Nicholas, who grew up in the Southern Tier and designed computer hardware for IBM. When I interviewed Nicholas, he was preparing a talk for the public on the search for life and its creation from inorganic materials, a subject of great personal interest. This gave him a unique view on the ecological risks of space exploration, "I think of debris as sort of garbage. Stuff that's out there, you don't know what to do with it so you just leave it laying around, it's like cluttering on a highway. You know?" For Nicholas, depositing leftover materials from missions, like the *Cassini* probe, on a foreign planet is about more than the technical junk itself. Even the most sanitized bit of space equipment might carry remnants of the living world it came from. Nicholas had pictures in his Facebook feed of tardigrades (or water bears), the peculiar microbes that seem capable of withstanding the vacuum of space. "To me that's one of the areas that you could contaminate, if you're searching for life, you don't want to contaminate it."

NASA scientists are aware of these concerns, which are normally glossed as planetary protection and were included as part of the Outer Space Treaty of 1967. This stipulates the necessity of protecting the Earth from organisms that might exist beyond it, and protecting other planets from contamination by human and nonhuman earthlings. For instance, *Cassini* was positioned to collide with Saturn so that it would not inadvertently contaminate life that might exist on one of the gas giant's moons (life which, many astronomical enthusiasts would be quick to point out, *Cassini*'s photographs had helped demonstrate might exist). And Nicholas was also not alone in thinking that enthusiasm for space exploration could lead to denial about its unforeseen consequences.[10] Not everyone agrees, however. In 2018, the SETI institute sponsored a debate over planetary protection between a member of NASA and founder of the Mars Society and author Robert Zubrin. During the debate, Zubrin accused planetary protection of being nonsensical, since planets exchange substances all the time on their own, and dangerous, since it could limit human exploitation and exploration of the universe.

Space debris is meaningful as both barrier and bridge to desirable futures. These hoped-for futures involve, for instance, further exploration and exploitation beyond LEO and into the very valuable and legally contested domain of geostationary orbit, where satellites can more easily analyze from and transmit data to the entire planet. This also includes NewSpace initiatives that seek to extend capitalism and empire beyond the limits of the Earth, whether to mine asteroids or colonize Mars.[11] Such initiatives demonstrate a clear motivation to clean up the polluted and risk-filled environment in the vicinity of Earth. From this admittedly interested perspective, the presence of space debris limits the utilization of LEO, MEO, and GEO, creating risks for any state and/or capital investment. Insofar as space debris influences assessments concerning the utilization of outer space for various ends, it directly mediates the futures that space agencies and industries imagine possible and desirable.

It may be that the risks of orbital debris are being somewhat amplified by filmmakers and the media more broadly. After all, most chunks of space debris burn up completely before descending to Earth, posing little threat to life on the surface. And only those nations and corporations powerful enough to summon the resources to escape the planet's gravitational pull, to operate the ISS for example, place themselves directly at risk. In this regard, space debris is somewhat analogous to floating Pacific garbage patches in the world's oceans (see chapter 6). While troubling and aesthetically striking, space debris and garbage patches are located in little-used borderlands rather than directly inhabited landscapes. They would seem to lack an affected public, that is, a collective of interested social actors directly impacted by the problem and thus likely to organize to bring the problem to light.

The analogy between the garbage patches and space debris is more than incidental. At the opposite side of the Pacific from the first garbage patch to be discovered is another dumping zone. Known as Point Nemo—the place in the ocean furthest from any land—this stretch of ocean has been used for decades as a convenient place to deposit space debris, when such a thing is possible for space agencies.[12] But debris does not always land where one would expect. And the threat of damage from orbital space debris is real.

Space debris represents a clear barrier to the continued use of orbital environments. The ISS had to perform approximately eight evasive maneuvers during its first decade of operation in order to avoid collisions with debris. Calculations are normally performed at least three times a day to determine risks of collision over the subsequent seventy-two hours; if the chance of collision with a large enough object is determined to be greater than one in ten thousand, then maneuvers are planned and executed. In late August of 2008, the ISS had to engage in a collision avoidance maneuver when it was nearly struck by just one piece of more than five hundred cataloged bits of debris that resulted from Kosmos 2421's planned fragmentation earlier that summer (see Johnson and Klinkrad 2009, 5). In this case, the ISS was not dodging anonymous debris, but the specific fragments that are attributable to a Russian spy satellite that was launched in 2006 and began fragmenting two years later. According to widely agreed-upon space policy, if old satellites cannot be sent to the "parking zones" above LEO, then they are sent crashing into the atmosphere to hopefully disintegrate.[13]

In some ways, concerns over orbital debris can be related to the discourse around climate change, sociologist and historian of science Lisa Ruth Rand argues, insofar as both are global in scope and have been associated with "tipping points" toward certain and perpetual disaster. "With no control over where surviving fragments might land, orbital space became a site from which pollutants could cross geographic boundaries and extraterritorial regions" (Rand 2016, 11). In this sense, orbital regions are not some sort of beyond, disconnected from terrestrial life. Like the atmosphere itself, planetary borderlands are dynamically entangled with life on Earth. Moreover, like the seemingly never-ending threat of nuclear annihilation, they are also associated with the rise of the national security state in the twentieth century.[14]

When specific entities generate fragments or are threatened by them, orbital space debris begins to resemble other pollution events where there is an alleged perpetrator and a documented victim. More often than not, it is not just any perpetrator accused. Discussions of space debris events frequently single out America's adversaries as being responsible, as in the episode above, despite the fact that Americans contaminate orbital environments as well and that other countries are frequently responding to and imitating the ongoing American militarization of space. Politicizing space debris in this way fits easily into previous Cold War–era assessments of risk and blame where it is only national rivals to the United States and Europe who break rules and incur risks, namely China and Russia, which implies that Americans are blameless by contrast.[15]

Space Debris as Military Waste

All of the information provided in the section above, outlining orbital space debris as a problem, can be considered entirely without reference to the US military. This not only leaves out an important part of the story of space exploration and exploitation; it also helps further distinctions between civilian science and defense projects, as if the two were completely separate spheres of social action and imagination. In fact, they are continuous.

The launch of *Sputnik I* by the Soviet Union was the beginning of space exploration and the age of satellites. It also set the stage for a new alliance between scientific experts, the federal government, and the DoD. Prior to *Sputnik*, it was widely believed throughout the US that its Soviet rivals were incapable of launching a satellite into space. When they did, it not only demonstrated a flaw in this chauvinist presumption, but made clear that the Soviet Union had the capacity to launch intercontinental missiles as well. Even though the Eisenhower administration knew, by this time, that there was no "bomber gap" between the two countries, this real embarrassment and virtual threat radically altered relationships between scientists and government and military officials, which had previously been strained by McCarthyism and the Korean War. At least some Americans felt vulnerable to attack, and Eisenhower, who had hoped to reduce what he regarded as wasteful military spending, reevaluated his position on the matter and helped foster the military industrial complex he would later name and criticize.[16]

If an interpretation of space exploration as militarization is often foreclosed from consideration, one of the reasons is that the intentions behind space discovery have been successfully represented in different ways over the course of NASA's history. Outer space and space agencies are more popularly represented in terms of discovery, invention, and wonder. This has been a deliberate effort on the part of civilian scientists, government officials, and media organizations to differentiate NASA from military projects. Though NASA was created to be a civilian space agency, the end result of the initial shock and panic surrounding the launch of *Sputnik*, this was not a foregone conclusion. At the time, all of the technology that might have been used for possible space exploration was in the hands of the US military; consequently, some prominent members of the government scientific advisory, as well as Eisenhower himself, were initially in favor of folding all space exploration within the DoD as part of ARPA. ARPA had itself been recently created in order to consolidate and reduce waste from interdepartmental competition. Consequently, it only stood to reason that it would also absorb the space agenda, which also had enormous implications for the future of defense. The reason NASA emerged, instead, was the result of fears of the militarization of space, both because of the dangers this would raise for people on Earth but also because it went against the utopian internationalism of many American scientists of the time. It was decided that there would be a civilian space agency, but one that would remain funded by and deeply connected to the military, for fear that the loss of military relevance in space missions would cause it to die on the vine.[17]

While NASA is a civilian agency, stories of its rise and contemporary relevance illustrate the longstanding relationship its people and projects have had with the DoD. Near-continuous war games in space go back to when the first satellites entered near-Earth orbit and generated ever more debris. According to Rand, "Both superpowers carried out high altitude and exoatmospheric nuclear weapons tests beginning in 1958 and ending in 1963 with the Partial Nuclear Test Ban Treaty" (2016, 10). Secrecy regarding military-related space missions (and the debris they have caused) is most clearly associated with the National Reconnaissance Office (NRO), the "other space agency" that was created in 1961 but kept a secret until 1992 (Paglen 2009, 20–31). As an author from *Wired* magazine puts it, debris is a legacy of militaristic statecraft:

> In 2007. . .China decided to de-orbit one of its defunct weather satellites...by firing a missile at it. That certainly took the sat out of its path—but it also created a flume of debris that flung toward the Space Station in 2011. In February 2008, the US Navy launched its own projectile at a spy satellite toward its own satellite. The government claimed to worry that if it let the satellite fall back intact, its hydrazine fuel could release toxic vapors at breathing level. But some, at the time and still, interpret the action militarily. (Scoles 2017)

Debris from the NRO was not necessarily from weapons testing, moreover, because weapons are not the only space projects of great military interest. As Rand explains:

> New kinds of satellites—from giant, shiny inflatable balloons to a ring of hundreds of millions of tiny copper fibers—tested the use of space for communications while spurring controversy over whether such satellites could interfere with astronomy, crowd the electromagnetic spectrum, or present a collision hazard to other spacecraft. (2016, 10)

Official histories of space exploration as civilian science tend to demilitarize its relevance. Moreover, when a cover story is needed—as with the U2 spy plane debacle—the official narrative can be called upon to distract or misinform inquiring Americans, allies or rivals.

The activities of ARPA and especially the NRO are shrouded in mystery, though that has not stopped amateur astronomers from successfully tracking their activity.[18] From the beginning of the space race, nation-states with property in orbit worked out the basic terms of space law (see Beery 2016), which among other things does not allow for the practices of salvage characteristic of maritime law. Instead of seeing these materials as property to be protected, astronomers were historically the first group to mobilize against the contamination of the planetary borderlands with space debris. *Sputnik's* launch also began a wave of UFO sightings of all kinds, which would continue over the ensuing decades. As Americans watched the night skies, it was as if their apprehension and mistrust of Soviets somehow turned on their own government. And why not? Space exploration was begun in earnest by competing US and Soviet militaries during the Cold War and continues to be central to the machinations of securitizing states today.[19]

The ability for anyone with a telescope to track near-Earth objects makes complete secrecy all but impossible. Most recently, space enthusiasts were the first to raise awareness about the possibility of China's Tiangong-1 space lab tumbling out of the sky, before the Chinese state admitted this was happening. In essence, it was amateur astronomers who first noticed that the space lab was acting more like space debris, against the wishes of a government hoping to keep this from public knowledge. The first story reclassifying the space lab as space debris appeared in June 2016, and was quoted from for the next year and a half by the *Guardian* and the *Washington Post*. Eventually the Chinese state admitted that it had lost control of the lab and that it would likely fall to Earth sometime in late 2017 or early 2018 (see David 2016).[20]

However, as I discuss in what follows, amateur astronomers are not always excluded from government or military space projects, or left to expose them from the outside. The apparent divide separating civilians and the military is not fixed but has been renegotiated over and over again along with the boundary between technoscience and politics more generally.

MISS SPACE DEBRIS

Space debris may lack a directly affected public, unlike other ecological crises, but it is not only a concern for space-related agencies, corporations, and projects. Space debris either circles above in orbit or falls to Earth, which means that civilian witnesses to their movement and descent are rare. This can make encounters with debris seem exceptional and noteworthy or merely annoying or unremarkable, especially if one is hoping to witness something extraterrestrial. This is important to consider, where the militarization/militarism of space is concerned, because it also lays out the basic problem with successfully witnessing space debris. This will become important as directly military-related projects are outlined below because this kind of amateur expertise in witnessing has played a role in military projects since *Sputnik* was launched.

Unidentified Objects

After a few months of doing research with amateur astronomers, I was sure that the so-called "Halloween Asteroid" passing close by the Earth would be the biggest astronomical event in the news in late October of 2015. I assumed, given events I had watched transpire previously, that some people would post information online about an apocalyptic collision with Earth, which others would then seek to debunk. I was wrong, but only about *which object* would generate this familiar discursive cycle. The asteroid was overshadowed, at least on astronomy forums, by reports of an unidentified object about to crash into the Indian Ocean. This led to speculation about covered-up alien spaceships, which was informally debunked within a day by the online astronomical community. Debunkers alleged that the object was no alien but mere space debris. As one online commentator put it:

> Let's be honest, it would be super awesome if aliens came to visit Earth. It would also be rather scary. And if you've browsed about Facebook recently, you may have noticed that a trending topic leads you down a virtual rabbit hole of terror. Reports assert that an unidentified object (a UFO, to be precise) is on a collision course with Earth. And this is at least partially true. On November 13th, something is going to smash into our planet over the Indian ocean. However, scientists note that the space-based object is neither aliens nor a comet. Rather, as the team behind the research states, it is a piece of rocket stage. Space junk. Remains from a previous high orbit launch. (Creighton 2015)

This author follows other online commentators, as well as the amateur astronomers I have known, in regarding space debris as a less exceptional or unmarked possibility when compared with more interesting nonhuman events, be they asteroids or aliens.

It can often happen that some object is "observed" only to be confused for space debris burning up in the atmosphere upon reentry. Nicholas has had this experience, and not only with space debris. "There were times that I saw stuff that I didn't understand and later on found out what they were." This can happen despite years of experience studying the night sky and learning how to describe and name what one is looking at. Nicholas described one recent incident:

> There's a little island in the Atlantic, just off the coast [Wallops Flight Facility, Virginia]... A lot of times [NASA] sends up suborbital rockets and it explodes a bunch of dyes in the upper atmosphere, and they're studying...how it expands out and how it moves into the top of the atmosphere...twenty, thirty, forty miles up...and then the thinnest part of the atmosphere. And I saw those happen once and I saw this purple sphere in the sky and a small dot that expanded out..."Hey, it's the first time I'm seeing a UFO!" Turns out it's a NASA experiment.

One does not have to be an astronomer to be startled and befuddled by debris. Nicholas added that the observatory and its volunteers and staff are routinely asked by family and members of the public to explain strange events they witness, especially peculiar lights in the sky. They tend to wonder, in particular, whether they are bearing witness to something not only new to them but new to the planet and to history, that is, whether the unexplained is a sign of alien visitation or of military experimentation. This is repeated often enough online and by people I've spoken with that it could be regarded something like the culturally default interpretation of strange nocturnal encounters with distant light. For amateurs, by contrast, anything difficult to recognize can normally be associated with some sort of artificial debris, whether from an intentional experiment or launch or from an unplanned reentry.

This may be disappointing news if you are less interested in capturing images of space debris than comets and aliens, and most people are. Other amateur astronomers I spoke with did not express uncertainty about the observation of space debris. Roy was born in Houston; his father studied physics at the University of Tennessee and got involved with North American Aviation right out of college. Consequently, he was involved in helping to track the shuttle missions to the moon, all of which had to be invented, Roy insists. His father then went on to work for IBM doing mission control, which meant Roy witnessed many launches for the space program growing up. He therefore knew that some of what goes up comes back down as debris. These early experiences sparked an interest in astronomy. At some point he got his first telescope, an important experience for many amateur astronomers. It was a Tasco

60 mm refractor, he recalls. His family eventually moved north, closer to IBM's global headquarters. Roy became involved with the Kopernik Observatory in 1978 because of an IBMer who lived across the street. As a high schooler, in the early 1980s, he began photographing and mapping the night sky for fun. And from 1988 on he has been involved in some way with the KAS or the observatory almost continuously to the present day.

As an employee of the Kopernik, Roy said he encountered space debris all the time, especially "looking through the twenty"—referring to the observatory's largest telescope, used especially for astrophotography. How did he know it was debris?

> Because of the way it's reflecting the light...when you're looking through the twenty-inch and you see something dimly go by, it's not a meteor burning up. It could be I guess... meteors, they're glowing more, I'm talking about reflected sunlight and they're just slowly moving through. It's most likely space debris.

The twenty-inch is so powerful that it reveals objects at many different orbits, moving at different speeds. Unlike other objects, space debris are distinct because of their reflection of the light and how quickly they move through the viewer, "You can't predict it. Once in a while you see something quickly move through it. Maybe it's two seconds." That does not mean it would be impossible to know if it was space debris for certain, or to map its progress across the night sky. Roy thinks this might be achievable, "We can see stuff randomly, and maybe if you had a bunch of people looking at the same time, you could figure some things out."

While Roy expressed confidence about identifying and tracking space debris more than some others did, that did not mean he wanted to accomplish this task. While unexpected things do happen, amateur astronomers get accustomed to knowing what they are looking at and looking for. And when the thing that enters their field of vision, natural or artificial, is not what they were seeking, it is usually regarded as a waste of time—one's own human time as well as the limited and limiting nonhuman times upon which one depends to observe, since all of these resources are finite (see Reno 2018a). From their perspective, space debris mistaken for a meteor is an insult to the intense practical and corporeal investment required to undergo astronomical observation.

Making a Meteor

Space debris can also impact lives more directly, as when the orbital environment "cleans itself" in such a way that debris tumbles out of orbit and crashes on land.[21] While rare, this does provide opportunities for ordinary civilians to engage directly with the material remains of the militarization of space.

Since the dawn of the space race there have been at least three recorded incidents of what is thought to be space debris crashing very close to people in the state of Wisconsin. Most recently, in late December of 2016, a large object came seemingly out of nowhere and smashed a man's van in Milwaukee (Lemoine 2016). Many comments on the incident joked about a fragment of Santa's sleigh, but the local police were reportedly baffled by the object, which they could not identify and which seemed to have dropped from a great height. The FAA was contacted for assistance, but did not respond. A week after the incident, a blogger for the site *Mysterious Universe* used satellite tracking data to point out that Milwaukee was on the projected path of a Russian military communication satellite, Molniya 3-51 (Molniya-3K-1), which was predicted to reenter the atmosphere around that time; the blogger went on to suggest it might be "a COP-V—a carbon overwrapped pressure vessel used on satellites and rockets" (Seaburn 2016).

Wisconsin is also where a twenty-pound fragment of *Sputnik IV* crashed down from the sky in September 1962, leaving a round impression in the concrete that still remains. As civilians had done since the first *Sputnik* launched, so-called "deathwatchers" in Milwaukee tracked the five-ton satellite as it descended and reported it to authorities for recovery (McCray 2008, 9). The occasion is still celebrated in Manitowoc as "Sputnikfest," which includes an annual pageant run by the Rahr-West Art Museum to determine the annual "Ms. Space Debris." Part of what makes this event worth celebrating is that many Americans alive today still remember the national embarrassment and public paranoia surrounding news of *Sputnik I*'s launch. As I will discuss in the next section, the shock of this incident was enough to completely transform American space and military policy. Possessing and displaying a chunk of this famous, fallen satellite also serves as a means of reckoning with the history of conflict with the Soviet Union, especially the space race and the Cold War, in a playful way. I spoke about this with Elaine, a member of the museum administration.

The Rahr-West Art Museum did not begin celebrating Sputnikfest until 2008, well after the Cold War had concluded. The decision to do so was, according to Elaine, to honor "the only place in the world that can say we have space debris that fell to Earth" and in order to attract people to the museum's impressive and nationally recognized modern art collection, much of which was donated by a local family that had made its fortune in the brewing industry and shipbuilding. The museum is a logical institution to organize the event since the satellite dented the street not far from its entrance. Museum staff had talked about doing something similar for years, but needed to wait for a museum director who was willing to commit to all the work. This involves organizing local bands, food vendors, volunteers, and running contests, including the beauty pageant, an alien pet dress-up contest, a quilt raffle, and others. The two-day event regularly draws huge crowds and brings people from all over the Midwest and beyond. In general, there is a sense in Manitowoc that the *Sputnik* crash put them on the map in a significant way (certainly one preferable to their notoriety as the location of the controversial true-crime docuseries *Making a Murderer*). In his 2011 presidential address, President Obama referred to America's "Sputnik Moment" which Americans could draw on to inspire change and innovation. He was scheduled to appear in Manitowoc shortly after, so people in the community thought he had chosen the imagery deliberately with reference to Sputnikfest and the debris landing.[22]

Most of the out-of-town visitors around during Sputnikfest reportedly ask, "Where's your Sputnik?," wanting to see the object that fell. They may be disappointed to find that the museum had to relinquish the original to the Smithsonian, which made two casts of it, one for the museum and one for the local police to keep as evidence. At the time, Elaine says, there was controversy about whether the satellite should return to Russia immediately. The Soviet Union had been arguing that any American equipment that crashed in its territory was no longer US property; most famously this was argued after the U-2 spy plane incident of 1960. Two years later, with the loss of *Sputnik IV* in the rural Midwest, Elaine said the Russians changed their position on the matter. Whether they did so is of course a matter of some debate, but the important point is that the fall of space debris to the Earth is not only a matter of epistemic uncertainty and a physical risk to property and safety, but also a matter of national security states fiercely guarding technological and military secrets, especially secrets about how to conduct surveillance to uncover the secrets of others.

In stark contrast to the seriousness with which Cold War rivals regard their outer-space secrets, the people of Manitowoc and the Rahr-West Museum consider Sputnikfest a joyful occasion for self-expression and unabashed silliness.

Many people dress up, as part of a "spoof on space," Elaine says. In addition to the contestants, the Wisconsin Garrison regularly perform at Sputnikfest. They are a branch of the 501st Legion ("Vader's first")—a global group of sci-fi and fantasy enthusiasts who dress up as characters from the Star Wars universe for events and appearances, with express permission from George Lucas (just so long as they do not use the words "Star Wars"). This is the biggest draw for children and families, Elaine told me, and normally includes a light saber duel and opportunities for pictures. The Ms. Space Debris pageant is similarly a "spoof on beauty contests." It began only for women but became more inclusive in recent years and, in 2017, the winner was a man for the first time, mostly because he sang well and provided good answers to the judge's questions (which are normally also meant to be silly, e.g., "Would you allow an alien to use your bathroom?" "What kind of makeup would you need to have with you if you were marooned on a desert island?"). The silliness of the occasion can also cause occasional controversy, however mild. They always have Sputnikfest on the weekend following Labor Day, which fell on September 11 in 2010. Some people objected in open mike forums that it was disrespectful to have such frivolity take place on a solemn occasion, but Elaine and many others disagreed.

If some people seek out the crash site of *Sputnik IV* to enjoy themselves while celebrating history, art, and fiction, others are drawn to the museum whenever new and unexplained phenomena appear. Like the Kopernik, the staff of the Rahr-West are used to the press and the public contacting them when there are strange lights in the sky. This happens, especially, when objects appear close by. In February of 2017, Wisconsin was in the space debris news again. Many homemade videos surfaced of a strange object that lit up the sky for thirty or more seconds over Lake Michigan. As often happens, the Museum in Manitowoc was featured in some news stories. Once again there were those who claimed it was extraterrestrial activity, as well as equally passionate efforts to debunk this claim; there were those who said it was a meteor, and still others who said it was nothing so remarkable as that, merely space debris.

As seen in chapter 2, a civilian-run museum becomes a place where people can experience and engage with objectual remains in creative ways. In this case, unlike visitors to the Pima, visitors to the Rahr-West Museum do not necessarily connect what they encounter to stories or understories of permanent war readiness. Perhaps if it were a chunk of the American *Challenger* explosion that landed in the middle of Manitowoc, or something similarly culturally charged, they would react differently to its display and memorialization. The important point is that there are opportunities for civilians to directly engage with space debris, though rare. In the next section, I will discuss even closer connections, where amateur scientists are actively recruited to assist in military programs having to do with space debris, or involve themselves without permission. Once again, any attempt to resurrect a clear divide between civilian and military worlds fails when the afterlife of military waste is followed closely.

SALVAGING THE COSMOS

Space debris can be dangerous to orbiting vessels and, as such, it represents an ever-growing hazard to human uses of Earth space. But these objects are hard to track and easy to mistake for something else, even for people who spend all of their time looking up at the night sky. Like space exploration itself, this is a difficult problem to solve, so it is not surprising that only the most powerful and prominent space agencies imagine they are capable of finding space debris, let alone clearing it from orbital environments. A core dimension of that power and prominence, moreover, is about having military ambitions that extend beyond the surface of the planet. And, from the very beginnings, doing so has meant enrolling amateur or civilian scientists in DoD plans for outer-space.

Historically, solving space-related challenges has meant getting funds and resources from wealthy and powerful nations. With the growth of a permanent war economy, such expenditure is very often tied to imagined or real military applications. Consequently, the history of space exploration has been and continues to be shaped by tensions and networks between civilian and military scientific objectives. But these seemingly opposed groups also align and become indistinguishable, especially insofar as they embrace a fascination with developing the latest technology and an unrelenting faith in its ability to solve all problems. This is also known as *techno-solutionism*. Evgeny Morozov (2013) developed this idea related to utopian appraisals of the internet. His account draws heavily on Hannah Arendt's *On Violence* (1970), a book which openly criticizes US administrations that thought they could solve global problems through technically ingenuous forms of death and destruction. Broadly defined, techno-solutionism is faith that technical fixes can solve any problem. . .even when they are targeting a realm like outer space, one that is already saturated with the leftovers of generations of technological problem-solving.

According to Gökçe Günel (2019, 129), any technical adjustment is not only about "functionality, effectiveness, or use, but rather the ways in which its materially and conceptually indeterminate existence mobilizes potential towards a technically adjusted future." In this sense, technical fixes for space debris are more about extending the possibility of future technical intervention in orbital environments, rather than, for instance, encouraging ethical reflection on whether people should create debris at all.[23]

Space debris is not just any problem, it is one that originated with and threatens space science and, as such, shows the limits of technical solution-making in general. If it is problematic to see space debris as a technical glitch, as noise in an otherwise perfectly rendered human design, that is because such a view can mislead us into thinking that all it takes is a little more ingenuity, a bit more mastery, to solve the problem entirely. But, following Virilio (2007), every new technical innovation and improvement brings a new disaster, an unprecedented act of contamination. If space debris represents inevitable traces that human artifacts and projects leave behind in the space beyond Earth, then, whatever the future may hold, this problem is unavoidable. If people want to continue to escape their earthly confines, space debris will have to be reckoned with. Space debris is a possibility that haunts all uses of space *tout court*, rather than an incidental by-product of space exploration and travel.

A focus on technical mastery links the cause of space debris with its proposed cure. As a counterpoint, I discuss how amateur astronomers and ham radio operators have engaged with space debris in a different manner and with altogether different goals. Specifically, they tend to look for ways to become attuned with and enliven debris that has been abandoned.

Militarizing Civilian Science

The possibility of a semiautonomous civilian space agency had defined space exploration from the start, but by the 1970s and '80s, funding had dropped precipitously from the heyday of the Apollo missions. By that time, NASA had come under widespread criticism as the country entered recession and other big programs (such as the CIA) and national initiatives (the War on Poverty, Civil Rights legislation, the Vietnam War) were attacked by political representatives and activists across the political spectrum. The prominent image that NASA members used to promote the organization during the 1960s was that of pragmatism, that space efforts would yield scientific benefits.

This failed to improve the prestige of the organization within the government, until the Reagan era, when there was a resurgence of nationalist and romanticist rhetoric from earlier in NASA's history. With the Reagan administration there was an effort, first, to block international efforts to ban weapons use in outer space and, second, to invest new symbolic importance and new financial resources in the militarization of space.[24]

Since that time, solving space debris has become a common pursuit of space agencies all over the world, both the more militarized and the more civilian among them. By the early 1980s, satellites were central infrastructure, particularly for the United States. The militarization of space had already occurred, in other words, and without extravagant laser weapons.[25] Consequently, among the most central issues of the time was the testing and development of antisatellite weaponry (ASAT). The use of experimental ASAT has been partly responsible for reorienting international attention to space debris, since ASAT is a spectacular technology, the goal of which is to transform working satellites into unusable waste.

Since satellites were so vulnerable to attack, and space treaties did not allow for the defense of particular regions of space as sovereign territory, satellites could be destroyed simply by sending "space mines" to collide with them. This constitutes one clear reason why DARPA and the Air Force are so intent on tracking space debris—they want to know whether satellites colliding with unidentified objects represent coincidental hazards or deliberate attacks. Being able to tell the difference between space debris and an actively launched space mine would be like knowing whether an ocean vessel sank because of an iceberg or a submarine. Even if one cannot capture space debris, being able to detect and identify it might be necessary to predict or avoid war. The ambiguities of witnessing discussed in the previous section, not knowing what one is seeing, therefore take on perilous consequences.[26]

While Reagan's "Star Wars" and Trump's "Space Force" have been heavily discussed and derided, other administrations have had similar designs. Perhaps most enduring has been the Clinton-era concept of *full-spectrum dominance*, first outlined in the United States Space Command "Vision for 2020" released in 1997. This relationship between outer space and defense and security has been so central to US policy that prominent advocates for science, notably Neil deGrasse Tyson, have authored reports suggesting that NASA could be restored to its former glory by becoming more like DARPA, that is, the militaristic organization it was partly created *not to become*.[27]

In many ways the DoD's Defense Advanced Research Projects Agency (DARPA) is the epitome of techno-solutionist practice. Though the term *defense* was only added to the acronym later (it was termed ARPA until 1972), the agency was always closely linked to military interests and problem-solving.[28] In management studies, the concept of problems that are "DARPA-hard" has become widespread, with websites baiting visitors to see whether their company's challenges would come close to qualifying. According to Leifer and Steinert (2011,159), there are four criteria for the agency to consider something DARPA-hard:

1. Technically challenging (beyond current limits);
2. Actionable (proof of concept or prototype);
3. Multidisciplinary (complex); and
4. Far-reaching (advances on a grand scale, radical).

At the turn of the century, DARPA clearly determined that solving orbital space debris met these criteria. Space debris fragments exceeded the capabilities of the Air Force's Space Surveillance Network (SSN), it would take work with specialists from various fields, and the achievement of a solution would be legitimately global in impact. The only thing missing was proof of concept.

Their first attempt at a solution was to work with MIT aeronautics labs to develop a specialized telescope to detect faint objects. In 2011, DARPA unveiled a massive new telescope, the Space Surveillance Telescope (SST), specially developed with MIT labs to identify space debris. In contrast with what DARPA spokespersons described as the "soda straw approach" of existing telescopes, the SST would allow wide-angle shots of the night sky, made possible by a much larger aperture and an advanced visual processing system. In at least one report provided to NBC, moreover, cleaning up space debris was linked directly with military objectives.[29]

Within five years of operation at the White Sands Missile Range in New Mexico, DARPA claimed its new model had been proven and turned it over to the Air Force to integrate into the SSN. At the same time, however, it was announced that the SST would be moved from New Mexico to an American military facility in western Australia. Moving the massive telescope was characterized as yet another DARPA-hard task that would take another four years to set up, with the SST not operational again until 2020.[30] It would seem that one solution only necessitated solving a brand-new problem and that simply witnessing space debris had become a goal two decades in the making.

These are the same problems that bedeviled scientists and officials at the beginning of the space race, that is, how to not only find but *track* satellites and other machines across the night sky. As one prominent scientist wrote a year before *Sputnik*'s launch, this was akin to following a golf ball's descent after it was dropped from a plane. When *Sputnik* was first launched, this required the involvement of amateur astronomers and ham radio operators, some using war surplus equipment and guidance from government scientists. In other words, civilians were encouraged to use leftover military equipment in order to assist in developing the military's latest capabilities in space.[31]

Much as was done in the early years of the space race, in 2012 DARPA proposed to enroll amateur astronomers in their hunt for space debris and put out a call for volunteers. The goal, they claimed, was to supplement the DoD's Space Surveillance Network by integrating the observations of independent amateurs into SpaceView. These would then be combined with observations from the SSN and SST in a new, data-managing program called OrbitOut-Look, which is still in development. DARPA may have first considered this possibility based on security reports from 2001, which mention the abilities of amateur astronomers to track orbiting objects to point out the risks that terrorists could pose to American infrastructure (see Albini 2001; Wilson 2001). The idea of amateur astronomers as a risk also raises the possibility of their being a resource, as they had been in the days of *Sputnik*.[32]

Recruiting amateurs is one thing. But how does one take all of the data they generate, which comes from different people with distinct technical and personal abilities, and compile it? How can one be sure to trust it? Space surveillance is not alone in this respect. There are similar problems with acquiring data to develop models of the global circulation, which is necessary to make meteorological and climatological predictions. Satellites have been increasingly central to these activities, though there are other means of acquiring climate and weather data. In the case of climatology, civilian data sets are increasingly incorporated in various ways, which involves coping with what Paul Edwards (2010, 317–19) calls *metadata friction*, that is, problems that arise from the heterogeneous, nonstandard ways that data is collected, processed, and produced by different people, in different parts of the world, at different times.

With their university and corporate partners, DARPA has prepared recent appraisals that assess SpaceView (created from the datasets of amateur volunteers) and its integration into OrbitOutlook (the central hub that combines data from the SST, from the DoD's SSN, and other sources) in order to produce a "Space Domain Awareness" of Earth's orbital environments and their hazards (see Blake, Sánchez, and Bolden 2016). Key to this is finding ways to smooth out differences between datasets and the friction that results. In a broader sense, it means making actionable—for civilian as well as military uses of space—the independent observations of amateurs, academics, and members of the armed services, much as occurred at the start of the space race.

Becoming Attuned with Orbital Debris

Finding space debris is only one half of a technical solution to the problem. So, along with other space agencies in Europe and NASA, DARPA has also proposed a way of capturing debris, once found, to prevent it from colliding with existing infrastructure or preventing new space initiatives. A systematic effort to reuse and recycle space debris is currently underway, with the European Space Agency (ESA), DARPA, NASA, and Japanese and Swiss space agencies all developing experimental devices that would capture debris so that it can be used for future space operations. Beyond the risk that space debris poses, there are economic reasons to do this. It costs roughly $10,000 per pound to send something into orbit, which makes it appealing to salvage some of the electrical components still up there.

Cleaning up space debris is also no simple matter, and some things are so DARPA-hard that even DARPA seeks outside help to solve them. In 2010, DARPA announced that it was investing in a new technology pioneered by Star Technology and Research, a small business based in South Carolina and run by former marine and NASA scientist Jerome Pearson. Jerome started the company in 1997 after retiring from working for the Air Force at the age of fifty-nine. He had contacts in government and the military and was confident that he could apply his ideas to get contracts despite the fact, as he told me in an interview, that it was much harder to compete for them at the time. Jerome had not set out to solve the problem of space debris, but to address a different one, which was how to maneuver vehicles in LEO. As mentioned above, objects in LEO are closer to the surface of the Earth and move much more quickly than objects in higher orbits. The problem this presents is with relative velocity.

Jerome's interest is primarily LEO. He credits one of his childhood heroes and famed science fiction author, Arthur C. Clarke, with the increasing utilization of LEO to place communication satellites in geostationary orbit, "hundreds now," he explained, "for Direct TV and such." For this reason, it is

commonly called "Clarke orbit." In fact, he and Clarke had a long correspond-
ence during which time they exchanged ideas that would lead to Jerome's space
elevator idea, one of the primary innovations that is credited to Star Tech and
a direct precursor to their space debris initiative. The key here was solving the
problem of "delta v" or change in velocity at Low Earth Orbit: "LEO is two
kilometers of altitude, the toughest regime moving around going orbit to orbit.
Up at GEO [it's] all in the same orbit, an equatorial orbit at the same velocity. . .[so] going between is easier. With LEO, there are different altitudes and
inclinations, differences in relative velocity." Jerome and his team began looking into developing an electro-dynamic vehicle, one that moves by using the
Earth's magnetic field to alter its orbit: "Like clipper ships of the nineteenth
century—you get a force of wind and angle the sale as needed. Tack against
the wind." An electromagnetic vehicle would work on solar power, with a current running through a long conductor. But the key innovation is that the force
of the magnetic field allows you to change orbit quickly and in subtle ways.

Jerome thought that this could be a way to service troubled or disused satellites and make them workable again. So the vehicle was called the Electro
Dynamic Delivery Express, or EDDE (pronounced "Eddy"). At the same
time, they realized, and convinced DARPA, that this could also help reuse and
recycle satellites. "Dead satellites can be repaired" using EDDE, "old satellites
with useful components can be reused. . .cut off antennae, cut off the solar
array." They had a NASA contract and were in the process of "working on
ground development of EDDE" but, according to Jerome, this all came to a
sudden halt due to internal politics. "They were excited about EDDE. The
problem was that NASA was afraid that the admin would say 'Oh, okay, start
removing debris.'" This is otherwise known, internally, as an "unfunded man-
date," which worries NASA staff that they are going to have to accomplish a
task with no additional funds and only their existing resources. According to
Jerome, this led to a negative response from the newest NASA administrator:
"NASA is not gonna develop any tech for space debris removal beyond lab
testing. It killed any follow-on for us."

I had wondered whether and how EDDE fit with DARPA's proposal to
use amateur astronomers to track space debris. When this announcement was
made, two years after they expressed commitment to EDDE, DARPA did not
mention Jerome but proposed its own recycling robot, called the Phoenix,
which the spokespersons claimed would be operational by 2017. The Phoenix
would find the debris identified by astronomers, they said, and use the parts

to support new space missions. But achieving space situational awareness in LEO is much harder. "You can service satellites. . .in GEO fairly easily," Jerome explained, and space agencies have managed to observe a few satellites. "EDDE is the secret to solving the LEO problem for recovery, reuse, refurbishment, refueling. . . If you've got a vehicle to move around there is a lot you can do. . .get close to any object, observe and see what condition it's in. It might be a failed satellite or it might have been hit by debris or a micro-meteoroid." The European Space Agency and NASA have announced a similar goal, without any mention of the use of amateur astronomers. The EASA and the Japanese, Jerome says, have looked into harpoons, nets, and tethers to capture debris. The appeal of recycling space debris, whatever the solution, is that it turns the threat into a resource that can make up for the enormous terrestrial funds and resources that are needed to launch objects into Earth's orbit and beyond. With the help of amateur astronomers, space debris would not only be a form of cultural resource to manage—as it is typically imagined within the archae-ology of outer space—but a material foundation for new and emergent futures. Jerome agrees. "We've got to fix it" and "stop creating new debris." He compared this to the "tragedy of the commons" popularized by ecologist Gar-rett Hardin.[33]

In New York's Southern Tier, at least, amateur astronomers are typically unaware of SpaceView, and many I spoke with were very skeptical that such a collaboration could amount to anything anyhow. Space debris makes for bad objects, which is saying something if you're into astronomical phenomena. The vast majority are in fragments; they are not whole machines, like old ships and planes. They are too small, move too quickly, break up or burn up in the atmosphere, blink in and out of existence. Unlike nebulous galaxies and gases, they don't usually have catchy Greek names and mythological credentials. Amateur astronomers are exceptionally good at identifying distant and blurry objects based on their relative luminance and position in the night sky. With the exception of the International Space Station, they are not interested in the tiny machines that stand in between the Earth and more distant phenomena. Space debris is just noise, like clouds or light pollution, that they are trying to see *past*.[34]

Amateur astronomers are not the same as ham radio operators, or ham-mies, however. If it takes billions of dollars of equipment to gather informa-tion on leftover satellites, you do not have to be a national space organization to reuse it. The radio room at Kopernik observatory is where Drew, the director, sneaks away to practice his favorite hobby, not astronomy but amateur ham radio. Like his father before him, Drew is a self-described "hammie": he enjoys communicating with people all over the world, exchanging postcards labeled with their individual callsigns, and trying to bounce signals off of the ionosphere and objects in space.[35] Unlike his father, Drew can track satellites on his computer display and identify their footprint using NASA tracking. When he is within the footprint, he can transmit and receive signals using his rotor controller by adjusting for the asmith (to indicate direction) and the elevation.

While I am there, he selects Oscar 7 (aka AO 7 or Amsat Oscar 7) on the monitor, and shows me its massive footprint, which it casts from almost a thousand miles up. With such a big footprint, Drew can transmit to Oscar 7 and communicate with someone as far away as North Africa or anywhere in Europe. The reason Drew brought Oscar 7 to my attention is that it was considered space junk until hammies recognized it was still working.

> This one was dead. It was dead for ten years. And then all of a sudden one guy happened to be just listening on the frequency and heard the sort of. . .a beacon frequency coming down from this thing, and then said, "That sounds like Oscar 7!" And sure enough it was, and then people continue to use it.

Oscar 7 was launched as a ham radio satellite in 1974 and worked for a decade until its batteries failed and it shorted. When it was unexpectedly recontacted in 2002, everyone realized that what they thought was junk was lying dormant only part of the time. Whenever its solar panels are illuminated by sunlight, it works, presumably due to an open circuit left behind.

Very different from this relatively passive recovery effort was the crowd-funded reboot project that targeted ICEE-3, a comet explorer launched in 1978, which NASA ceased contacting in 1997, after its technology had become obsolete. Unlike Oscar 7, ICEE-3 is in heliocentric orbit, though still moving close to Earth, as it was designed to by NASA. In 2014, two-way communication was established with ICEE-3 by a collection of NASA watch bloggers, entrepreneurs, and engineers. They managed to crowd-fund $125,000 for the purpose, though some were still skeptical they could succeed. Since the technology to contact and command the satellite no longer existed, they adapted basic radio technology and borrowed dishes in Puerto Rico and the Mojave Desert to enhance the signal. For almost three months, in a widely publicized affair, they managed to recontact the satellite and adjust its path. They were the first nongovernment group to command a spacecraft outside of Earth's orbit. A similar project involved English scientists funded by the EU to identify and repurpose the Beagle 2 Mars lander (see Bridges et al. 2017).[36]

If Oscar 7 and ICEE-3 are still functional, it is not hard to imagine how much usable hardware is floating up there for the taking, how much rubbish may turn out to be reclaimable material. But these are not just any machines, nor is this just any cleanup. According to Article 8 of the Outer Space Treaty, any salvaged debris still belongs to the agency that left it there—an economic investment, a state secret, and a piece of cultural heritage. Legal scholars point out that even before such issues are dealt with, there needs to be an agreed-upon definition of what constitutes space debris, which is still used in rather flexible ways. If Oscar 7 and ICEE-3 can be recovered, are they debris? Were they ever? If the technology to contact these devices has been forsaken, as was the case with ICEE-3, is this a matter of planned obsolescence? These are issues waste scholars are very familiar with, and they are not easily resolved.

What is noticeably different about these waste recovery activities is that they respond to the conditions already present and find passive and relatively inexpensive means of reusing debris. The problems are not DARPA-hard, but still require ingenuity. They do not create more debris, but reenliven what debris already exists. This is not recycling as technical mastery, but a form of attunement to conditions beyond their control. Attunement is openness to activity-without-action, at least as normally defined. Therefore, it need not assume instrumental activity or techno-solutionism, where a human agent masterfully shapes the world toward a predetermined end. Instead, attunement is a process of growing together to achieve emergent and open-ended outcomes.[37] In this sense, attunement is very different from the ambitions of empires, which seek to predict and develop a future for warfare in orbit. That future demands a form of control and certainty that amateur astronomers and hammies normally learn to forgo to some degree.

TO BOLDLY SLOUGH. . .

Should the emancipation and secularization of the modern age, which began with a turning-away. . .from a god who was the Father of men in heaven, end with an even more fateful repudiation of an Earth who was the Mother of all living creatures under the sky?

—Hannah Arendt (1958, 2)

Hunting for space debris unites some military and civilian actors, but I have argued it can also divide them in terms of how they relate to interactions with outer space. Within the literature on military tactics there is an analogous divide between those who advocate for a technocratic approach to victory and more population-focused counterinsurgency methods. As explained by Laleh Khalili (2013), the former emphasizes technological superiority and carefully selected, precise attacks, while the latter is more focused on understanding the contextual nuances of the people who are ideally being protected from the insurgency and persuaded not to join.[38] My point has not been to claim that the military should enroll more amateurs in its efforts, or make its efforts of debris recovery and recycling more sensitive to orbital environments per se. Instead of making warfare more humane or more successful, I would argue that it is better to reflect on the purposes of war and war preparation in general, with the militarization of space one of its aspects. Similarly, I hope that the efforts of amateurs will raise questions about how orbital environments have been and continue to be used, making the space debris problem a different one than it is normally assumed.

Outer space has long been a source for fantasies of pure war and future war. While Eisenhower opposed participating in the space race as a potentially wasteful expenditure, a generation later, war in space would be enthusiastically pursued by the Reagan administration through the Strategic Defense Initiative (SDI), more popularly known (and criticized) as "Star Wars" in reference to the famous film franchise. Supporters of the SDI said it was inevitable that the Russians would get there first if the United States did not beat them to it, echoing the line that had been used throughout the Cold War and since to justify the militarization of space. The SDI included plans to target objects in orbit from the ground and vice versa. The tens of billions spent on the program correlated with a large increase in defense spending relative to GDP in general, which had otherwise been steadily declining since World War II.

What SDI promised—war waged at a distance with more precision and less risk—is still highly sought after by the defense establishment. One of the more recent examples, and a popular source of discussion in technology and military online forums and publications, is the so-called "Rods from God" program (also known as Project Thor): tungsten rods the size of telephone poles which, when dropped with precision from space, could have the effect of a nuclear detonation, but without the fallout. Most recently, Donald Trump suggested the possibility of adding a new branch to the military—which he dubbed the "Space Force"—in an address to members of the Marine Corps in San Diego. Though this remark was mocked in some quarters, it came barely a week after Lockheed Martin's media day, when the company's CEO excited reporters with talk about new laser weapons and hypersonic planes. Or consider the secretive "space plane" that the Air Force has already been experimenting with, according to online space enthusiasts. These are among the reasons why the Pentagon and the armed forces are so invested in tracking and solving space debris.[39]

Jerome explained that, given his history, he was "comfortable working with the military" and it was much easier to work with compared to NASA, which "has a lot of complicated things to go through and demands on contractors." On the other hand, Jerome's team also includes some who are "pacifists at heart, with problems with the military." This is not an issue when they set their minds on fixing a problem, he insists. The problem with the techno-solutionism currently pursued by entities like DARPA is not, to echo Morozov, "that solutions proposed are unlikely to work but that, in solving the 'problem,' solutionists twist it in such an ugly and unfamiliar way that, by the time it is 'solved,' the problem becomes something else entirely" (2013, 8). The problem with endeavoring to "solve" space debris, I would argue, is that it is no replacement for reflection and debate on continuing to interfere with orbital environments, especially for the sake of military dominance and experimental warfare.

In December of 2017, there was a familiar news story. The Pan-STARRS initiative of the US Air Force had detected a new object entering the solar system from a great distance. It was named 'Oumuamua from the Hawaiian for "first messenger" because, given its peculiar shape and coloration, it was unclear whether it was an asteroid or possibly of alien invention. As reported in *Scientific American*:

> 'Oumuamua might be shaped rather like a needle, up to 800 meters long and only 80 wide, spinning every seven hours and 20 minutes. That would mean it is like no asteroid ever seen before, instead resembling the collision-minimizing form favored in many designs for notional interstellar probes. What's more, it is twirling at a rate that could tear a loosely-bound rubble pile apart. Whatever 'Oumuamua is, it appears to be quite solid—likely composed of rock, or even metal—seemingly tailor-made to weather long journeys between stars. (Billings 2017)

Or, the article was quick to point out, it could just be a random, intergalactic flotsam. The greatest minds and nations are not yet in a position to tell the utterly insignificant from the significant, despite millennia of experimentation with one of the oldest scientific practices: looking up. This might be taken as a call for greater humility, rather than techno-optimism. Space debris exists because of the space race and the Cold War, the primary motivations for which have not gone away in the intervening years. But even human contamination of the world can only occur by working in concert with earthly forces and forms independent from us. Arguably the more successfully human beings trash the environment, terrestrial or otherwise, the more we depend on help from these planetary powers to do so. This is critical to realize because, even if the local problem of space debris is "solved," and people and their machines do enter space en masse to colonize and exploit its resources, further space debris will arise from the impact these activities leave behind on nonterrestrial worlds and beings. Contamination is never entirely under our control, making it an all-but-inevitable accident of space exploration.

If people manage to address the "local" problem of space debris, in other words, then we are no longer the exclusive victims of our own waste and are free to share it with others beyond our planet or solar system. Judging from science fiction film, television, and literature, it would seem humanity has more to fear from an uncaring universe than vice versa. Annihilation by means of aliens or asteroids implies a vision of life on Earth, and human civilization in particular, as vulnerable to what might arrive from above. The relative fragility of our species and our planet is not simply about our failure to predict or prevent what the future may bring, however, but our very cleverness. Space debris is a constant reminder of that, provided you can catch a momentary glimpse, and bring yourself to care.

CHAPTER 5

Domestic Blowback

Several hundred million guns are now in circulation in the United States. That is more than the number of registered passenger vehicles, nearly one for every adult and child. According to a 2012 *New York Times* column, "more Americans die in gun homicides and suicides in six months than have died in the last 25 years in every terrorist attack and the wars in Afghanistan and Iraq combined" (cited in Gusterson 2013, 1). Many scholars have tried to find *the reason* for all of these guns and gun deaths. They could be a consequence of:

1. a culture of honor passed on since the days of duels and slave patrols (Nisbett 1996);

2. a gun culture that associates personal independence and property ownership with adequate self-defense (Bellesiles 2000);

3. a moral and legal discourse that emphasizes liberty to protect against government control or curtailment of rights (Burbick 2006, Anderson 2017); and/or

4. the continuing influence of white supremacy and the legacy of settler colonialism (Dunbar-Ortiz 2018).

In this chapter, I am not adding another possible explanation to the list. Instead, I want to consider a generally unacknowledged parallel: the same country with a heavily armed general population also has the world's largest military and security apparatus. Put differently, there are even *more guns* in the United States if you count those in the hands and holsters of police departments, the FBI, the CIA, the NSA, the Coast Guard, and branches of the military.

This correlation between a large military and a large supply of guns could exist for any number of reasons. Yet it rarely receives any consideration. It is as if guns and gun violence on the home front exist in total isolation from the war front. Like orbital space debris, discussed in the previous chapter, these incidents tend to be demilitarized in popular discourse. This is arguably the case even when mass shootings occur at military facilities, as happened at Fort Hood in 2009 (and again in 2014). The public discussion of the first incident resembled that of other mass shootings even though it involved a military base as a target and a service member as a perpetrator. There were still discussions of the motives of the perpetrator and their individual psychology (see Moskalenko and McCauley 2011); there were still discussions about improving security or preventing attacks by making guns more readily available or regulating them further.

This chapter approaches guns and gun violence as the excess leftover, the waste, of American militarization and militarism. This is admittedly a difficult connection to demonstrate empirically. It is easier to see military wastes in the form of literal planes stored in the desert or naval vessels being dismantled. But objects like these, on which the earlier chapters of this book focus, do not exhaust the by-products of permanent war preparation.

Mass shootings are an extreme form of gun violence. Though far less common than other forms of gun-related deaths, especially suicides, mass shootings are still more of a problem in the United States than elsewhere.[1] According to Roxanne Dunbar-Ortiz, both American warfare and mass shootings are made possible by *militarism*:

> Public mass shootings. . .parallel the rise of the gun-rights movement and ramped-up militarism. This suggests that it is not only the sheer number of guns in the hands of private citizens or the lack of regulation and licensing, but also a gun culture at work, along with a military culture, matters more difficult to resolve than by imposing regulations on firearms. (2018, 131)

The social production of militarism is not something that can be documented as easily as the amount of money spent on the military, or the number of guns, planes, ships, and satellites in circulation. Militarism is a way of being, of thinking and acting, that privileges violent confrontation as a way to resolve conflict and, more broadly, as a way to demonstrate strength (Bachevich 2013, 2). Militarism is apparent in the motives of mass shooters, who would use violence as a means to take revenge, to gain fame, to act out fantasies, or for some other purpose. But it is also apparent when proposed solutions to mass shootings include using violence to stop them, for instance arming teachers or school staff. Militarism is apparent during wartime, of course, as a way to justify the need for military buildup. But it is also apparent when a preemptive military strike or invasion is used to prevent further war. In all of these cases, violence is the preferred option and nonviolent resolutions are either downplayed or foreclosed from consideration altogether.

The broader culture of American militarism predates the military industrial complex, and is also its condition of possibility. While current forms of militarism could be traced to the late twentieth century, especially national responses to the war in Vietnam, their origins could also be identified much earlier, in the British colonies and their use of civilian militias. Many of the so-called "little" or "savage" wars fought against Native Americans in the first two centuries of the settler colony were fought, not by the formal military, but by organized militias armed with guns. As Dunbar-Ortiz (2018) argues, this ideological and material reliance on civilian guns to wage war on native peoples was formally acknowledged in the Second Amendment and its reference to a "well-regulated militia, being necessary to the security of a free state."[2]

Currently, the military establishment invests in militarism at the level of policy, political discourse, and mass entertainment. Beyond the DoD's relationship with politicians and policymakers, it has made sure in recent decades to invest in popular sports (the NFL), in video games (*America's Army*), and in films (the Marvel Cinematic Universe) that privilege militarism in one form or another. While militarism has long been a part of civilian life in the United States, what Bachevich calls the new American militarism "is a little like pollution...the perhaps unintended but foreseeable by-product of prior choices and decisions made without taking fully into account the full range of costs likely to be incurred" (2013, 206). Varieties of gun violence can be seen as the pollution-like seepage of militarism into the home front, an ideology underlying everyday life as well as permanent war readiness.

I begin this chapter by describing some of the origins of this "polluting" militarism, especially its association with guns. First, I argue that militarism is entangled with histories of settler colonialism and white supremacy in the US. The first mass shootings on this continent were those committed against indigenous communities by settlers and colonists from Europe. And it is pre-

cisely in the excess of violent expenditure that white identity has been peril-
ously shaped, often through confrontations with *others* who have been empowered and armed and (many whites believe) should not be. What I call *guns in
the wrong hands* is the common thread that connects settler colonial violence
with US military interventions abroad and mass shootings, mass incarceration, and police killings on the home front.

One way to study militarism empirically is by documenting its role in stories and storytelling. Here I follow David Pedersen's (2013) argument that an
analysis of storytelling can reveal larger, open-ended wholes beyond empirically observable events. Broadly speaking, storytelling about violence draws on
the perspectives of people directly involved, but tends to do so in ways that are
meant to make the violence matter to others who were not. This can make
representations of violence ethically fraught and politically controversial.
Many accounts of an act of violence endeavor in some way to understand what
seems empirically given: who used violence and their possible motives, who
was targeted by this violence and their experiences, and the accounts of witnesses.[3] To use Keane's (2016) terms, actual witnesses to violent acts may have
the most reliable "first-" and "second-person" observations about what actually
happened in an interaction or the feelings and thoughts of those involved. But
when violent acts appear to have larger significance for others in the community, in the society or in the world, it may be that the interpretations of people
who bore direct witness can be overridden by those of others, people with
what Keane (2016: 63–67) calls a "third-person perspective" on the broader
ethical and political implications of the event.

For example, while some people may want to give public platforms to survivors of shootings, others may accuse them of seeking to benefit from this
publicity and, by extension, being unreliable narrators. This was the fate of the
Sandy Hook and Parkland school shooting survivors, whom some right-wing
commentators accused of manufacturing events that did not happen or of
using their newfound fame for their own political ends. On the other side of
the political spectrum, people on the left tend to be suspicious of the first-
person perspectives reported by police after unarmed civilians are shot. Ideological divides over who really acted violently in a given situation (i.e., whether
a specific action should be interpreted as aggressive or defensive, for instance)
ultimately fall back on questions concerning whose experience really counts
and which witnesses can be relied upon to interpret events. With both police
shootings and mass shootings, moreover, video footage and other collateral

information may be used to impeach the credibility of direct witnesses to violent interactions, based on the assumption that these media will offer a neutral, third-person perspective free of any bias (Bui 2017).

My intention is not to equate these events beyond pointing out the shared processes of ethical generalization they undergo. Whether for police shootings or mass shootings, storytelling about gun violence reassembles empirical facts, rearranging perspectives and actions, assigning blame and credit, constructing a timeline and a history, all to process what has happened and put things back to normal. Often this draws on the direct experiences of participants to an event, but it may not.[4] In the wake of any mass shooting, a collection of influential media actors, from journalists to expert pundits and politicians, work with and against each other to shape public perceptions of the event. The reason that third-person accounts can take precedence, though they may not represent situations from a perspective of direct involvement, is arguably due to the broader significance of such events. In the contemporary United States, police shootings and mass shootings are random incidents that only happen to some people but could in theory occur anywhere, anytime, to anyone.

Militarism informs storytelling about American violence, offering an underlying and unifying thematic that makes sense out of seemingly random events. In keeping with militaristic ideas, participants in violent events may be described in ways that resemble stories about warfare. As a result, the specific decisions they make are reduced to a familiar and accessible repertoire of militaristic behaviors. While Trump openly criticized an officer at the February 2018 mass shooting at Parkland High School as "a coward" for not acting to prevent the attack (and bragged of his own heroism, had he been there), the intrusion of militarism into narratives of shootings can be subtler. To take one example, schools where mass shootings take place are occasionally described by scholars, journalists, and politicians as having become like "war zones." This provides a meaningful analogy, because people generally have some sense of what war zones are supposed to be like (even if based only on media representations), or at the very least what makes them different from schools. The collapse of this difference, between military experience and civilian life, is meant to be horrific, but it also makes traumatic events somewhat legible. That does not make mass shootings any less disruptive or damaging, but may serve to demonstrate normative assumptions about how things ought to be by highlighting the degree to which things are not as they should be. According to Patricia Molloy (2002), war zones and schools are also analogous in that they are explicitly governed by sovereign power, following Agamben, as states of exception. As I will explain, this creates a "hidden curriculum" (Webber 2003) in schools that may perpetuate damaging personal experience (for instance, bullying) and encourage the use of militaristic storytelling to make sense of it. That being said, when warzones and schools are made too much alike through events like mass shootings, the limits of sovereign power are exposed. This is arguably one of the primary objectives of such a violent performance.

But there are limits to militaristic storytelling, slippages where they fail to represent events or offer possibilities for alternative accounts to emerge. Pedersen also discusses the possibility of "transvaluing" stories in new ways, by turning them on their heads. Specifically, he defines transvaluation as "the capacity for the same form or sign to shift or expand its immediate object and therefore its meaning" (2013, 24). In this chapter I discuss two unusual mass shooting incidents in the Southern Tier of New York State, one of which was planned but not carried out, and the other which was carried out yet tends to be ignored in the national media. I argue that these two out-of-the-ordinary incidents challenge what is normatively expected with mass shootings, transvaluing the dominant form of storytelling about such violence in the United States.

BY-PRODUCTS OF MILITARISM

The age of Colt was the age of the gun, an age when a youthful nation first dreamed of glory and empire.
—William N. Hosley (1996, 67)

Before discussing mass shootings, it is important to recognize that how Americans relate to guns has been shaped both by histories of settler colonialism and white supremacy and by their realization through militarism and militarization. This is what ultimately led to a nation that has borne witness to mass killing time and again. There is not a period of US history that has lacked civilian slaughter; it is just that some people are recognized as legitimate targets or collateral damage in a just cause. In brief, Americans were at war with themselves long before they participated in or planned for global conflict. In the first two centuries of the settler colony, organized violence was normally carried out by militias and volunteers. They recaptured and tormented escaped slaves, fought and slaughtered indigenous tribes for control over land, and later would enter into formal conflicts against French and English imperial forces.

And yet the capacity for violence was still in the hands of a relatively few. Americans did not become heavily armed until midway through the nineteenth century, largely because guns were expensive and difficult to maintain. The issue was not only the weapons themselves, but their treatment. Belleslies explains that military leaders "complained of the indifference with which Americans treated their weapons" and that "many state governments discovered that their armories were full of useless firearms" (1999, 23–24).[5] Neither machines nor men could be depended upon. It was military investment that changed all of this.

The first attempt to mass-produce arms with interchangeable parts actually dates to the beginning of the nineteenth century, when Thomas Jefferson sought to reproduce manufacturing processes he had observed as ambassador to France. More reliable arms, he and others believed, would make up for the routine problems that afflicted America's armies. In response to Jefferson, Eli Whitney, notable inventor of the cotton gin, was one of the first to attempt the process. Whitney was unsuccessful, but his efforts inspired later would-be industrialists like Samuel Colt. Colt not only introduced new forms of precision mass production, but also transformed what guns meant to Americans and what they could do with them. As a popular saying went on the American frontier, "God made men; Colonel Colt made them equal." At the same time, it was not individual entrepreneurs alone who armed the nation, but a militaristic settler colony looking toward continental expansion. Like Eli Whitney, or the Wright brothers with their airplane (discussed in chapter 2), Colt was primarily interested in selling guns to national militaries, at home or abroad. Like later gun manufacturers, he would sell to civilians as a secondary market.[6]

Between the Civil War and the Spanish-American War, the US military began changing into what it is today. First, this was a period of increasing military professionalization. This transition was not inevitable, since many Americans and their representatives resisted fully professionalized armed services until well after the Civil War. Second, during this period the US government transitioned from occasional, disorganized "little wars" against native peoples to systematic, total war. Third, there was a transition in tactics away from the mass formations that had characterized infantries for centuries toward more dispersed troop formations. All three of these changes were associated with changing weaponry. It would not be a stretch to say that it was not until this historical period that guns became guns as they are known today, rather than small and ineffective cannons. In 1873, the Colt Single Action

Army Revolver and Winchester Repeating Rifle had been released, both of which are said to have "won the West" for the settler colonists (provided they were in the right hands, i.e., those of whites). Breech-loading weapons replaced muskets with powder and ball, and "besides ease of loading and rapidity of fire, the metallic cartridge permitted greater velocity and accuracy" (Utley 1973, 69). This made mass formation lines (in which it was typically pointless to aim when shooting) all but obsolete, which also encouraged professionalization by making it necessary to train infantry to wield new and improved guns.[7]

All of these trends converge in the infamous Battle of Little Big Horn in 1876. The reaction to this event is worth reviewing in some detail, because it demonstrates the entanglement of ideas concerning settler colonialism, white supremacy, and militarization, which are still evident in the stories we tell about guns and mass shootings today.

Custer's Revenge

In the early nineteenth century, the US Office of Indian Affairs, based within the War Department, had treated the lands just to the west of the Mississippi River as Indian Country. This was easier to do when the Great Plains were considered a barren desert and gold had not yet been discovered. But after the acquisition of Oregon settlement from Great Britain, and ceded territory resulting from the war with Mexico, the continental United States now existed on two coasts, divided in the middle. Around this time, Indian Affairs was transferred to the Department of the Interior, which was staffed by people even less sympathetic to Native Americans. This led, in turn, to the creation of Nebraska and Kansas territories in Indian Country. During the Civil War, soldiers went back east and volunteers with less experience (and typically more animus toward Native Americans) were put in charge of forts in the West. Yet this created an opportunity for indigenous tribes. Just as World War I and II strained the ability of European empires to keep their global colonial possessions in order, the war between North and South provided a chance for some tribes to regain lost territory from white settlers and reassert their autonomy to roam beyond the boundaries of reservations.

Even after the war, northern soldiers were kept in the South for Reconstruction, and the funding and ranks of enlisted soldiers shrank considerably, leaving smaller parties to return west to secure the creation of railroads, conduct geological surveys, and confront native resistance.[8] All of these events culminated in warfare when gold was reported in the sacred Black Hills and encroaching settlers increasingly pressed their way into lands in direct violation of government treaties. The gold was found by the Seventh Cavalry Regiment of the US Army, under the command of George Armstrong Custer. The Seventh Cavalry had been surveying the area for scientific purposes in order to establish a military base. When large numbers of native peoples wandered beyond the Great Sioux Reservation, partly in response to repeated treaty violations, Custer was sent to intercept them and bring them back. At Little Big Horn, the Seventh Cavalry was confronted by a larger force and overwhelmed.[9]

One of the most dissected military conflicts of all time, "Custer's Last Stand" was a decisive moment in the Sioux Wars between Plains Indians and encroaching settlers. I am not interested in why the Seventh Cavalry lost this battle, which has been debated and dissected ever since. In a way, it is the very fact that this rather minor episode has stirred up so much discussion that is far more interesting. Prominent stories told about Little Bighorn represent tensions surrounding changes in warfare and American settler colonialism at that time. Such tensions materialize in the form of what I call *guns in the wrong hands*. By this I mean, most obviously, normative assumptions about who should have guns and who should not, which relates to the foundational projects of settler colonialism and white supremacy. But I also mean the obverse, that is, stories about guns misused or misfired due to human or mechanical failure, guns mishandled, poorly produced, or neglected. Most often, stories about misused or misfired guns indicate who should and should not be equipped with guns and skilled at using them.

Surveying reactions to the Battle of Little Bighorn, all of these senses of guns in the wrong hands are in evidence. One popular narrative that emerged surrounding the battle was that the Indian guns had been better, or they had been used more skillfully. By implication, this makes the weapons in the hands of Custer's men, or the men themselves, inferior. Guns in the wrong hands were wielded by Sioux warriors when, according to white perspectives, they ought to have been in the hands of white soldiers and settlers. Guns in the wrong hands were also those wielded by US cavalry with poor training or suffering from fatigue as a result of military mismanagement after the Civil War. Even good weapons were likely to be misused, according to this story, by men who were overworked and underprepared. Some have also claimed Custer's loss was due to malfunctions in carbine machinery (see Utley 1973, 70; for reasons to doubt this, see Fox 1993). Not only had weapons possibly malfunctioned, but American cavalry had been outgunned: "The anomaly depicted by survivors of Little Big Horn (not without considerable exaggeration) of Sioux warriors armed with single-shot Springfields dramatized the need for a military repeater. Shortly after the Custer disaster, Colonel Mackenzie formally applied to have his regiment's Springfields replaced with Winchesters" (Utley 1973, 72). It was as if whites had somehow been denied these guns and skills while Sioux had somehow managed to acquire them.

Through successful storytelling, Little Bighorn was represented as a battle that should not have been lost. And this had important historical consequences for the growth of permanent war readiness. Republicans at the time, following President Rutherford B. Hayes, urged increases in military spending (ostensibly during peacetime) for added troops and better equipment. Generally speaking, after the Civil War there was considerable public and political support for shrinking the army to a negligible size and relying more on civilian militias once again.[10] The military as a whole was looked on with suspicion and widely unpopular. For this reason, the Battle of Little Bighorn was dramatized by political and media elites, who used stories about the ill-fated Custer to draw public support for replenishing, rather than reducing, military might.

White supremacy and settler colonialism link these developments, both ideologically and materially. According to popular storytelling motifs within and beyond the American South, the widespread value of white pride and honor had been under attack since the Civil War. Republican storytelling won out at least in part because of Custer's humiliating defeat. Congress authorized an increase in troops as a "temporary" measure to deal with the perceived crisis on the frontier. These proposals were strongly opposed by Democrats, who had only lost the 1876 election by allowing their opponents to claim twenty contested electoral college votes. This agreement, also known as the Compromise of 1877, required that the government withdraw troops from the South, effectively ending Reconstruction. In essence, troops were not only removed from the South to ensure Republican power in the federal government, they were a bargaining chip that simultaneously ended Reconstruction and ensured that troop numbers could be increased even further to win the West (and later the world) for whites. In one fell swoop the government empowered Southern militias to restore racial hierarchy and emboldened the US military to defeat indigenous tribes domestically and colonize others abroad. All of these projects were arguably part of an effort to overcome white humiliation.

Total war against Native Americans was therefore directly made possible by and connected with the beginning of the Jim Crow era of black disenfranchisement, terror, and segregation. Not long after the military spending bill, Congress passed the Posse Comitatus Act (1878), which barred the federal government from using the military to interfere with state policies. It is no accident that troops would return to the South to ensure voting rights and desegregation during the Civil Rights era. With contemporary gun violence, the scars from this period continue to shape both white male subjects (who are more likely to engage in mass shootings) and black male subjects (who are more likely to be the victims of the new Jim Crow and excessive policing and mass incarceration).[11]

This might have happened anyway; a different Custer might have been mourned and scrutinized. But it is significant that it was through fear of natives massacring white troops that consensus on permanent war preparation was reached in a still-divided republic. Furthermore, this moment of debated militarization links the absence of protection for nonwhite civil rights with the presence of soldiers to conquer indigenous lands, not only in the homeland but in colonies abroad. Like the Alamo, Pearl Harbor, or 9/11, the story of Custer's Last Stand has been puzzled over ever since. And like these other incidents, Little Bighorn also represents the beginning of a turning point in the American way of war. This began with the Civil War, with a shift in military strategy toward total war and victory (which was part of the reason that southerners and Democrats looked unfavorably on the US military in the first place). In the late nineteenth century, finally defeating native resistance was made a primary goal. Custer's Last Stand helped inspire the US military to strive for professionalization and modernization in order to eliminate any and all native resistance to the growing American empire (see chapter 6). The predictable result was the mass shooting of nonwhite civilians. At the turn of the century this culminated in the 1890 massacre of more than 150 Lakota at Wounded Knee in South Dakota and the less well-known 1906 massacre of nearly a thousand Tausug Muslims in the "Battle of Bud Dajo" in the Philippines. In both cases, total war meant using modernized soldiers and munitions to systematically slaughter nonwhite men, women, and children in the name of defeating native insurrections.[12]

The increasing professionalization of the military, to do away with guns in the wrong hands by eliminating the figure of the inexperienced, unequipped soldier, would lead to more focus on producing professional killers. It has been pointed out that Custer's troops not only were inexperienced, but lacked training. For instance, they were not given ammunition to practice with their assigned weapons. If a shooter could not develop familiarity with his gun, then how could the two form the murderous cyborg that modern war seemed to demand? In this way, an underused weapon supposedly goes to waste regardless of its accuracy or reliability. The gradual rise of sharpshooters within the armed services represent the opposite extreme, eventually leading to a public embrace of this kind of soldier (as in films like *American Sniper*). Between Custer and the sniper of the twenty-first century is not only better equipment, but a concerted effort to train soldiers to kill more efficiently and effectively, to produce usually white, male subjects who are good at killing, and in whose hands guns will not go to waste.[13]

What is sometimes described as the first mass shooting in the United States was the University of Texas tower shooting of 1966. The perpetrator: a former marine who excelled in sharpshooting.[14]

Gunfighters

Debates surrounding Little Bighorn echo contemporary divides surrounding guns in the wrong hands, where each violent episode leads to arguments about guns that should be in the right hands (i.e., the hands of "good guys") or guns that should be more regulated so they are not misused by hapless fools who will only shoot the wrong people if armed (i.e., accidental shootings, police killing of unarmed civilians). Whether gun regulation is considered insufficient or excessive, many seem to agree that guns are in the wrong hands. These concerns are critical ingredients in militaristic storytelling.

Stories about people good at killing with guns became a powerful motif in the twentieth century. This is associated most strongly with the cultural figure of the gunfighter, also known as the ranger, the frontiersman, the militiaman, the Indian fighter. This was a person (most often white and male) with the ability to kill effectively with a gun. But he did not kill just anyone. In the young republic he was surrounded, confronted by wave after wave of Europeans, Mexicans, Native Americans, and escaped slaves. The figure of the gunfighter does not dominate his surroundings; rather, he is imagined as if perpetually outnumbered and outgunned, continually forced to defend civilization (and usually, by extension, the white race) against ceaseless attacks and threats from others.

It is for this reason that the gunfighter became an especially important cultural figure during the invention of the western genre in the early 1950s. According to Richard Slotkin, who deserves the most credit for elaborating upon the significance of the gunfighter for American history, this figure is the "embodiment of the central paradox of America's self-image in an era of Cold War, 'subversion,' and the thermonuclear balance of terror: our sense of being at once supremely powerful and utterly vulnerable, politically dominant and yet helpless to shape the course of crucial events" (Slotkin 1992, 383). With both the Cold War and the War on Terror, Gusterson argues (2004, 21–47), war and war preparation were both justified by conjuring purportedly un-American, nonwhite others who might gain weapons they should not. If whites once agonized over Springfields in the hands of Sioux riding horseback, now this anxiety shifted to cultural others with weapons of mass destruction.

What Slotkin does not mention, in his otherwise impressive compendium of American pop culture, is that at the same time that the gunfighter was purportedly invented in popular fiction, so was the serial killer. The popularization of serial killers fits within an ideology of militarism, which reduces all social relations to acts of implicit and explicit force. However, the primary target of the serial killer, in reality and in fiction, tends to be women and children, not the "workers, Indians, and freed slaves" that Slotkin argues are the primary obstacle standing in the way of civilization and the marketplace (1992, 19).[15] Yet, arguably the rise of postmodern westerns, such as Clint Eastwood's celebrated *Unforgiven* (1992), deliberately blurred the distinction between gunfighter and serial killer. They are not only persons good at killing, but white men compelled to do so by their true nature.

In this way, the gunfighter remains a prominent cultural figure of white-masculinity-at-risk in the post–Cold War era. Today, mass shooters and serial killers are often imagined in the same way: they cannot be reasoned with or expected to stop themselves, they can only be identified and stopped before they do what they are meant to. Storytelling about serial killers and mass shooters share another feature in common. They are often depicted (and depict themselves, see Seltzer 1996) as humiliated subjects. Ordinarily white and male, they have been denied pride and honor by others and seek to restore it. This sense of individual humiliation, real or imagined, is frequently associated with child abuse and bullying in popular accounts. Horror films and television shows rarely portray a killer who has not been unfairly traumatized in some way. In the case of mass shooters, bullying is commonly referred to but not always present. Even so, it is possible to identify a continuum of male humiliation that goes from direct bullying and abuse to more indirect or implicit denial of power, especially by women and people of color.

Not simply rising gun ownership and a growing military, but the continued mass production of this white masculine trope has co-occurred with mass shootings over the last half century. In a nation forged by the gun and settler colonialism, innocent civilians are not only collateral damage, but sometimes considered worthy targets. And not everyone will agree on the difference— one person's innocent victim will be another's threatening menace, a legitimate target because they trouble prominent forms of white masculine selfhood.

A FORGOTTEN MASS SHOOTING

Vigilante killing as an antidote to male humiliation is not a new phenomenon, but has its historical and cultural origins in white supremacy, especially the overthrow, partial reconstruction, and reinvention of the institution of slavery (see Wyatt-Brown 2014). The way they talk about themselves and are talked about and remembered by others, it is as if contemporary serial killers and mass shooters collect and repurpose fragments of America's troubled history. In fact, the trope of the male gunfighter is pliable enough that nonwhite men and boys have also relied on this cultural figure to restore their pride and honor through mass killing. When a nonwhite perpetrator's path to mass murder is narrated, by themselves and others, white supremacy is often blamed, implicitly or explicitly, for their personal trauma. But these stories are less frequently told in general, precisely because they do not fit within the storytelling pattern of white male grievance.

In mid-September of 2017 I was at Strange Brew, a café in downtown Binghamton where much of this book was written. In the background, I could overhear a conversation between three middle-aged white men in suits. They mostly discussed local development, but their conversation devolved into signs that their community is in decline. To my surprise, one of them complained that Binghamton is never mentioned alongside other cities that have had a tragic mass shooting—Columbine, Sandy Hook, Aurora, Orlando, Las Vegas—even though the one "we" had, in April of 2009, was "just as bad." For the man speaking, this was evidence of the fact that nonlocal media tend to ignore what happens in Binghamton. This fits with anxieties that one can often hear voiced by residents in any city or town that has lost manufacturing jobs in recent decades, the sense of having been forgotten and cast aside by the economy (see chapter 1). In a society that so values wealth and prosperity, this is tantamount to having been cast aside by the country as a whole, to having been denied the opportunity to be truly fulfilled, to be *real men* who provide for their families.

But there is more going on. The shooting is one of the only recent mass shootings on US soil to primarily claim the lives of noncitizens. It happened the morning of April 3 at the American Civic Association immigration center when a naturalized citizen, 41-year-old Jiverly Antares Wong, barricaded the rear door of the building and began firing at people inside, wielding two handguns. Entering the property, he then began shooting people in an ESL classroom where he had previously been a student. He took some people hostage and, once the SWAT team arrived, eventually shot himself. In total, thirteen people died, including Wong. President Obama made public comments about the tragedy and it received widespread national coverage, as is typical. But this did not last, which betrays normative expectations about mass shooters and their victims.

In various reports and studies, "the first" mass shooting is normally characterized as the 1966 clocktower shooting at the University of Texas.[16] But such historiography deliberately leaves out centuries of white massacres of Native Americans as well as enslaved and free African-Americans. One might object that "mass shooting" is supposed to be about civilian attacks on others. Even so, for centuries civilian militias carried out public attacks on slaves, freed blacks, and Native Americans. The only possible objection to characterizing these as the nation's first "mass shootings" is that they were conducted with the implicit and explicit approval of government agencies and were therefore not clearly illegal. First of all, one could respond, with philosopher of war Jeff McMahan, that "what matters in the justification of violence is not whether a goal is *political* but whether it is *just*" (2009, 83, emphasis in original). Second, this counterargument about legality would only prove Dubar-Ortiz's (2018) point: militarism is deeply woven into American history and society, which has meant that murdering civilians with guns and racial politics have tended to go together.

Surrounding mass shooting narratives there is often reference to a sense of white pride in jeopardy. This jeopardy may be experienced by victims or those who worry about becoming victims, who understandably may conclude that arming themselves is the only way to feel safe. It is also experienced by many shooters themselves, or would-be shooters, who frequently see themselves as beleaguered and bullied. Like the mythical gunfighter discussed above, a narrative of violent white masculinity is predicated on shooters overcoming others *different from them* who nevertheless have *power over them*. Even where shooters and victims are broadly similar, as with the Columbine attack, shooters try to separate from their intended victims, to represent themselves as distinct, godlike, unique. In this way, the act of violence is not only a way of bringing order to their world, getting revenge on those who have slighted them, for instance, but more precisely as a means of creating themselves anew by overcoming the imagined domination of others.[17]

One might even characterize mass shootings as a form of suicide. By this I not only mean that the perpetrators normally intend to take their own lives at the conclusion of their act of violence, or expect to be shot by police. I also mean to distinguish between suicide as the ending of one's own physical life and suicide as bringing to an end one life story and beginning another.[18] Whether or not a mass shooter dies in the incident, the shooter's old self most certainly does. So powerful is the enactment of a school shooting, that it can be recognized even if no one is actually shot. Furthermore, just because people are shot does not guarantee it will be similarly dramatized if it does not conform to the trope of the gunfighter mythos. This is arguably the case with the mass shooting in Binghamton. A recent immigrant killing mostly other recent immigrants does not clearly conform to an imagined confrontation between an aggrieved, white self and bullying, oppressing, dominating others.

I am not alone in this interpretation of the relative neglect of the Binghamton shooting. This is a dominant theme in a *Boston Globe* article that appeared in November 2017, one of the only national stories to report on the shooting in the time since:

> Not long after the massacre, Binghamton receded from public memory. Some residents are upset by this. It's as if the horror they endured together is being minimized or passed over. Others don't mind; they would rather their community not be associated with the murders. People here are somewhat reluctant to say it, but many believe the Binghamton slayings get overlooked because most of the victims were immigrants from distant shores. (Arsenault 2017)

This is also how some of the family members of victims of the shooting explain why it is rarely if ever listed alongside mass shootings at Fort Hood (2009/2014), Aurora (2012), and San Bernardino (2015), though it had as many or more fatalities. According to the son of one of the victims, the fact that the victims were mostly immigrants, rather than citizens, is the only reason it appears to have disappeared from public attention: "That's the only reason I can think of in terms of why people didn't care as much as they do about some of the others" (King 2015).

The question for social scientists is not only which mass shootings occur, how many, where, how often etc., but also which mass shootings people tell the most stories about and remember. And Americans seem more attracted to those stories that echo the racial politics of the gunfighter mythos, that is, stories that involve predominantly white victims and/or villains confronted by a world that seems beyond their control. If the absence of the familiar trope of white griev-ance is why the Binghamton shooting is rarely discussed, this is also unfortunate because it involved an act of nonviolent heroism. One of the first people shot was Shirley DeLucca, who pretended to be dead and crawled across the floor, wounded, to call 911 and get help. Given that the rampage only ended when Wong reportedly saw that the police had arrived, DeLucca's brave actions likely saved more lives. But that kind of bravery is rarely heralded, for the simple rea-son that it does not fit with narratives of militarism, which tend to credit those who use violent means to respond to violent attacks, or blame those who fail to.[19]

A SCHOOL SHOOTER WHO DID NOT SHOOT

Solutions to mass shootings typically focus on some combination of preven-tion (identifying people who might commit them, limiting their access to weapons, or getting them professional support) and preparation (readying institutions with active shooter drills, arming more members of the public, or providing additional security measures at vulnerable locations). What all of these answers presuppose is that people will continue to become mass shoot-ers. Americans hope the shooter will fail or strike elsewhere whenever the next one appears, but know they cannot avoid *him* indefinitely. It is easy to forget that committing a mass shooting did not always appear to so many as an avail-able option. Put differently, it is important to remember that no one has to become a mass shooter. And this is true, surprising as it may seem, even for people who decide to carry out a shooting.

When I First Met Jeremy

Looking back sixteen years ago, I don't know whether I was fortunate or foolish. As a college student I thought I could explain why school shootings were happen-ing, or at least discount the reasons many gave. To do so, I interviewed people involved in a highly publicized school shooting that almost happened in Elmira, New York. In 2001–2, I conducted my honors thesis research on the so-called *Columbine Effect* that appeared to be spreading across American suburbs and small towns in the late 1990s. I was fascinated and disturbed by public debates over proposed causes and solutions to the crisis, not least because they implied that nonwhite, urban violence was unworthy of similar consternation and often concluded that schools should become more like prisons. Nearly two decades later, the debate has remained much the same. But at the time, entranced by my relatively recent introduction to critical social theory, I believed that the way mass shootings were being represented was helping contribute to their repeated performance (much as reporting on suicides is known to make the suicide rate increase).[20] In order to make my argument, I drew on conversations with those associated with a near–school shooting that occurred in Elmira and its aftermath.

Like nearby Binghamton, Elmira grew dramatically during the 1940s with military contracts. Both are small cities that suffered over the last several decades as a consequence of epic floods and plant closures. Both are left to remediate the toxic TCE plumes left behind by the industrial giants—IBM in Binghamton, Remington Rand in Elmira—that once employed thousands of local workers and now threaten to contaminate local water supplies.

On Valentine's Day 2001, a young white man named Jeremy went to his high school on the south side of Elmira with two guns and over a dozen homemade bombs. His plan was to kill as many people as he could and then himself. But when he arrived, something unexpected happened. The details are debated. The way he tells it, Jeremy suddenly realized that he did not want to hurt anyone. What is generally agreed on is that he was convinced by a friend (a young female student who did not know he was armed) to deviate from his plan and sit in the cafeteria and pray. He was apprehended quietly and peacefully by the school officer and the whole community went into shock at what had almost happened. According to Jeremy, his lawyer, family, and supporters, shock and horror about what *almost happened* made it so that many people lost sight of what *did happen*, which was that everyone involved acted nonviolently.

In my honors thesis, I explain my relationship with a school shooter who chose not to shoot:

I first met Jeremy in November of 2001 at the Chemung County Jail in downtown Elmira, almost nine months to the day that he had been arrested at school. . . My interviews with Jeremy progressed through three stages and three forms of communication. In mid and late November we spoke across a wire mesh locked into our adjoining rooms, but with a considerable amount of privacy given the circumstances. For those sessions, Jeremy was accompanied by his lawyer. . .who was kind enough not to intrude into the interview process, or prevent his client from releasing

information. Our second period of contact was administered through e-mail with
the help of. . .Jeremy's GED instructor at the Jail, until Jeremy was sentenced and
transferred to a prison in Fishkill, New York in late December of 2001. Since his
move to Fishkill and his final transfer to a Correctional Facility in Dannemora. . .
Jeremy and I. . .remained in. . .contact through letters.[21]

In what follows, I provide Jeremy's story, as he told it to me and others. I also
explain the dominant story that he resisted and, in a way, is still resisting as he
tries to make a new life for himself. I am not capable of dissecting the inner
motivations of this or any would-be mass shooter. What interests me here is
the extent to which competing narratives reflect, recycle, or resist (that is *trans-
value*) the tropes of militaristic storytelling.

A school shooter who does not shoot offers something like a test case for
the proposed link between mass shootings and American militarism. Because
there are thankfully no victims, no dead or injured, it takes more effort to make
Jeremy's story fit in with the militaristic narrative of white male grievance I
have described up to this point. The only immediate evidence for anyone to use
to dramatize the incident are the motivations and methods of those involved,
which makes it potentially more open-ended how actions might be represented
and dramatized. I show how Jeremy's actions are represented variably as an
ethical choice, a failure of masculinity, or as a military defeat. To the extent that
the latter narratives become more dominant, this betrays a close association
between mass shooting incidents and militaristic storytelling. That is, whether
or not anyone actually shoots or is shot, stories about violence planned and
thwarted take precedence over alternative accounts of what happened, even if
they are witnessed first-hand. Jeremy's was an unfamiliar nonviolent decision
embedded in an all-too-familiar narrative of nationwide violence. For this reason, it was his potential for violence that the prosecutor emphasized, that the
local and national media focused on, and that eventually swayed the judge during the sentencing hearing. But another story is possible, one that transvalues
and repurposes the familiar tropes of militarism in unexpected ways.

"I Decided I Didn't Want to Hurt Anyone"

Not surprisingly, I was not the only one interested in speaking with Jeremy. He
said the following during an interview with a local TV channel:

> A lot of the articles I've read in the newspaper seem to almost give the impression
> that like before I could have hurt anybody I was stopped, or that thanks to the
> school's quick action no one was hurt. I was the one with the gun. I had a window

of ten to fifteen minutes where I could have hurt a lot of people, and I didn't. It's not because the school acted quickly it's because I decided I didn't want to hurt anyone.

This was aired several days after his sentencing in what was a fairly large media event, perhaps as significant to the Elmira community as the sentencing itself. After his imprisonment in February of 2001, Jeremy worked with the media to express his narrative in a variety of ways. Aside from the segment with channel 18, Jeremy conducted interviews with local newspapers, other local television stations, NBC's *Dateline*, and CBS. This was largely due to the efforts of his attorney, who realized early on the value of media exposure to his client's case. Since Valentine's Day 2001, counteracting negative publicity has been a matter of necessity. According to Jeremy: "A lot of the media, especially locally, makes me seem to be some kind of monster, which I'm not. If I was half the monster the media is portraying me as then I wouldn't be sitting here." Clearly by fighting his portrayal as a "monster," Jeremy was hoping to improve his chances within his socio-legal context.

At the same time, Jeremy had other motivations beyond his impending hearing in the courtroom. For one thing, interviews with the media provided Jeremy a break from the tedium of prison life. At that time Jeremy enjoyed contact with different people, curious about his life. Whether that person was a student anthropologist from Cornell, Anne Curry from *Dateline*, or Allison Collins from ETM 18, Jeremy was eager to have a discussion and these interviewers, myself included, were equally happy to provide one. These interactions are important to keep in mind because, as linguistic anthropologist Sabina Perrino (2007) puts it, oral self-narratives are not purely about what happened in the past, but coexist (or are "coeval") with storytelling interactions in the present, including the audience a storyteller recruits to hear a tale.[22] As Webb Keane puts it, "Talk affects not only how one person interprets another but his or her self-perception as well" (2016, 244). With that in mind, an additional motivation was Jeremy's desire to show others *and convince himself* of the good in himself. According to letters he has sent me, Jeremy wished to show other angry adolescents that violence is not the answer and that they should talk to someone about their feelings of loneliness and aggression. At one time, Jeremy had even begun writing a book, tentatively called "The Negative," to show other troubled youth that there is a way out of their emotional pain other than violence. In other words, Jeremy framed his narrative to counter militarism: violence is not necessary, nonviolence is an option.

If Jeremy's story was told in part so that he could represent himself as something other than a monster, in certain respects it conforms to many other oral narratives associated with mass shooting, as well as the historical figure of the gunfighter. For instance, he describes himself as isolated and cut off from others who made him feel miserable and should not have. The use of gun violence offered a chance for him to make things right, to correct this perceived imbalance. This way of thinking is also present in the Columbine massacre, about which Jeremy knew a great deal. According to media scholar Mia Consalvo:

> In considering this evidence, Harris and Klebold, along with The Trench Coat Mafia, were in a precarious position at Columbine High. Although as white males they were supposed to be in a privileged position (relative to adult men at the school), they were instead shown to be at the bottom. The group tried to evade this positioning by denying potential identities ("we're not a homosexual group") as well as by trying to opt out of the system itself—they said they wanted mostly to be left alone. Yet, school culture, as noted previously, tends to celebrate and reward some masculinities and punishes or discourages others. (2003, 35)

When asked why he picked February 14 as the day he would attack Southside, Jeremy offers the following interpretation:

> I figured it was Valentine's Day, a day that cheerleaders would be with their boyfriends and when everyone shows each other love and appreciation. I guess I thought it was kind of ironic that on a day when they were all supposed to be happy I would show them what I usually felt, which was fear and anger.

Jeremy tried to explain to me the fantasy he often envisioned of his attack on the 14th, an inversion of what he went through on a daily basis:

> I saw all them, all the people who always focused their bullshit on me... I saw kids running out of Southside with emotions like I had all those years, like with fear. I never really saw them as dead, like corpses, just afraid and running. I guess it never really hit me, until closer to that day, that someone was going to die.

While not all school shooters experience bullying directly, all tend to be familiar with the role of hierarchy and competition in school environments. Like the gunfighter, as described by Slotkin, would-be school shooters see themselves as aggrieved and humiliated, surrounded by people who threaten their sense of a masculine self. Unlike Harris and Klebold, the infamous Columbine duo, Jeremy never singled out people either in writing or, he claims, in his mind that would be his victims. He only imagined types of people: "The plan, overall, was not for one specific person. The plan I had written up started with going to this area of the school that was right outside the upstairs bathroom. I was gonna go there and put my shotgun together. Lots of popular kids used to hang out there."[23]

At the same time, it seems that Jeremy both experienced a difficult adolescence and drew on what he had read about the typically difficult experiences of would-be school shooters who came before him. When he told his story to me and to others, Jeremy did not need to lie or exaggerate to be influenced by all the other stories told about mass shooting. Given how new I was at interviewing at the time, when I look back I am proud of the extent to which I made clear in my thesis that the story I recorded was not simple Jeremy's. I repeat that same point here from over 15 years ago:

> Between February 14, 2001, when Jeremy was arrested, and November when he and I first spoke, his personal narrative had been rehearsed and reconstructed countless times. First with his initial interrogation by local and state police which lasted for many hours, next through interviews with his own attorney and District Attorney John Trice's office, television interviews with Dateline and more "local" stations like ETM and ENY, his encounters with other inmates, his interviews with three different psychologists including James Garbarino, Dr. Richard Ciccone, and Dr. Jeffrey Donner, and finally through his own writing. With this in mind, it is to be expected that by November Jeremy had begun to sound a little bit like a psychologist, a lawyer, an attorney, a celebrity, and a prisoner. Also not surprising, his multiform narrative is conflicted and occasionally uneven. This is not to suggest that Jeremy's narrative is in any way fabricated. . .rather that, like any story (or, arguably, any memory), Jeremy's depiction of his own life maintains certain silences for the purposes of dramatization. He knows, from constant questions, interviews, debates, and interrogations, which details in particular are of interest.

Since Jeremy was an audience for his story as much as its narrator, he relied for its telling not only on his sense of who he really was, but also on his understanding of how a "person like him" (that is, a school shooter) could or should be. Writing about homeless women in an outpatient drug treatment program, anthropologist E. Summerson Carr (2009) discusses how they learn to anticipate their interpellation as people who act and talk "like drug addicts." Jeremy and other would-be mass shooters also arguably talk with anticipatory reference about the type of person they are or will become. Mass shooter is not only a type of person that naturally exists, in other words, its adoption is informed and expected by mass media and legal institutions that will eventually tell and shape stories about this person. This is a story for an imagined "America as a whole" long before it is a story shooters can tell themselves about themselves.

Just as there is a significant difference between Jeremy as narrated and Jeremy as narrator, there is a gap dividing Jeremy's account of his actions leading up to his planned attack and the familiar school shooter story. Despite his exposure to bullying, by his own admission Jeremy still had to convince himself to carry out his plan. Much of Jeremy's preparation, after he had finished constructing bombs in secret, involved readying himself for what he intended to do. "By the time I was within single-digit numbers every day I tried to convince myself 'I *have* to do this.'" Jeremy described the single-digit days in a computer file called "the final nine," his daily countdown to the attack—part journal, part explanation/justification for his intended actions. "I thought...I knew the police would look at all that stuff, I had the floppy disk on me when I went to the school. I thought I would answer as many questions as I could."

Like many other would-be mass shooters, Jeremy spent a great deal of time meticulously planning and fantasizing about what would take place. From his computer, Jeremy produced maps of the architecture of the school hallways and strategically chose his point of entry and the most effective plan of attack. In his own words, Jeremy was obsessed with the shooting: "there was not a single day in the months leading up to that day that I didn't think about bringing this shit to school." Leading up to the final nine, Jeremy recalls how deeply immersed he still was in feelings of depression and loneliness. This was made all the more oppressive by Jeremy's complete emotional and psychological distance from his parents. While in the midst of the final nine, Jeremy thought a great deal about his upcoming death and the effect it would have on them. He pictured his parents sad at the loss of their son, but liked to imagine that they would understand his motivations.

Within two days of the upcoming attack, Jeremy found himself telling another friend about his plans, something for which he has no explanation.[24] And despite the plans he had drawn, the layout he had written up, and the bombs he had constructed, Jeremy says he went to bed the night of February 13 unsure about what would happen the next day. Throughout the "final nine" Jeremy had felt sick and disoriented as he prepared for his attack. The morning of that Valentine's Day he recalls being so nervous he was shaking with fear. When I asked him if this was, perhaps, an adrenaline rush, he was clearly uncomfortable with that idea. What he felt wasn't a rush at all, he told me, but a "sick feeling...in [his] stomach."

When Jeremy's parents left for work that morning, he gathered as many bombs as he could (18 total) into a gym bag along with his father's disassembled shotgun. Along with ammunition, Jeremy also packed into his jacket his father's .22-caliber Ruger pistol. Before entering the school, Jeremy approached his closest friend, Mike, with a note for his parents, which explained his actions, apologized, and said goodbye. The previous night, he had spoken to Mike and another friend, who "were cool with it." But Jeremy remembers Mike being shocked that morning. Jeremy thought to himself, "they honestly didn't believe...didn't think I was serious." He remembers Mike whispering to him, "you're never gonna get away with it." From that point, Jeremy explains what happened with clear detail:

> I entered the school, according to plan, up the back stairwell. I chambered a round in the pistol and unclicked the safety. I remember standing there, and a kid started walking down the stairs toward me. I couldn't see his face yet, but I raised the pistol at him. The kid didn't see the gun. I was standing there for a while, just pointing the gun up at him and then it hit me like a flash, "I can't shoot this kid." I put the safety back on. He kept walking by; he still didn't see the gun. I still don't know who he was. I kept going up the stairs, towards the upstairs bathroom, where I planned to assemble the shotgun. I remember walking down the hall and I saw a group of kids hanging out by the bathroom talking. I thought, "I could throw a bomb in the middle of the group." Before I did anything, a couple kids stepped out and I saw they were people I knew, kids I liked. I just sat there thinking, "I could have hurt someone I liked." I walked past the bathroom carrying my bag. At this point I had stopped following the plan I wrote up. I ran into Stacey [a friend from Christian youth group]. She had heard from Mike that something was going on and she came up to me. She said, "I know you're upset, if you're gonna kill yourself I don't want you to, but make your peace with God first." We walked to the cafeteria together and talked a little. I told her what I had planned to do, but she wasn't worried...she wasn't even scared. She just sat there with me. Five minutes later I heard the cafeteria door close and the school officer was walking toward us. He came in with a smile on his face (he didn't know I was armed) and sent Stacey to the principal. He asked, "Do you have anything you shouldn't?" That was when he saw the gun. He was still nice at that point. Then he looked in the bag and found all the bombs. Then he was like, "Oh no," really loud, and all of a sudden he looked really worried. That's when I realized that I knew him, I hadn't noticed until then. He was my D.A.R.E. officer in sixth grade. He called the police and we waited there.

The policeman who approached Jeremy was a Chemung County sheriff's deputy who worked as a resource officer in the school. After apprehending Jeremy, Hurley notified the office and called the proper authorities. The local Elmira newspaper, the *Star Gazette*, was at the school fairly quickly. The next day the paper provided a concise description of what occurred after Jeremy's arrest:

Southside administrators ordered an immediate lockdown of the school, and students were ordered to remain in their classrooms. A short time later, 30 buses arrived to take students to the EFA gymnasium, where they remained until they were picked up by a parent or driven home by a school district official. As soon as Southside was empty, officers from the Chemung County Sheriff's Department and the Elmira and Southport police departments began to comb the school for additional explosives or weapons. They found none. Investigators summoned members of the New York State Police bomb squad, who were training in Albany. The 10-member team and four trained bomb- sniffing dogs flew into the Elmira-Corning Regional Airport in Big Flats and were at the school by 12:15 p.m. The bomb squad used a portable X-ray machine to determine the contents of the pipe bombs found in the bag. Outside the building, emergency response teams waited as the bomb squad worked. A container used to transport explosives sat in a trailer outside the school's main entrance. Southport volunteer firefighters pulled their rig up to the school's front doors and dragged their hoses into the school. Paramedics with Erway Ambulance parked near the school, ready to rescue the bomb squad members if anything went wrong. A bomb disposal team member, dressed in a protective jumpsuit, brought explosive devices out of the school in heavily padded bags and placed them in the container outside. The bombs will be transported to a lab in Newburgh, N.Y., where they will be dismantled. After clearing the school of explosives around 3:30 p.m., the bomb squad headed to [Jeremy's] home, where it removed more bombs and bomb-making paraphernalia. Police also seized two computers, books and other written materials. Members of the bomb squad and ATF team continued their investigation into the evening. Murnan, with the ATF, said he couldn't recall the last time a situation of such magnitude took place in a school in New York. (Quinn and Phillips 2001)

By the first newspaper account, the special investigator with ATF (who had witnessed nothing) had already positioned the near-attack within the militaristic school shooting narrative with two key statements. First, he established its proper placement within the national trend by evoking the crucial referent, "This could have been Columbine." Second, before undertaking a full investigation of the incident, he was quick to report that "Quick action by Officer Hurley helped to avert a major tragedy... He's the real hero in this situation." In this often-reprinted quotation, the ATF investigator attempts to stabilize the narrative surrounding the situation: Jeremy was prevented from attacking the school, which he surely would have done without heroic action stopping him. Those held responsible for the absence of any violence are people deemed most appropriate or likely given assumptions about mass shooting and mass shooters.

This initial proclamation would carry over into the national press as well: in a special issue of *Time* (Bower 2001), all the shootings in the two years following Columbine were diagramed as part of what the magazine called the "scorecard of hatred." Jeremy is shown with the word "FOILED" stamped across his portrait, a brief mention of Officer Hurley's intervention, and no account of Jeremy's actual *behavior* on that day, or Stacey's, or Mike's. According to this version of the story, he is just an unsuccessful school shooter.

"He Chickened Out, Basically"

In militarized societies war is always on our minds, even if we are technically at peace.

—Hugh Gusterson (2007, 156)

As discussed above, explanations and justifications of mass shootings in the United States have long relied upon the trope of white male humiliation and grievance. Committing violence involves real, fleshy bodies overflowing with affects, bodies that get exhausted and feel stress, remorse, panic, and pain (like a "sick feeling...in my stomach"). A would-be shooter's relationship with potential victims is not merely conceptual, in other words, but corporeal. Drawing on research on what it takes to make effective killers out of military recruits, John Protevi argues that part of what enables shootings like Columbine to occur in practice is a shared system of judgment that pervades school environments and that would-be shooters learn to embody:

> The secret of the Columbine killers, the answer to "how?" is the vast disinhibiting effect of finally operating the judgement machine for their own benefit, of being the trigger points of all that desire. The somatic marker of the scenario of the victim's death must have been that of the sheer joy of finally being the judge after having been judged so often, a rush that raised the threshold of inhibition and allowed them to enact the unthinkable. (Protevi 2009, 161)

Judging and being judged are part of the routine trauma and humiliation of attending public school: whether or not one is physically "bullied," it links social relations to felt experiences of weakness, shame and embarrassment.[25] It also provides the embodied grounds for a reversal whereby white males can overturn their perceived inferiority through violence.

For these reasons, Julie A. Webber considers militarism to be part of the *hidden curriculum* of what is taught at American schools, even the vast majority that never have a shooting. In critical pedagogy, hidden curriculum refers to the practical experience children have of schooling, rather than the formal knowledge they are tested on. If schools are coercive institutions, by definition, mass shootings serve as their antistructural opposite, yet both would form part of the "domestic blowback" of America's permanent war readiness:

> In a democratic society, leaders have to justify the use of force. One way to avoid having to rationalize imperialist behavior is to mobilize the population by inciting it into a violent and competitive disposition. As if war were inevitable, as if someone like a fellow citizen causes harm, or as if someone undeserving or unqualified might get the job or college degree at the expense of someone else. In short, as if there were no alternative to this zero-sum view, and as if there is no other way to deal with it, save for intense competitive behavior. (Webber 2003, 5)

Such a hidden curriculum shapes the choices a person makes, from ordinary to extraordinary violence, bullying to mass shooting. And yet, these realities of contemporary schooling can only be relayed to lawyers, reporters, courts, ethnographers, or any audience through language and, specifically, the narrative tendencies that the person speaking shares with these audiences. In this way, militarism is not only arguably felt and embodied as part of the implicit first-person perspective of the hidden curriculum; it also frames, from a third-person perspective, how these actions are interpreted by others (see Keane 2016).

With militarism tacitly shaping available storytelling strategies, even decisions to act nonviolently may not register as such. All that people do in schools, as teachers, students, or would-be shooters, is readily narrated in terms of competition and resentment, strength and weakness. If schools are assumed to be divided into weak and strong, unpopular and popular, as if by a hidden curriculum, then unpopular individuals—like Jeremy—are defined primarily through that violent antagonism, which effectively circumscribes their actions. Put differently, the tropes of bullying and white male grievance are not merely literal causes for student behavior, but also influence what counts as relatable, third-person interpretations of what happens in schools.

My conversations with Jeremy focused on his story leading up to his decision to commit a mass shooting and his mindset after his arrest, as various actors struggled over his narrative and decided his fate. In addition to interviewing him, I spoke with his GED teacher, his lawyer, a prison guard, some of his friends, and his family. I observed court proceedings and followed local media debates. What I determined was that some persons and institutions in Elmira and nationally wanted to portray Jeremy as a thrill-killing psychopath who was "foiled" before he could carry out his plans. Others, especially those who knew him best, thought he was a depressed child who was hurt by social ostracism and teasing and, as a result, made a horrible plan that, for some reason, he could not carry out.[26]

The public defender assigned to the case visited Jeremy in jail shortly thereafter. The person he saw did not seem like a monster, but someone horrified at his own actions.

> He was distraught to the point of being crippled. It was virtually impossible to even communicate with him. I have never seen anyone that depressed in my life. Not even close, nothing even compares to the level of visible depression. It didn't take a psychiatrist to pick this out. He looked terrible, his speech was so slow and deliberate. He was utterly confused.

According to the defender, Jeremy did not decide to act nonviolently, exactly, but could not bring himself to go through with it: "he chickened out, basically." This is a very different interpretation, one which takes nonviolent action to be equivalent to inaction. More specifically, it represents Jeremy as overrun by his bodily affects, like fear and panic, rather than as making a purely agentive decision. One could just as easily offer this kind of physiologically reductive explanation for those who carry out their planned attacks, by arguing that they were overcome with affective rage. Either way, subjective acts are represented as if they were less than fully agentive by rooting them in embodied impulses and sensations. The defender was so impressed by Jeremy's fragile physical state, in fact, that he initially went to a psychiatrist from the University of Rochester to ask about a possible insanity plea.

The prosecuting attorney investigated and publicly presented the opposing view. "Did he abandon the plan? The evidence says no. Was the plan stalled perhaps, or adjourned until he...you know we don't know what would have happened if [the student] who stopped him would have said 'okay, see ya, I gotta go to class.'" The prosecutor credited others for stopping Jeremy. "The community realizes that tragedy was averted because students acted in a concerned and responsible manner and the Southside High School staff took appropriate action." And he breaks down Jeremy's actions into a minute-by-minute structure in order to cast doubt on his moral decision-making, "Some will say that the defendant chose not to go through with his plan...that he stopped himself that day... But he did not stop at 9:40, he did not stop at 9:50, or 10:00..." Jeremy's subjective control over his behavior is here placed front and center. His actions are the product of purely rational intention, as if each moment he was committing himself over and over again to being a mass shooter. During the sentencing, the prosecutor explained Jeremy wrapping the shotgun in tape, loading his bombs, not once choosing to turn himself in during this timeframe. He also talked about all of the possible dead. The prosecutor had, as support for his version of Jeremy's story, the popular representation of other prominent shootings (ones that were actually carried out), most notably Columbine.

In characterizing Jeremy's actions in ethical terms, both lawyers are faced with a similar dilemma. Neither was there on that day as a direct, first-hand witness. More to the point, both intentionally downplay the first- and second-person perspectives and words of some of the people who were there to provide an ostensibly impartial perspective from outside. The prosecutor's listing of empirical facts, as if detached from any person's feelings or perspective, is done in the service of replacing such accounts with what is meant to be a purely objective, third-person view on what happened. Taken in isolation, the facts that he built the bombs, made plans, and carried the bombs to school reduce Jeremy's actions to either/or propositions, as each individual choice would serve to make him either a mass shooter or the reverse.

In Michael Lambek's (2015) terms, the alternative story offered by Jeremy and his attorney characterizes Jeremy's actions instead as "practical judgment," which "begins with the idea that the good or right thing to do in a given set of circumstances, or how to do it, is not always obvious" (2015, 14). The first-person and second-person accounts of Jeremy, Stacy, and Mike support this interpretation, that whatever else he was planning, Jeremy was not completely sure of what he was doing and was weighing his options accordingly. Whereas Jeremy's lawyer wanted to present him as someone who was capable of learning from his actions, changing course and selecting alternatives, the prosecutor wanted to depict Jeremy as someone acting with clear moral intentions, entirely responsible for what the facts show *he almost did*.

A legal hearing is arguably premised on an ethical interaction between lawyers, the people they represent, and the judge. And, in the end, the defense attorney told me that he misjudged the judge on Jeremy's case, thinking he would be more lenient than he was. Jeremy was sentenced to eight-and-a-half years in prison. The judge focused on what made Jeremy *the way he was*, casting Jeremy as a type of subject, not a distinct person with practical judgment. As was said at the sentencing:

> One has to ask the question: Why? What motivated the defendant to do this?... Defendant had a history of being bullied that reached back to his early years in primary grades. He hated school because of the harassment by other students—students in school picked on him, called him names and threw things at him as he walked down the hallway. Defendant felt self-hatred, could not recall a time when

he felt happy—he did not want his parents to know about his depression. The depression worsened as he got older with feelings of inadequacy, worthlessness and guilt with suicidal intentions. He had a feeling of daily unhappiness and emptiness, isolated and unsupported.

This characterization fit with the story that Jeremy's lawyer had hoped to encourage. But it arguably draws, implicitly, on two sources: first, the hidden curriculum as a frame for understanding school environments; second, the longstanding American cultural figure of the gun-toting killer—an irreparably aggrieved and threatening character—neither of which allows room for a person executing practical judgment, someone capable of changing his or her mind and acting nonviolently. Deciding to forgive is not supposed to be what bullied schoolkids do; deciding not to shoot is not supposed to be part of a school shooter's nature. Even though he never shot anyone, or even tried to, Jeremy was prosecuted and sentenced like a school shooter.

WEAPONS TRANSFER

Once, I came across a picture, of a strange-looking violin.
The caption said, that it was made out of a rifle.
I thought to myself, "someday that could be me."
—Rudy Francisco, a line from "The Heart and the Fist"
(www.youtube.com/watch?v=8IHYA1l7Yew)

Someday I may inherit guns that belonged to my late grandfather, some of which he acquired during his service in World War II. Many Americans inherit guns in this way, which makes it more difficult to count the number in circulation. People in the United States do not only inherit literal weaponry, however, but ways of narrating the kinds of people we once were, are, and want to be. In the poem excerpted above, Rudy Francisco begins by describing small arms melted down and remade into musical instruments, an image he uses as a model for himself and his efforts to unlearn the violent conception of masculinity that dominated his childhood.

I have argued that mass shootings can be thought of as the unanticipated outcome, the waste, of American militarism. These horrible events are caused not only by the availability of actual guns but by the fears and fantasies that have haunted their use for centuries. Popular representations of these violent events tend to invoke the figure of guns in the wrong hands. If the guns used in these attacks are too readily available, then there are more in circulation than should be. If, on the contrary, more guns would solve the problem, then *the wrong people* are armed and unarmed. Across the political spectrum, people accuse politicians of wastefulness when it comes to guns. Defenders of gun rights accuse proposed regulations of being excessive and unnecessary; proponents of gun regulation accuse politicians and the NRA of corruption and passivity. Both see time wasted rather than wisely spent. If, on the other hand, it is believed that shooters are motivated by violent fantasies, then there is more violent television, music, and gaming content than there should be. Whatever causes and solutions are proposed, they tend to involve identifying a surfeit of something, a corresponding lack of something else. Things are somehow out of balance, and mass shootings are the symptom.

Another way to approach the problem of mass shootings is to consider who benefits the most from the status quo. One answer is gun manufacturers. After all, they make more money the more guns are purchased by Americans and the uniformed personnel who ostensibly serve them. Most analyses have tended to downplay or ignore the role of gun manufacturers when gun violence is discussed, even though they are the missing link that connects ordinary gun-owning civilians with gun-owning police officers and service members. Mass shootings most often raise debates surrounding *gun ownership*—people argue either that more guns (armed teachers, for instance) or more gun restrictions are the solution. Police shootings, by contrast, most often raise debates surrounding *gun use*—people argue either that officers suffer from racial bias (and use their guns too readily) or that those they shoot are legitimate targets (and might be about to use guns themselves). If one set of circumstances leads to debates about guns as property, then the other leads to debates around guns as a tool. While gun manufacturers are typically left out of the discussion altogether, it helps to think about guns instead as a commodity, one whose exchange value would otherwise go to waste were it not possible to market them to civilians. For example, gun sales went up dramatically after the Sandy Hook school shooting of 2012, and each shooting thereafter, in part because gun sellers and organizations like the NRA routinely stoked fears that the Obama administration was pursuing radical restrictions on gun ownership.[27]

The history of gun manufacturing in the United States is not only about corporate profits, however, but as we have seen is complicated by its connection to militarization and militarism, which have not only made guns and gun violence possible in a historical sense, but continue to directly influence both in the present. If the permanent war economy means that military objects are manufactured which outlive their usefulness, it also means that industries have to exist to supply these objects in sufficient quantities. Since the very beginning of the United States, there has been an effort by the federal government to support gun manufactures so that they can supply armies in times of need. That is why the government was an early investor in the mass production of guns with interchangeable parts: "the government's participation was vital in this as in many other early industries; the federal government provided capital, patent protection, technological expertise, and the largest market for guns" (Bellesiles 1999, 32).[28] Having gun manufacturers producing abundant weapons for the military means that they are likely to sell *excess weapons* to others markets, namely ordinary consumers and uniformed government employees. There has been a continuous weapons transfer, by way of gun manufacturers, from military to other uniformed personnel and civilians. As argued by Peter Kraska (2001, 2007) and others, this transfer has consisted of literal weapons, the excess that is necessary in order to keep the American military supplied with weaponry.

In August of 2017, Trump lifted a ban that Obama had introduced which prevented surplus military equipment from being transferred to police departments. Obama's administration had done this in response to what was perceived as excessive police reaction to protests in Ferguson, Missouri, which had begun in response to the police shooting of unarmed, eighteen-year-old Michael Brown, one of a series of highly publicized and tragic shootings of young black men and boys. In fact, a year prior to the actions of the Trump administration, the previous administration had also considered lifting the ban in part or entirely. Echoing some of the same arguments, Trump's former Attorney General Jeff Sessions described this as an act of recycling: "Assets that would otherwise be scrapped can be re-purposed to help state, local and tribal law enforcement better protect public safety and reduce crime" (quoted in Johnson 2017).

Police departments do not always want this weapons transfer to be widely known. I contacted the Crime Prevention Unit of the City of Binghamton, and the lieutenant on duty would tell me where to find the budget for the police department, but would not tell me from whom they purchased their guns, only that it was one of an approved list of companies provided by the New York State Department of Criminal Justice. The lieutenant also expressed frustration with my question regarding military equipment. People might be frightened by the presence of military vehicles or weapons in the hands of police, he said, but if you are responsible for patrolling an area that floods, as does Binghamton, then more durable vehicles like military Humvees might be necessary to get around. For this reason, he said, the local sheriff's department had participated in a program that provided local departments with surplus vehicles from the military. He did not express concern about what message this might send to the people of the community.

With each chapter, I have tried to show the unexpected and creative ways that people make do, living with the remains of military waste, in the midst of a permanent war economy. There are creative responses to gun violence that mirror the forms of repurposed waste discussed in previous chapters. For instance, there are companies and artists that acquire guns from conflict-torn regions all over the world and recycle them into products, like shovels and jewelry, the sale of which can lead to the collection of even more guns (Froelich 2015; Raphael and Zwillich 2016). In a similar vein, Jeremy's story has received the most attention because this story potentially repurposes, or transvalues, stories of militarism. Told one way, it is about a would-be shooter foiled before he could really act. Told another, it is about people who actively used nonviolent solutions to prevent anyone from being physically hurt, including the would-be shooter himself. The latter version is worth telling precisely because it takes the familiar tropes of mass shootings and reveals alternative possibilities. I call this transvaluation or repurposing because no new elements are involved: the same are present in any similar situation, merely reconfigured to achieve a different outcome.

Guns make mass shootings possible, but so too do the stories people tell about mass shootings, because they give us a sense of what is possible, what actions might be taken. Sensible gun regulation, improved mental health care support, and better emergency preparedness are possible and necessary social policies to implement. But troubled people, young and old, arguably also need to hear shootings talked about in a particular way in order to think that becoming a shooter is an available and attractive option. This may sound odd, but it is as necessary for American gun violence as guns themselves. If military manufacturing helps make guns more readily available, militarized stories about what it means to be a man or an American help *make up people* willing to use those guns against groups of innocent civilians. Put differently, *both* the abundant consumption of guns today *and* the production of people willing to use them to kill innocent civilians are the unintended outcomes, the wastes, of America's troubled history as a settler colony and imperial power.

Since it does not seem like people will stop talking and thinking about these incidents, the best that Americans might be able to do is find new stories to share, or new ways to tell the ones we know. If Americans feel helpless to stop these events from happening over and over again, they can learn to talk about them differently at least, and this may give rise to future Jeremys, Staceys, Mikes, and Officer Hurleys by providing people with a sense that there are more options available to them for how to act in such situations. This might involve looking for more examples of first- and second-person accounts of nonviolent action to admire and follow, which could start by recognizing nonviolence as legitimate and sincere action, rather than the absence of a will to act. Nonviolent action would include people who are talked down from committing acts of violence or who change their minds out of an ethical compunction, not cowardice. Americans might look to acknowledge and reward police, service members, and civilians, adults and children, who use nonviolent means to solve problems. Even militaries need not be so militarized, Cynthia Enloe writes, "A less militarized military would be one less imbued with an institutional culture of masculinized violence" (2007, 79). Care for others, in times of emergency, is often celebrated in commercials aimed at military recruitment, but it is less often reported on or celebrated in public culture (in films, for instance). The alternative is to continue to endorse militarism and deny the reality and necessity of nonviolence.

CHAPTER 6

Island Erasure

Waste has been a critical part of US imperialism from the start and continues to be. Yet the role of wasting is not always acknowledged, partly because of the peculiar character of US power. This is not a chapter about what makes America historically exceptional, however, but how purportedly exceptional circumstances, sites, and substances can be marshaled in the exercise of power, both to justify military force and to conceal it.

Two seemingly separate events coincided in 2009. First, in his last month in office, President Bush established the Pacific Remote Islands National Marine Monument. This banned commercial fishing and deep-sea mining around the United States Minor Outlying Islands of the Pacific and Caribbean. The United States had accumulated these islands during a little-known period of imperial expansion in the mid-nineteenth century, which is why it possesses the world's largest exclusive economic zone (EEZ). Also in 2009, the United Kingdom attempted to do the same thing for the British Indian Ocean Territory (BIOT), which includes the disputed Chagos Archipelago. The largest Chagos island, Diego Garcia, is where the United States maintains what is arguably its most important overseas military base. The decision to establish a monument in the BIOT was encouraged by the Chagos Conservation Trust (CCT); it was also supported by the outgoing Labour government and conservation specialists. But it soon generated controversy. Then, in a diplomatic cable released by WikiLeaks in 2010, it was revealed that turning the BIOT into a marine preserve was also a calculated move to contest the claims of dispossessed Chagossians:

HMG would like to establish a "marine park" or "reserve" providing comprehensive environmental protection to the reefs and waters of the British Indian Ocean Territory (BIOT), a senior Foreign and Commonwealth Office (FCO) official informed Polcouns on May 12. The official insisted that the establishment of a marine park—the world's largest—would in no way impinge on USG use of the BIOT, including Diego Garcia, for military purposes. He agreed that the UK and United States should carefully negotiate the details of the marine reserve to assure that United States interests were safeguarded and the strategic value of BIOT was upheld. He said that the BIOT's former inhabitants would find it difficult, if not impossible, to pursue their claim for resettlement on the islands if the entire Chagos Archipelago were a marine reserve.[1]

While the United Kingdom is no stranger to using military environmentalism (Woodward 2001, 2004), it is no accident that political and environmental management of the BIOT should resemble American marine preservation efforts in the Pacific. Island erasure, the dual process of deeming islands useless or unusable and their inhabitants as invisible or irrelevant, has been characteristic of American imperial formations since the mid-nineteenth century, most recently in the occupation of Diego Garcia. Erasure is evident, for instance, in the very use of terms *minor* and *outlying* to refer to these islands, and is rooted in a longstanding relationship between American imperial power and *wastelanding*: a mode of power and a representational practice that devalues and wilds landscapes for destruction and reclamation.[2]

Wasteland can mean many things: a place wasted through overuse, a wilderness gone to waste as a result of abandonment or underuse, an opportunity for reclamation. John Locke mobilizes each of these senses in the chapter "Of Property" in his *Two Treatises of Government* (1689). At a critical moment in the history of British governance, Locke uses the ethics of waste to argue that there is a natural right to both own private property against sovereign usurpation and usurp indigenous lands owned in common. If it would be a waste to allow privately held goods to spoil, with the introduction of money it becomes possible to hoard wealth without diminishing its value. In fact, once money exists to stand for all temporary value forms, Locke argues, it is now those who hold property in common who are being wasteful, for private industry can make more productive use of their possessions for the betterment of all. Through the enclosure movement, Locke's ideas were implemented by the British Empire, first at home and then abroad, over the ensuing centuries.[3]

This specific rhetorical move, in terms of wasteland lost and recovered, has become characteristic of moral and economic arguments used in support of

American colonization and imperialism over the ensuing centuries, to govern indigenous inhabitants, former slaves, and white and nonwhite settlers alike. In Traci Brynne Voyles's words, wasteland is "a racial and a spatial signifier that renders an environment and the bodies that inhabit it pollutable" (2015, 9). Places and people can be rendered pollutable through direct planning or simple neglect. As John Beck argues, wasteland "is a powerful enabling discourse for the redefinition of habitat as empty and useless" (2009, 126). On this basis, habitat can be appropriated, protected, and/or polluted with impunity.

Processes of ruination are arguably implicated in imperial formations in general (Stoler 2013), which can make ethnographies of empire difficult. This is the only chapter of this book where I forgo ethnography and explore military waste through historical documents, environmental discourses, and science fact and fiction. This is in keeping with Stoler's argument, echoing those made by Fernando Coronil (1996, 1997), that studying empire requires looking beyond "the actual connection of things. . .at the conceptual interconnection of problems and who and what are made into them. . .not only how things are assembled, but also how they are disassembled, conceptually and politically severed from the conditions that made them possible" (Stoler 2018, 478). In the examples I discuss, American empire is premised on civilizing that which has been wilded through a "double erasure" (Davis 2007, 2015)—it is by first claiming, destroying, abandoning, and reclaiming wastelands, and then denying and forgetting that this was done and for what reason, that successive American imperial formations have grown atop one another.[4]

The Pacific Remote Islands National Marine Monument and its equivalent in the BIOT are recent examples, where wilding a purported wasteland appears apolitical, even inactive. In this way, the creation of a marine monument fits with a broader strategy by the Pentagon to embrace the scientific claims and ideological aims of environmentalism, and particularly climate change discourse (see Havlick 2007; Coates et al. 2011; Marzec 2016). However, the wild is not a preexisting domain to be appropriated, but a heterotopic space constructed through political and technical intervention. As historian William Cronon (1995, 47) writes:

> Wilderness is not quite what it seems. Far from being the one place on earth that stands apart from humanity, it is quite profoundly a human creation. . . It is not a pristine sanctuary where the last remnant of an untouched, endangered, but still transcendent nature can for at least a little while longer be encountered without the contaminating taint of civilization. Instead, it's a product of that civilization, and

could hardly be contaminated by the very stuff of which it is made. Wilderness hides its unnaturalness behind a mask that is all the more beguiling because it seems so natural.

Natural preservation projects like marine reserves are political projects that endeavor to frame "the natural" in accordance with existing logics and techniques. This is clear, for instance, when decisions are made regarding which species count as native, invasive, and so forth. The less-than-natural constitution of protected areas becomes apparent if one examines the historical acquisition of the Pacific "outlying" and "minor" islands that gave the United States authority to wild them in the first place. As a consequence, US empire starts to appear less like a fixed transoceanic assemblage, and more like a continuous process of disassembly and reassembly, of imperial ruination through a transnational legal regime that has made atolls and islands wastelands, uninhabitable and wild.[5]

Previous chapters attempted to complicate the separation between home front and war front by showing how war preparation leaks into the former domain whether or not war happens. In this penultimate chapter, my goal is to go further and demonstrate that *the home front is not what it seems*. Rather than a clearly demarcated territory, coextensive with the fifty sovereign states and Washington, DC, the nation-state is actually a massive territory, an exclusive economic zone, stretching across oceans, including "minor" and "outlying" islands, some inhabited and some not, none with the autonomy normally expected of American-held lands. This extended territory is not normally recognized as such because of repeated wastelanding. As a result the EEZ is the product of a double erasure—the leftovers of forgotten moments of imperial ruination.

Beyond its territorial holdings, contemporary US empire is premised on a global network of bases, which represent an "urbanization of the ocean": Diego Garcia is a key node in a global infrastructural project that exploits "the connection medium of the geographic itself" and is therefore "capable of conducting force to local expressions of power across the depth of the ocean and extents of the atmosphere" (Bélanger and Arroyo 2012, 74; see also Bezboruah 1977). It is as if the very nature of the globe, its thickness and shape, were made to serve American power. But processes of capitalist urbanization, as Marx and others have pointed out, inevitably become implicated in their own undoing, exacerbating metabolic rifts as country is divided from city and the conditions for human survival become unstable, acting against human designs. It was such terrestrial rifts that led to the US acquisition of Pacific and Caribbean islands in the mid-nineteenth century, as part of a search for guano, a natural fertilizer to restore soils exhausted by capitalist overexploitation. This peculiar and forgotten moment of American history is worth recounting because it made possible the imperial formations that followed, as well as their internal contradictions. The shift toward fossil fuels made guano islands irrelevant, and this very excessiveness made possible their exceptional and experimental (re/dis)-use. At the same time, exceptional islands are also vulnerable to new metabolic rifts, including rising sea levels and oceans filled with plastics, and it is partly in response to these marine crises that military environmentalism has developed.

In addition to providing a comparative genealogy for successive imperial imaginaries premised on wasteland, and their constitutive metabolic rifts, in the last section of this chapter I explore the instability of ocean urbanization more speculatively. One way to do this is to highlight the awkward fit between strategies of imperial control developed for the Pacific when applied to the Indian Ocean. Another way to provincialize power, and the method I pursue in this chapter is to strategically reuniversalize oceanic forces to serve as a counterpoint to the universalizing project of the American empire. I do this in order to use the oceans against military occupation, or to show how strategic island bases may become untenable. This is so because the vital forces of planetary oceans and atmospheres represent an unconquerable totality, the taken-for-granted, antecedent conditions for any power that seeks global reach. As I discussed in relation to orbital environments in chapter 4, planetary forces have their own conditions of emergence and causal impacts that must be reckoned with, especially by the largest military power the world has ever known.[6]

WASTE ISLANDS

If American colonization was in part premised on recuperating land that would otherwise go to waste as common property, by the early nineteenth century it appeared as if private industry was instead creating wasteland. With the ascendance of the British Empire and a coal-fueled revolution in transportation via steam, Lockean-style liberal capitalism was taking hold and the world's first integrated world market emerging. At the same time, settler colonial soils were losing their fecundity in a crisis that lasted from 1830–70, a symptom of "environmental overdraft" in relation to which global markets were both cause and cure (Clark and Foster 2009).[7] It was the perception of this agricultural crisis and nascent revolutions in trade and chemistry that inaugurated what is arguably the first moment of American imperialism, to guarantee the productive use, in private hands, of lands that were meant to have been rescued from going to waste by settler colonists, not ruined by them even further. What followed were successive experiments in American democracy and imperialism, where the two became interconnected in ways that would later be forgotten.

Nitrogen Democracy / Guano Imperialism

Timothy Mitchell's *Carbon Democracy* (2011) begins by differentiating sources of energy derived from agriculture from those derived from coal that emerged after 1800. He does this in order to account for the carbon-based origins of contemporary democracy and imperialism. Tellingly, the United States is left out of this account until the 1870s. The reason for this is that, prior to the rampant industrialization, urbanization, and migration of the Gilded Age, and the miners' strikes that would follow, American society was predominantly agricultural throughout the nineteenth century. And it was during the alleged soil crisis that the relationship between energy demands, democracy, and imperialism began to take root in American geopolitics, which would provide the preconditions for the carbon democracy and fossil fuel imperialism that followed.

The so-called soil crisis is now often retrospectively described as the beginnings of the "second agricultural revolution" in soil chemistry. But scientists at the time were not optimistic. Most notably, the German chemist Justus von Liebig used soil exhaustion to warn of a broader crisis associated with the growth of cities, the unchecked activities of industrial agriculture, and the failure to reproduce soils that both rely upon. Socialists, from Victor Hugo to Marx and Engels, related the exhaustion of the soils to the wasting of sewage that arose from the division of industrial workers and urban denizens from the land that fed and clothed them. Since urban sewers were wasting human effluent and fossil fuels would not be utilized in the production of artificial fertilizer until the early twentieth century, shit would have to be imported.

The best source of nitrates, at the time, came from seabird guano. And the best source of guano came from the South Pacific, off the coast of Peru, where entire islands were coated with heaps of it, as if waiting for someone to take possession who recognized its true value. Guano imperialism left enduring scars on Pacific landscapes and lives. Peru used the guano trade to pay down its debt to Britain, owed due to the latter's support during the war for independence from Spain (Clark and Foster 2009, 319). The guano trade also precipitated a massive labor shortage, which resulted in the importation of as many as one hundred thousand Chinese "coolies" and the enslavement of Polynesians. For a time, local narratives held that Polynesian slaves, mostly from Easter Island, were kidnapped and forced to work under horrendous conditions in the Peruvian guano mines. While archival data indicate that Polynesian slaves were instead used largely for agricultural and domestic labor, the connection people now make between their abduction and the global guano market is no mere historical error. Archaeologist Grant McCall (1976) is generally credited with refuting the idea that Polynesians were used for guano mining, yet he also argues that the guano trade helped create the labor shortages that led slave traders to Polynesia in the first place. The story of Polynesian enslavement to farm bird shit, while likely historically inaccurate, could be seen as an evocative attempt to conceptualize the abstract yet real domination of Polynesians and Peruvians by capitalist value relations, or a transvaluation of capitalist storytelling that is meant to counter alienation and erasure (Pedersen 2013).

American farmers, desperate to keep their soils fecund, lobbied to address the Peruvian monopoly over the guano trade. In response, the United States passed the Guano Islands Act in 1856, which gave any individual or organization the right to take possession of unclaimed islands and atolls with guano deposits. Around sixty guano-covered islands in the Caribbean and the Pacific became (hitherto unappreciated and unproductive) wastelands for the taking, whose use value would benefit the ailing soils of the homeland and whose exchange value would break the Peruvian-British monopoly over the global guano market.

One can characterize the energo-politics that prevailed during this period, contra Mitchell, as *nitrogen democracy*. As with the carbon democracy that would follow, this is not to claim that material relations and practices simply determine ideal concepts of government; rather, it means "establishing connections and alliances that do not respect any divide between material and ideal, economic and political, natural and social, human and nonhuman, violence and representation" (Mitchell 2009, 7). While nitrate-rich guano did not make American democracy what it was, the connections and alliances of which it was a part did represent a critical mutation of American democracy and settler colonialism.

Prior to the Guano Islands Act—from the Louisiana (1803) to the Gadsden (1853) Purchases—it was expected that any newly acquired territory would become settled and, in time, rise to statehood. Production of wealth from fertile lands was thereby linked to the reproduction of a citizenry to rule it. The Guano Islands Act assumed acquisitions of territory intended solely for the accumulation of wealth through the exercise of force, not the expansion of popular sovereignty. American acquisition of territory during the Spanish-American War would follow suit: Puerto Rico, Cuba, and the Philippines were not sovereign states in the making, but administered colonies with economic value. This did not preclude the use of violence in their colonial administration (Balce 2016), or indirect economic colonial relations with territories in the future (Vine 2018), but it was different from the previous century of settler colonialism.

According to radical historian William Appleman Williams, the Old Northwest and the West were also colonies for northeastern elites in the early years of the republic, but in these cases American and British capital was still moored to the Lockean bundle of property and sovereignty. The improvement of wasteland rightfully acquired was supposed to go hand in hand with labor-producing and rights-bearing individuals. The guano islands, by contrast, were extensions of American sovereignty realized through military reach. Long after their guano had been mined and organic had become replaced by artificial nitrogen, the guano islands were still claimed by the United States under the powers of the Guano Act, with Coast Guard and military residents serving as proof, where necessary, of "permanent population" (O'Donnell 1993, 58).

Islands under Erasure

It is important not to overstate the novelty of the Guano Islands Act and its subsequent implementation in the Caribbean and Pacific. Prior to the guano rush, settler colonists and the US government exploited ambiguities in legal treaties and territorial boundaries to seize more indigenous-held lands than would have been possible otherwise (Saunt 2014, 23–28). In the first decades of its existence, the newly created American navy was meant to combat Algerian corsairs in the Mediterranean and defeat English pirates in the Caribbean, both in the interests of American commerce (see chapter 3). Moreover, American influence continued to spread in Hawaii, Japan, and China through this growing naval power (O'Donnell 1993, 45; see also Davis 2015). It is neither the exploitation of legal ambiguities nor the backing of global commerce through force that mark the guano islands as a turning point in the American imperial formation, but the legal-juridical strategy which, faced with an exceptional circumstance, detached sovereignty from settlement.[8]

The guano islands were justified as an *exceptional* acquisition because of the extraordinary crisis of soil exhaustion, but remained so after this particular emergency passed. The Guano Island Act had included the promise that the United States would give up control of the unincorporated territories once the guano was exhausted, but this was not the case. For twenty of the guano islands (most notably Baker Island, Howland Island, Jarvis Island, Johnston Atoll, Midway Atoll, Kingman Reef, and Palmyra Atoll), private claims were made that would help build the military infrastructure to establish dominance over Pacific water, land, and air, leading up to the confrontation with Japan in World War II. As with the creation of the nation's first navy in the late eighteenth century (chapter 3), the modernization of the army a century later (chapter 5), or the building of the space program (chapter 4) and nuclear arsenal during the Cold War, an exceptional circumstance was used to justify a military solution that would become permanent. After the Spanish-American War, there were efforts to create global bases as the operation of American empire became more formalized, and again this was resisted. Despite a close vote in 1901 surrounding the so-called Insular Cases, this would provide the constitutional basis for US colonialism in formerly Spanish-held territories.[9] From the late 1930s to the early 1940s, naval air bases were constructed at Wake, Johnston, and Palmyra, while airstrips were created at Howland and Baker. Wake is the only site that continues to host a military base, as many were abandoned following the conclusion of the war. Instead, this has largely fallen to islands like Guam, which was acquired from Spain in 1898.

The guano islands became excessive, by definition, when the cause for their acquisition abruptly vanished as a result of innovations in soil science. Consequently, the episode has largely been forgotten. The only remnants of it are the United States Minor Outlying Islands themselves, as the guano islands are now referred to. Their exceptional administration places many of these sites outside of national and international laws and the legal and environmental "black holes" that result have proven useful for experiments in securitization and secrecy. Yet all of the previous and ongoing activity on these remote islands has left lasting impacts, including threats to the bird populations that once thrived on the guano islands and gave them their namesake, as well as the surrounding coral reefs.[10]

Wastelanding has generally shifted away from the liberal strategy of justifying improvement through private industry (except, perhaps, in fantasies that still cling to oceanic and space exploration as wild "final frontiers"). If farmers and industry previously spearheaded wastelanding at home and abroad, in the twentieth century wasteland became valuable in and of itself for the purposes of imperial statecraft. These exceptional uses include the storage of radioactive materials and weapons, and the testing of nuclear devices. Most notably, Johnston Atoll was used as a site for seventy-one nuclear weapons tests as part of Operation Hardtack I (1958) and Operation Dominic (1962). The lasting radiation from these tests can still be detected in coral as far away as Guam (Andrews et al. 2016). Since the Partial Test Ban Treaty (1963), the atoll has been used for chemical weapons storage, including containers of sarin, sulfur mustard, and VX that were transferred there from Okinawa in 1971.

At the same time, these exceptional sites have contributed to the development of various biological and environmental sciences. As waste islands, they serve both as founts of public knowledge and black holes shrouded in military secrecy. Their involvement in environmental science did not begin with the Pacific Remote Islands National Marine Monument; in other words, this is only the most recent form scientific-military collaboration has taken. From 1963 to 1970, these exceptional sites provided a unique opportunity for scientists to observe migratory bird patterns as part of the Smithsonian's Pacific Ocean Biological Survey Program. This eventually led to a controversy surrounding alleged collusion between the scientific and military establishment, especially as some of the guano islands became used for weapons testing and waste storage, for which notable scientific projects provided a degree of cover.[11]

The guano islands serve these many purposes because they were wastelanded, constructed to be heterotopias outside the limits of normal territorial democracy and capitalism, an illiberal exception to liberal freedoms and their alleged condition of possibility. During the Cold War and since, America's waste islands largely became places to store waste rather than mine it, to destroy rather than build, to conserve and observe as wilderness rather than to settle and populate.

Carbon Democracy/Oil Imperialism

In the mid-nineteenth century the US government intervened abroad to shield farmers from the guano market. Decades later, however, Lockean concerns about the production of wealth through labor were seemingly displaced by a shift toward value extraction associated with the modern nation-state. By the twentieth century the United States and many other states had transitioned to *national capitalism*, meaning they became reliant more on the extraction of rents from natural resources.[12]

The year after the Guano Islands Act was passed, for example, Jarvis Island and other guano-rich acquisitions began to serve as coaling stations to enable overseas transportation (Vine 2011, 48). Fossil fuel eventually replaced guano altogether, not only as an artificial fertilizer ingredient, but as a purer object of capitalist desire and imperialist strategy. After World War II, the world's biggest commodity was typically purchased using American dollars, and "the value of the dollar as the basis of international finance depended on the flow of oil" (Mitchell 2011, 111; see also Jones 2012). The strategic island strategy was developed by the Pentagon at the start of the Cold War as a means of ensuring American influence in an era of postcolonial independence and global oil markets: "The premise of the plan was...that in an age of decolonization, local peoples and governments of newly independent nations were increasingly endangering the viability of many of the Navy's overseas bases" (Vine 2011, 41). The viability of these bases was crucial as part of the formation of a "technological zone" to control the supply and circulation of oil, "a set of coordinated but widely dispersed regulations, calculative arrangements, infrastructures and technical procedures that render certain objects or flows governable" (Mitchell 2011, 40).

The location of Diego Garcia made it logistically suitable for this purpose, providing the Navy with spatial proximity to the oil-rich post-colonies that ring the Indian Ocean. If geography makes the location of the Chagos optimal for the US military projects, the base on Diego Garcia is only made possible due to the legal contrivance that has allowed the UK Foreign and Commonwealth Office (FCO) and the US government to claim that the BIOT falls outside of international human rights conventions and environmental agreements. For this reason, Peter Sand (2009a, 2009b) suggests that Diego Garcia is a black hole in legal theory. This does not so much reflect an absence of law, as a strategic manipulation of it in the practice of asymmetric warfare. Like Israel, the United States generally engages in warfare while deploying an explicit "discourse of legality," demonstrating that they both have "borrowed and learned significantly from previous colonial counterinsurgencies, especially from the asymmetric or small wars of the British Empire" (Khalili 2013, 64).

The native inhabitants of the Chagos are the descendants of slaves and indentured servants who were brought to the archipelago by Franco-Mauritian colonists in the late eighteenth century. At the time the French and British empires were engaged in a global conflict that would secure for the victor, among other things, control of the Indian Subcontinent and Ocean. Chagossians won their freedom in 1835 (a generation earlier than American slaves), only to be forcibly removed over a century later by the United Kingdom at the request of its now-more-powerful ally, the United States. The United States sought to acquire Diego Garcia as early as 1960 and convinced the United Kingdom to cut off the BIOT from other colonies, with designs to use it for military purposes as well as economic ones (Vine 2011, 185–87).

The acquisition of Diego Garcia occurred in the midst of worldwide decolonization and rising Cold War tensions, including the Cuban Missile Crisis. For these and other reasons, this legal transfer was carried out with great care. Vine explains how this transpired:

> On December 30, 1966, the U.S. and British governments confirmed the arrangements for the base with an Exchange of Notes. By doing so, they avoided signing a treaty requiring Congressional and Parliamentary oversight. According to the Notes, published months later, the United States would gain use of the new colony "without charge." In confidential agreements accompanying the Notes, however, the United States agreed to secretly pay the British $14 million. The money was, as other documents show, to be used to establish the territory, to pay off Mauritius and Seychelles "generously" to avoid "agitation in the colonies," and to take "those administrative measures" necessary to remove the islands' inhabitants. (2011, 331)

Displaced Chagossians, many of whom are languishing in the margins of other African island nations, have spent decades appealing to American, British, and international courts to have their mistreatment and their claims to the archipelago recognized, with varying success.[13] The main barrier preventing them from doing so is precisely the BIOT's exceptional legal status. Occupied by the Americans by federal order (which can only be legally challenged by citizens of the United States), but technically administered by the British crown (creating a barrier to Parliamentary appeal), the BIOT is a legal black hole, much like the guano islands. Within the global human rights infrastructure, the occupation of the Chagos is thus difficult (though not impossible) to register as a legal violation, even as it serves as a cornerstone of American empire.

Wilderness as Imperial Strategy

The Chagos Marine Protected Area, proposed in 2009, was finally declared illegal in March of 2015 by the Permanent Court of Arbitration at the Hague.

The reasons given had to do with UN recognition of the legal rights of people from Mauritius to fish in the waters surrounding the Chagos and not, significantly, recognition of the rights of Chagossians. While it is nothing new for British or American powers to dispossess native inhabitants and deny their land claims, they no longer do so by claiming that they will improve Diego Garcia with private industry, as they had done in the age of Lockean liberalism. And yet, the idea that the military presence on the BIOT is not only lawful but a responsible caretaker fits very well with the liberal roots of American and British warfare over the last century. As Laleh Khalili puts it, "This insistence on legality of action goes hand in hand with the will to improve that is inherent to liberal imperial invasions, occupations, and confinements" (2013, 241). As the recent efforts at marine preservation make very clear, the goal is to withdraw the island behind military secrecy, to make it invisible as wilderness. In a fantastic claim—used also as part of the marine preservation of the guano islands—the exceptional biodiversity of these transoceanic territories was used as a justification for their removal from global commerce and, by extension, from (re)occupation.[14] Such dual-purpose occupation, both public and scientific and secret and militaristic, echoes American uses of guano islands throughout the twentieth century.

The Chagos Conservation Trust has argued that marine preservation of the BIOT is critical to protect its rare and endangered coral reefs. The released Wikileaks cable, mentioned at the start of the chapter, suggests that this is also supported as part of a strategic ploy to maintain military occupation. This does not mean that the CCT is merely pretending to care about marine preservation, only that its proposal does not preclude continued US occupation or enable Chagossians to return to their homes. In response to the CCT, Peter H. Sand (2009b, 295–96) has challenged it to address the environmental impacts of the military base, including:

1. "the massive jet fuel spills (totaling more than 1.3 million gallons) at the US military base on Diego Garcia in 1984, 1991, 1997 and 1998";
2. "the 31% observed increase in alien plant species unintentionally introduced in Diego Garcia since 1988 as a result of US military construction and naval operations, including *Leucaena leucocephala* (listed by the IUCN among the top worst invasive species of the world)";
3. "radiation leakages in the Diego Garcia lagoon from US nuclear-powered naval vessels and submarines regularly transiting or permanently stationed

there since 1979, and from the transit of 550 tonnes of low-grade uranium in the lagoon in 2008"; and

4. "harm to marine mammals caused by the US Navy's continued low-to-medium sonar used for submarine monitoring and long-distance underwater sound propagation programs at its Diego Garcia Ocean Surveillance Station since 1974 (the Chagos Archipelago is part of the International Whaling Commission's Indian Ocean Sanctuary)."

As has happened at many other bases throughout the world, the United States is leaving a scarred environment behind as a result of its long occupation. But Americans are not the only ones responsible, since the United Kingdom, Mauritius, and Seychelles were paid to make this occupation legally (if not morally) defensible.

Depictions of the Chagos environment by the CCT also differ from those of the displaced Chagossians themselves. For Chagos islanders, there are yet other problems than these with the state of their homeland. After being in American and British hands for decades, it is not just the abstract environment that has declined, but the dwelling places they remember. One hundred Chagos islanders were permitted to visit the Chagos by the British government in 2006, the first ever such large-scale trip. Laura Jeffery describes reactions of those she interviewed upon their return from visiting:

> Their main complaint concerned the abandonment and dereliction of their former pathways, houses, school buildings, clinics, chapels, and cemeteries. They described coconut palms lying over the sea and blocking the routes through the interior of the islands, and overgrown vegetation causing damage to the remnants of the human settlements on Île du Coin and Île Boddam in particular, but also beyond the confines of the military base on Diego Garcia, including the former settlement at East Point. Such changes were routinely described as a change from a "clean" (*prop*) to a "dirty" (*sal*) environment. (Jeffery 2013, 308)

Importantly, Jeffery also points out that Chagos islanders do not all share the same environmental perceptions and priorities. But beyond their varied concerns (and the many others that would likely emerge were the Chagos to come under further international scrutiny), one could also point out that the greatest threat to marine biodiversity, including coral reefs, is not a small collection of Chagossians returning home, but the changing ocean itself. This includes its increasing depth, acidity, warmth, and nitrification, brought about by anthropogenic climate change.

If military strategy is closely tied to global oil markets, then American carbon democracy and oil imperialism are ultimately responsible for the greatest threat to marine life, with or without a military base leaking oil and radiation, or introducing invasive species. Guano was sought to address a symptom of metabolic rift (soil exhaustion); however, its replacement (fossil fuel–based nitrogen fertilizer) has helped usher in yet more rifts, and they not only threaten the argument made on behalf of turning the BIOT into a marine preserve, they may also threaten the military operation it was partly conjured to disguise.

THE OCEAN-IN-ITSELF

After all, the question is not *whether* these meteorological and geological forms of existence are playing a part in the current government of the demos. Clearly they already do, economically, politically, and socially. The question is what role has been assigned to them as they emerge from a low background hum to making a demand on the political order.
—Povinelli (2016, 142–3, emphasis in original)

The guano trade destroyed the habitats of oceanic seabirds, but competition for guano ended only for seabirds to become popularized victims of plastic pollution and oil spills, and therefore emblematic of the excesses of the fossil-fuel age. Climate change is but one of the many environmental crises ushered in by the embrace of fossil fuels. Both plastics and nitrogen fertilizers (the latter a direct replacement for guano) rely heavily on the productive consumption of oil; both are spilling into the ocean, accumulating on ocean surfaces and in the bodies of marine creatures. These consequences are the collective product of the distinct metabolic rifts created (and risks taken) by successive imperial formations. If guano and oil imperialism were actively developed geopolitical strategies, their polluting effects were no more expected than the radical democratic movements to which they gave rise. And their impacts are made more difficult to predict and manage, despite their anthropogenesis, due to the mediating influence of oceanic forces. To characterize this influence properly, following Povinelli's (2016) analysis of contemporary geontopower, is to recognize how the ocean emerges from the background of human projects, in specific ways, to make demands on the political order.

For the remainder of this chapter, I focus on two effects of the oceanic Anthropocene—plastic garbage patches and sea-level rise. I chose these crises, following Eugene Thacker, because they help represent the world *in itself* rather than the world *for us*: "Even though there is something out there that is not the world-for-us, and even though we can name it the world-in-itself, the latter constitutes a horizon for thought, always receding just beyond the bounds of intelligibility" (2011, 5). Something can be tangible without being wholly intelligible. Thacker relates the world-in-itself to the specter of human extinction, which he finds productive insofar as it challenges human mastery and anthropocentrism. But human extinction is only one, and the most extreme, tangible possibility the future holds. Many other endings can be imagined, including a possible end to the current American imperial formation.

In order to approach such things as future calamities, it is helpful to explore not only the known and experienced, but the emergent science fictions and facts that are bubbling up along the horizon of oceanic energies. "Science fact and speculative fiction need each other," writes Donna Haraway, "and they both need speculative feminism" (2016, 3). Haraway combines (or "composts") these ingredients in the form of what she calls *string figures*. These figures are not so much found as followed: "the string figure is not the tracking, but rather the actual thing, the pattern and assembly that solicits response, the thing that is not oneself but with which one must go on. . . It is becoming-with each other in surprising relays. . .a figure of ongoingness in the Chthulucene" (2016, 3). The transforming ocean-in-itself is my own string figure, one which solicits response by finding troubling tangles of water, empire, and island.

The examples I provide include scientific assessment, satire, and speculative fiction, which represent attempts of *nonislanders* to remember a perilous future for the ocean.[15] I have focused on these representations because they offer a glimpse into how an emerging ocean-in-itself is encouraging responses among those (like most of the informants of this book) much closer to the center of empire than to its hinterlands. Their representations could therefore be appropriately characterized as forms of neocolonial fantasies of wastelanding: gleefully imagined endings and new beginnings for people and places elsewhere, whose coeval political struggle is potentially denied and erased further. In this way, sea-level assessments, comic books, and online humor are not unlike the designs of the DoD and national security state; they seek opportunity in oceanic crises. They can and should be critiqued, but these stories of endtimes might also be repurposed to new ends.[16]

Sea-Level Rise, or Climatic Rifts

According to Clark and Foster (2009), the market in guano constituted a global system, unevenly redistributing environmental repair and destruction. If so, then climate change represents a similarly uneven process on a planetary scale, that is, one whose impacts extend far beyond the limited horizon of human designs and imaginations.

As the atmosphere fills with carbon dioxide, oceanic energies respond in ways that are difficult to intelligibly predict. Even those organizations that pride themselves in prediction insist on accepting a level of unavoidable uncertainty. In the IPCC's fifth and most recent assessment of climate change impacts, an entire chapter is devoted to ocean systems, including a subchapter outlining "Key Uncertainties" (IPCC 2014, 465). These include changes in microbial function and primary productivity, deleterious effects of ocean warming, depleted oxygen, and acidification on marine resources and, most significantly for the present argument, increases in sea-level rise. On the one hand, sea-level rise represents a dimension of oceanic anthropogenesis that appears relatively more predictable. It is, after all, a description of a seemingly straightforward parameter that can be measured and assessed on any coastline. In the same IPCC report, it is predicted that sea level will rise anywhere between .17 and .38 meters by 2065, depending on how much the relative concentration of carbon dioxide in the atmosphere increases before that time. At the same time, the potential impacts of such changes are hard to predict with any certainty, both because sea level is mediated by distinct regional variations and because human uses of coastline and resilience to change vary to an even greater degree.

On small islands, more human occupation and infrastructure is concentrated near the coast and is therefore in greater danger than on larger land masses. And yet, there is an ongoing dispute over whether sea level has been rising in the Chagos. At the Royal Geographical Society meetings in May of 2011, members of the CCT claimed that sea level was rising in the Chagos by 12 mm a year, which according to some critics would place the Chagos underwater in less than fifty years. Prior to the failed attempt to establish a marine preserve, the imminent sinking of the Chagos was used by the FCO to cast doubt on the affordability and practicality of resettling Chagossians (see Dunne 2011). In its report, the IPCC did not quote these dire predictions, but chose instead the more modest assessments of Dunne, Barbosa, and Woodworth (2012). The IPCC argues, against the FCO and CCT, that the location of the Chagos relative to the Indian Ocean makes its variable sea-level fluctuations relatively stable, and will continue to do so for the foreseeable future. This suggests that the physical environment poses no meaningful barrier to reoccupation. It is worth noting that Richard Dunne, a coral scientist and key contributor to this alternative study, is also an advocate for Chagossian rights and explicitly links these predictions to their cause. At the same time, unlike his opponents, Dunne (2011) cautions against anyone who would claim to know with certainty what the future of sea level in the Chagos will be, given the limited data available. That depends on the unintelligible ocean-in-itself.

Beyond the Chagos, it is vitally important to attend to the sea-level rise now impacting small island nations and coastal areas, which are inhabited by some of the world's least powerful people. Not only do they face the greatest risks, with limited access to political and economic resources, but their voices and fates are all too readily appropriated as wasteland in political struggles between global elites over climate science and policy, that is, as doomed locations whose people are erased from consideration. My lack of attention to their perspectives is not meant to discount the significance of the plight of Pacific Islanders and others, but rather to *reappropriate* the rhetorical move by which vulnerable others are made to appear as hapless and tragic victims— canaries in coal mines whose sole purpose is to conjure privileged imaginings of ecological endtimes.[17]

Let us instead bend these imaginings to consider the hapless victimhood of American military bases as they fall into wasteland. Whether or not sea level has been stable in the Chagos for the last two decades in which this has been closely studied, changes are happening there and are expected to continue. It is therefore worth speculating whether this will threaten military occupation within a few decades. It would be fitting, in some ways, that as Americans and British conspire to make Diego Garcia vanish into an exceptional wilderness, the ocean is swallowing it up. This clearly concerns the DoD, which is actively involved in speculating on negative scenarios as a result of climate change. For Andrew Bickford (2015) and Robert Marzec (2016), this means that it is important to attend to the unspoken relationship between environmental researchers and advocates and American military interests.[18] This is plainly apparent in the dispute over the Chagos' environment, whether it is considered stable and worth fighting for or vulnerable and in need of saving. In fact, the timing of potential sea-level rise could coincide quite nicely with the expiration of the UK-US agreement for continued occupation of the BIOT, which was renewed for another twenty years, after the initially agreed-upon fifty-year period came to an end in 2016. In 2036, the US is meant to leave anyhow. It would therefore be a mistake to miss connections to military interests where they exist.[19]

But it would also be a mistake to imagine that the United States, no matter how powerful, can legally and tactically outmaneuver a changing and unpredictable ocean. In addition to confluences of climate power and knowledge in the present, can one usefully imagine the American and British navies being forced to evacuate an island form that betrays its formless origins, i.e., its constitutive emergence from the surrounding ocean? For one thing, reduced land area would curtail the ability to dock and launch ships and aircraft. Attempts by the military to counter these limitations, with new logistical and technological innovations, would be expected in this instance. Yet one can also expect they might ultimately fail against the receding horizon of intelligibility that is the ocean-in-itself. They would then have to abandon the Chagos.

Nonmilitaristic human occupation (by Chagossians, for example) arguably requires considerably less land and could theoretically subsist on the (admittedly contaminated and altered) spaces thus abandoned. This would not constitute a mere return, moreover, but a form of what archaeologist and paleoethnobotanist BrieAnna Langlie (2018) refers to as an act of *ecological resistance*, where human-ecological relating serves as a moral project against hierarchical, especially imperial, authority. But achieving justice for displaced people means something more than acquiring physical land. The fact is that a Chagossian story of a hoped-for return could just as easily be facilitated as prevented by oceanic forces turning against imperial designs for the ocean. As Vine (2011, 192–96) explains, Chagossian suffering can never really be undone or healed fully, and something approximating true justice would mean not resettlement alone, but reparations and assistance rebuilding the lives that were taken from them. Even if sea-level rise makes occupation no longer possible, if the archipelago finally sinks for good, then the loss of Diego Garcia could still be used to justify reparations to Chagossians. After all, they would no longer be merely dispossessed but now permanently displaced, and in part because the United States failed to curtail its carbon emissions, for the same reasons it insisted on meddling in Indian Ocean affairs, out of a dual commitment to carbon democracy and oil imperialism.

Like the American empire itself, Chagossians and other island-dwellers seek lives with value, not simply wealth and territory. The task is parallel to but different from the metabolic rifts connecting ocean and land. It is about landless people regaining lives with dignity from the landed. Some have benefited from their loss and have land to spare, going to waste in excessive and forgotten territories, where the distinction between hinter- and homeland begins to dissolve. The empire's influence stretches far beyond acts of occupation and counterinsurgency. In addition to military operations, Diego Garcia is one of only four monitoring stations that are part of the global infrastructure of GPS, specifically used as control facilities on the ground which help coordinate orbiting satellites (along with Ascension Island in the Atlantic, another British protectorate). This not only changes the stakes of what happens to these occupied islands, it also demonstrates a relationship, generally unacknowledged, between American military power and ordinary American life, between the militarization of hinterland and homeland. Diego Garcia is better known for making possible the flight of pilotless drones, not the navigation of driverless cars, but it is part of the critical infrastructure for both.[20]

Oceanic Gyres, or Waste Is Land!

An oceanic gyre is a relatively stable area at the center of circulating wave and wind currents. Gyres are where the ocean collapses in on itself, a vortex that draws materials in. One could not imagine a more appropriate counterpoint to the networked, urbanized warscapes of the American empire, which are designed to harness wind, water, and electromagnetism to monitor and access the entire globe. Gyres, by contrast, are regions of ocean that generally fall outside of shipping lanes, flight paths, and satellite imaging.

There are five major gyres known throughout the world. All of them have multiple accumulation zones for the world's plastic waste, which gradually drifts to these areas over time, a fact only recently discovered.[21] The resulting "garbage patches" of the gyres remained out of virtual and actual reach for decades, a reality of the ocean-in-itself not yet recognized. Not only are they distant from dominant seafaring routes; the existence of the patches did not easily fit within prevailing models of environmental impact and regulation. Marine scientists predicted that such accumulation zones would exist before they were visited and officially documented, beginning in 1997, but in many ways they still remain a mystery. It is unclear, for example, who is responsible for the plastic waste, and how far and how long the debris has traveled, the degree to which waste has impacted and altered marine ecologies, and whether this affects human consumers, and what strategies and techniques, if any, can be called upon to mitigate and manage gyre wastescapes.

The Indian Ocean's main gyre is located just to the west of Australia, though the primary source for its marine debris is estimated to come from Southeast Asia and Indonesia further away to the north. It is also estimated to be one of the least polluted of oceanic gyres, though the Bay of Bengal is a major accumulation zone for debris, due to extensive coastal development and boat traffic.[22] Given its comparatively greater size and proximity to imperial homelands, more people are aware of the Pacific Garbage Patch, located roughly between Alaska and Hawaii. The plastic debris in this area has been estimated at over three million tons, distributed over an area roughly the size of the state of Texas. While these are preliminary figures, they have been successful at attracting the imaginations, not only of scientists and environmentalists, but of artists, fantasists, and satirists. Consequently, I will use the Pacific as a model for the Indian Ocean, imitating how models of marine conservation have been replicated across these respective oceans in service of imperial formations. But my model is meant as a counterformation to empire, one that turns the wastelanding strategy against itself.

In February of 2014, a satirical online journal published an article claiming that the Pacific Garbage Patch would be transformed by the United Nations into a floating island to serve as a refuge for those displaced from climate change:

> This agreement has been heralded as a victory in most developed nations, with the United States already pledging 30.5 million more tons of wreckage by May of 2014. "We will not stop consuming," President Obama told reporters this morning. "The road will be long, but we must not give up our insatiable lust for material goods until each and every climate refugee has their very-own milk-jug house." (SpeculumPaper WorldNews 2014)

While not directly referenced by the satirists, an actual design for exactly this purpose had already been proposed by Rotterdam-based WHIM Architecture, a nonprofit organization. In 2010, the Netherlands Architecture Fund awarded them a grant to develop Recycled Island NPG, a "research project on the potential of realizing a habitable floating island in the Pacific Ocean made from all the plastic waste that is momentarily floating around in the ocean" (https://architizer.com/projects/recycled-island/).

Whether or not this is feasible—especially given that most of the waste suspended in oceanic gyres has photodegraded into small plastic fragments—

it appeals to the imaginations of both satirists and architects in a specific way: as a new source of land recovered from waste, engineered for those climate displacees who are losing land. The satirists make more apparent the geohistorical irony that this turn of events would bequeath to the victims of climate change: a *terra nullius* literally expended by those who have contributed most to rising sea level and plastic pollution. In other words, what both have collectively imagined is that those most responsible for global injustices and metabolic rifts might transform symptom into cure. Another example comes from the British social media and entertainment site LADbible, which proposed applying to make the Pacific Garbage Patch an official country in 2017, beginning an online campaign to find citizens and form a government, with the idea that this would finally get other countries to pay attention to the problem of plastic waste in the oceans (see http://www.ladbible.com/trashisles /welcome).

A less optimistic portrayal of this process of nation-building is provided in *Great Pacific*, a 2013 graphic novel written by Joe Harris. In this neoimperialist fantasy, the disgraced son of a wealthy industrialist fights to establish sovereign control over the settlement of New Texas, founded on the debris of the Pacific Garbage Patch. In the two volumes, "Nation Building" and "Trashed," the white male protagonist and his competitors are modeled on familiar tropes of the American West, with their foundations in the acquisition of order and Lockean sovereignty through private property and the improvement of wasteland. Unlike in related science fiction fantasies, such as *Star Trek* and the exploration of the "final frontier" therein, *Great Pacific* simultaneously offers new lands for the application of imperial designs and highlights the artificiality and absurdity of a moral logic based on wastelanding.

Similar fictions and facts have not yet developed around the Indian Ocean garbage patch, nor, if they eventually do, will they necessarily resemble the American-Pacific Garbage Patch model presented thus far. It is unclear whether oceanic conditions or geohistorical imaginaries will allow for wasteland to be symbolized in the same way, despite the moral and political forces that have taken hold in the Chagos. It is tempting, of course, to imagine new islands, made out of plastic, for Chagossian occupation. Compared with the Pacific, the Indian Ocean's gyre appears to be more interconnected with the rest of the ocean, allowing the materials it has accumulated to travel further faster and gradually spread plastic debris along coasts, from the Persian Gulf to East Africa to the Straits of Malacca. Garbage patches are not solely a pollutant or a resource, but part of the peculiar stratigraphy of what I call the Polemocene; they are the technofossil record left behind by human occupation in the age of oil imperialism and carbon democracy. In Navaro-Yashin's terms, this ruination would serve as the representation of "an abjected political system" (2012, 160). As such, the question is not only what can be made of the plastic debris, but what alternative, non-Lockean stories it will tell about moral and geopolitical relationships.[23]

According to a recent report from the nonprofit Ocean Conservancy (2015), for example, China, Indonesia, the Philippines, Thailand, and Vietnam are the world's leading contributors to plastic pollution, accounting for over half of the plastic waste dumped into the ocean. As a result of framing the problem in this way, the Ocean Conservancy's policy recommendations largely focus on these five nations. Yet, the production and purchase of plastic in any one region cannot really be separated from more global, geohistorical relations, including US economic influence and military presence in the Indian Ocean, particularly given how much the United States and other nations have relied on Southeast Asia as a destination for their plastic waste exports. As with the so-called soil crisis and competitive guano market of a previous century, the distribution of wastes and assets is not random but shaped by geoimperial histories. As the production, consumption, and recycling of plastic in Southeast Asia continues to increase, it is likely that the Indian Ocean garbage patch will grow in size and global awareness.

And if Diego Garcia begins to disappear under the ocean waves, the remains of American military occupation will accumulate in patches as well. What stories will then be told, what studies done, what moral narratives proffered, if these traces begin to accumulate in the Indian Ocean garbage patch? Compare this to the revelation that Bluie East Two, an abandoned US Air Force base in Greenland, may begin to leak toxic waste as a result of melting ice. Greenlanders have complained about the "American flowers" left behind for decades, but climate change has brought it renewed attention. Imagine if climate change not only made it visible but mobile. "And when the empire declines and falls, as it inevitably must," W. J. T. Mitchell writes, "it leaves behind nothing but objects—relics and ruins, inscriptions" (2005, 155).

The trace evidence left behind of war preparation, and the stories that can be told from them, matter. As we have seen, the political strategy of island erasure operates in part as "double erasure" (see Davis 2007, 2015), in that making the history of an island and its people invisible also enables a forgetting of the geoimperial relations that make such wasting possible. If the ocean cannot be predicted, at the very least it might serve as an undeniable record, a counterimperial archive of sorts to aid in decolonization and allow us to see interconnected histories that have been denied and forgotten, whether through wastelanding or some other means. In the same way that subaltern, island-dwelling people should not be made to stand in only as token suffering subjects, to shock a global elite into action, it should not only be their task to remember what they have lost and why. This can begin with the United States and the United Kingdom assuming full responsibility for what they have done, both symbolically and financially.[24]

HOPE IN THE POLEMOCENE

By not embracing resignation we can turn down catastrophe—even if we cannot escape watery perturbations.
—Jeffrey Jerome Cohen (2015)

Whatever the outcome of this ongoing struggle, my point is that oceanic energies are not on the side of the powerful, any more than the powerless, and the current plans and projects shared by climate science and centers of calculation cannot possibly anticipate all the creative destruction that a radically altered planet is capable of. There is obviously a risk associated with environmental optimism, especially with hoping for nature to right wrongs. William Cronon reminds us:

> As we gaze into the mirror it holds up for us, we too easily imagine that what we behold is Nature when in fact we see the reflection of our own unexamined longings and desires. For this reason, we mistake ourselves when we suppose that wilderness can be the solution to our culture's problematic relationships with the nonhuman world, for wilderness is itself no small part of the problem. (Cronon 1995, 47–48)

A pristine nonhuman nature will not heal the wounds Americans and British have left behind. My aim is more modest, to suggest that an anthropogenically manipulated nature-in-itself will prove to exceed the walls put up to contain it and sustain global hegemony. This is against the CCT and its claims to bound this ecosystem outside of human interference, to wild it in such a way that disguises its history and protects American military interests from native interference.

Wilderness and wasteland have been the tools of American settler colonial and imperial formations. From western expansion through the great guano rush to the dispossession of the Chagossians, the reuse, destruction, and reclamation of lands has recurred, again and again. But ocean is not land; there cannot be an equivalent "waste-watering" strategy. Forming and sustaining permanent occupation in the midst of the ocean only occurs—whether through geological perturbations or coral reef accumulations—with great time and effort. Should anyone be so confident in the power and ingenuity of the American military that it can withstand progressive sea-level rise in Diego Garcia? No more than we should be so confident in Western engineering and artistry as to imagine brand new lands being formed out of degraded plastic flotsam.

US empire is built atop waste. This is so not only historically, as a result of the guano rush, or metonymically, through the representational practice of wastelanding, but also because its rise to global hegemony literally depended on laying waste to Japanese and German cities, loaning money to those who survived, rebuilding and occupying them with bases. Nor did this end with World War II or the Marshall Plan. Leah Zani (2019) explains how this was also the strategy employed as part of the Secret War in Laos, from 1962–75, which laid waste to the country with explicit aspirations of later economic exploitation. And insofar as American global hegemony is structured around the threat of nuclear destruction (the twin needs to protect against it and be capable of it), it is also premised on the possibility of turning the entire world into a wasteland at the push of a button. The virtual threat of wasteland is official US policy.

Such instantaneous and universal destruction can make the gradual creep of anthropogenic climate change seem less important and more speculative by comparison, but both are equally real and deeply intertwined as part of what I have called the Polemocene (see chapter 3). If the Polemocene is worthy of being classified as a timescale all its own, it is worth considering in more detail what makes it distinct. Terms like Anthropocene, Capitalocene, and Polemocene encourage us to focus on distinct, tangled compositions of beings, places, and forces (string figures, as Haraway calls them), as well as different beginnings and endings. The Capitalocene has been premised on the use of violence since its inception, and not only environmental destruction. American capitalism and its military are thoroughly interwoven enterprises— to speak of one is to assume the other.

From another perspective, the destructive possibilities of nuclear war over-shadow the capitalist forces with which they are mutually dependent. Unlike nearly every other form of violence concocted by human beings, for instance, no one profits from all-out nuclear annihilation. And, consequently, the time horizons within which national security states dwell tend to extend deep into the future. This was famously lampooned at the end of the satire *Dr. Strangelove* (1964), when token heads of the military industrial complex take a few minutes, after the accidental start of a nuclear apocalypse, to logistically plan humanity's rebirth over many generations and thousands of years. This kind of planning can make the timescales of capitalism (and anticapitalism) appear shallow by comparison, yet military and capitalist horizons regularly converge. In reality, in the mid-'60s American elites were working out how to secretly pay off Africans and the British to usurp an island in order to have a base strategically close to oil-producing nations.

It is important to understand the distinct problems presented by the Polemocene so that national security states and their allies do not have the last word on its management and meaning. They tend to favor what Dan Brockington (2002) calls *fortress conservation*, as in the Pacific Remote Islands National Marine Monument, which restricts access to areas in the name of environmental protection, while furthering the interests of securitization. Given the close relationship between environmental disaster and environmental management (see Marzec 2016), understanding the Polemocene means investigating the virtual futures imagined and planned for by those shepherding empire through a time of perceived crisis.

For those hoping to unmake the military, imagining the Polemocene does not inevitably lead to despair, but can be a revolutionary act. As Slavoj Žižek (2010) has said many times, paraphrasing Frederick Jameson, it often seems easier to imagine the end of the world than the end of capitalism. It is arguably just as difficult to imagine the end of the American permanent war economy, with which global capitalism is so interconnected. Many have attempted to unmake capitalism and create something new in the last century, but normally this has been accomplished by *intensifying* militarism and militarization, rather than unmaking them as well—this despite Rosa Luxemburg's (1971) insistence that they go hand in hand. What would it mean to imagine an end to permanent war preparation? Would all of those bases and satellites and warheads need to become something else (as do labor and machines in a communist revolution), or does imagining such an end require that they cease to exist entirely?

One possibility of an ending is in the form of antibase activism, which increasingly draws attention to American presence around the globe and has threatened the network of bases established over the last century. In this chapter I have explored other imagined endings, where Polemocene and Capitalocene meet. Like islands birthed from ocean plastic, wonder at miraculous techno-fixes proliferates in the Anthropocene (see the techno-solutionism of chapter 4), but so does nihilistic despair. In fact, the latter is increasingly accepted as the appropriate response to foretold global environmental disasters, especially phenomena like sea-level rise or plastic pollution. Speculating about foretold oceanic futures, can projections of lost and polluted seascapes be used to entertain hope as well? That is ultimately the question behind my analysis in this chapter, whether nonhuman, planetary forces might work against rather than for American imperial formations and inspire the telling of new stories about land, water, and waste.

There are other stories about the future of the ocean, these from Pacific Islanders and other island-dwellers, including Chagossians who continue to struggle for return and reparations, despite the enormous odds stacked against a few thousand people confronting a global empire. Where this chapter attempts to parallel and converge with those stories is in searching for radical and unexpected opportunities for hope. Here I follow Hirokazu Miyazaki, who argues that "reclaiming a place for hope. . .demands more than a strategy of delayed provisional engagement with an emergent world. . .one should make explicit one's own hope retrospectively via replication of others' hope *on a new terrain*" (2006, 139–40, my emphasis). Vine begins and ends his book, *Island of Shame*, in conversation with eighty-year-old Chagossian displacee and activist Rita. She expresses both the depth of her people's suffering and hope to one day return home: "'I will never give up the struggle!' Rita told me. 'I've suffered, suffered, suffered so much. And I'm still suffering.' But when they finally do win, she said, she'll write a sega [popular musical celebration] so that everyone can remember the victory" (Vine 2011, 196). Compare Rita's call for recognition and reparation, one day to be commemorated, to the more privileged imaginings that a depoliticized and dehistoricized ocean affords, one where islands of plastic can be recolonized by wealthy Texans and sea-level rise is a neutral quality to be objectively measured by government-backed scientists. What Rita, graphic novel writers, and climatologists do share in common is that, for them, the Polemocene—the epoch of militarized environmental transformation—is not only a source of risk, but of imaginative possibility.

Creating or reusing wastelands may involve repressive or revolutionary political action, liberating or neocolonial governance, science fact or fiction, hope or despair. The Polemocene does not respect boundaries, any more than the Anthropocene does, but this open-endedness offers chances to politicize and dramatize the contamination and loss that result. Not even the imagined boundary between homeland and hinterland is safe. During the heyday of nuclear testing in the Pacific, the remains of radioactivity did not stay on distant islands, but were brought back to bases on the mainland, making the US military network a vector for the spread of toxicity.[25] These are important narratives to explore because it will be all of us, not only the Navy and island-dwellers, affected by the Polemocene.

Conclusion

I have described unintended consequences of permanent war preparation, glossed as "wastes." Even if they end up being productive in various ways, in the first instance they involve excesses, accidents, collateral damage. Beyond that similarity, military waste takes form within alternative but interrelated contexts or, following Gusterson (2004, xxi), microworlds of action. To explain these distinct relationships to military waste, I made use of different theoretical terms (reflexive practice, affordance, world-making, attunement, transvaluation, and wastelanding), all of which share a sense of indeterminacy, possibility, or open-endedness. This is arguably at issue whenever people relate to that which is deemed rubbish (see Thompson 2017), but with military waste these flexible relationships can have greater moral and political stakes.

Such open-endedness also usefully contrasts with the idea of permanence—while few Americans openly question the seeming necessity of permanent war readiness today (despite a long tradition of doing so), the by-products of such readiness produce endless questions, not to mention uncertainty and doubt, debate and imaginative experimentation. Some of the people in these chapters sought out connections with military discards for profit, artistic enjoyment, or other reasons. Some avoid contact with military waste, which flashes across their vision like so much unwanted dust from the heavens, getting in the way of what they really want to witness. Some find themselves living out their own or other people's militaristic fantasies, trying to carry out or survive shootings made possible by an abundance of guns. Some, finally, are trying to imagine relationships with wasted places that have been withdrawn from reclamation and scrubbed from official history.

The structure of this book was intended to facilitate ever more challenging forms of comparison as the chapters progressed, so that odd resemblances were foregrounded between things as seemingly different as disused warplanes, mass shootings, and wilderness areas. I have focused primarily on the wastes of war preparation, but I want to take a moment to discuss military waste *in general*. To do this, I will compare it with something else seemingly different—automobile accidents—in order to reveal the peculiar ways that Americans tend to relate (and to not relate) to being both permanently ready for and perpetually engaged in war.

Automobile accidents are everyday events, meaning they happen to some Americans every day and tend to happen to everyone at least once at some point: over a million die in automobile accidents each year, and many millions more are injured or permanently disabled. Moreover, Americans arguably exert a great deal of effort in day-to-day life averting and imagining possible car crashes. Warfare is very different. To begin with, only a select few Americans are ever directly implicated in it, specifically those who volunteer, while the vast majority of Americans never experience war for themselves. Since the end of the Vietnam War and the draft, American civilians have become more distanced from warfare (even as the rest of the world has seen a rise in civilians targeted by conflict and a corresponding increase in refugees; Desjarlais et al. [1992, 25–26]). Moreover, growing inequality means the costs (and benefits) of war are not shared equally by all. Whereas 12 percent of Americans served in the armed forces during World War II, in 2013 the figure was as low as .05 percent, leading some to fear a growing gap between civilians and service members (Eikenberry and Kennedy 2013).[1]

When faced with a car wreck, one can imagine the bodily sensations and reactions that led to the destruction one is witnessing, to put oneself in the position of drivers and passengers. This could account for a common expression used when people want to refer to generic human interest in the misfortune of others, that people are "unable to look away" as they pass a car crash. You drive by a wreck on the side of the road, according to this idiom, and you cannot help taking a peek at what unfortunately transpired, no matter however terrible or gruesome. This is such a familiar expression that people will describe other events by comparing them to witnessing vehicular wreckage, "it's like watching a car crash, I just couldn't look away." In my experience, this might be used to describe the speaker's irresistible fascination with watching people suffer or humiliate themselves as a result of their own failings. When faced with things related to the military, by contrast, it can be hard to establish a similar connection or sense of empathy or judgment. This is compounded by a further moral quandary. At least with random automobile wrecks, onlookers normally do not think themselves responsible for the fate of the victims. At most, they might think how lucky they are by contrast, since anyone who has traveled in a vehicle can certainly imagine this happening to them.

In the case of the incredible military wreckage left behind, it is the opposite. Most Americans do not know what it means to be involved in or suffer from warfare, unless they have worked in or fled from somewhere less fortunate. Even if one considers structural inequality a debilitating form of quasi-warfare against marginalized groups (see Puar 2017), that still would arguably exclude a large number of Americans. People may know terrible, interpersonal violence in their everyday lives, without understanding war. Those Americans are likely aware that a global empire is perpetually assembled in their name; even if they are sometimes encouraged to forget what wars are being fought and how, they know global warfare is possible. Even so, they also may have noticed that the familiar wars of previous centuries, fought between the militaries of two states, are rare and short-lived. At the start of this book, I said that a third world war never happened and the military built to fight it became obsolete. From another perspective, this war did happen, just not for most Americans. Since the end of the twentieth century, what some have called a "third world war" (Neitschmann 1987) has been fought between states and indigenous people, rebels and marginalized groups within (often contested) state borders, often involving American-made weapons (Custers 2007; Feinstein 2012). For the United States, the open-ended "War on Terror" that ostensibly began in 2001 only represents one recent example of a worldwide rise in "low-intensity" conflicts going back decades (Desjarlais et al. 1995, 117).

In this sense, relationships with a (now truly global) military are like waiting in anticipation for a car accident about to happen, knowing it will likely involve people whom one does not know, with lives and backgrounds one does not fully comprehend, which will entail future consequences one can scarcely imagine. And even those critical of American attacks in various parts of the world might not find it possible to look away. This is one way to explain the bizarre reaction of famous NBC news anchor Brian Williams in April of 2017, while reporting on a US attack on Syria: "We see these beautiful pictures at night from the decks of these two U.S. Navy vessels in the Mediterranean."[2] Or the distasteful 2013 *New York Post* headline—"Bride and Boom!"—which was used to depict a drone attack on Yemeni civilians heading either to or from a wedding (not the first or the last US drone attack on a Muslim wedding as part of the supposed global war against terrorists).[3] Arguably only people so alienated from the military created in their name could watch from a distance and find enjoyment in bombs dropping and missiles firing, traumatic experiences they don't really understand undergone by people and places they don't really understand.

When faced with warfare, usually impacting people "elsewhere," Americans may be forced to reflect on how they allowed this to happen or what they might have gained from it. Partly because of the real and virtual separation of military from civilian worlds, those belonging to the latter may assume that the only proper thing to do is to honor the sacrifices of veterans. Sharing endless statements of support "for the troops" could be seen as a reaction to the distance that most Americans feel from the actual experiences of service members and victims of war and the sense of alienation this causes. In a society so dedicated to the automobile, car accidents arguably have a special significance because a machine intended for one thing, a means of comfortable and safe passage, ends up becoming something else, an instrument of death and destruction. Encountering the waste of the permanent war readiness is, in a way, the inverse of looking at a car crash: instruments of death and destruction that, in wreckage, offer up new, spectacular, and sometimes horrifying possibilities.

If most Americans ever come across a rebuilt car that they can purchase that was once involved in an accident, it is doubtful that they will think of it the same way as when they come across the kinds of military waste discussed in this book. In the case of military waste, they may hesitate to ascribe new meanings and possibilities to it and disagree on what forms of reuse might count as worthwhile or offensive. Like looking at vehicular wreckage, coming across military waste means reckoning in some way with the fate of the people entangled with it. Many of the people in this book had to reckon with an absent presence—service members and nationalist histories of war and peace—with which these objects are entangled. Meditating on the sacrifice of service members is one way, and certainly the most common, to make sense of military objects of any kind. But other ways are possible. Some of the people in this book were more interested in reusing military waste to explore alternative affordances or to communicate forgotten understories, even to question whether the military should exist in its current form. Others, such as the employees of the DoD and Lockheed Martin, saw military waste as part of their job and, by keeping it in check, hoped they were doing it well. Rubbish need not concern anyone, which is part of what makes it rubbish.

Car accidents and wars do have one thing in common, in addition to being life-threatening: most of the car accidents and military battles that Americans will encounter (including those who drive *and* those who volunteer for military service) are experienced from a relatively safe distance, mediated through a screen (windshield, monitor, television, smart phone). This is another way of saying that Americans are inundated with virtual violence and destruction on a regular basis—violence that is performed for their viewing pleasure and violence that is planned for in simulated war games, ostensibly to defend them against all manner of unseen dangers. Just as direct experiences of warfare are becoming less common in general for Americans, militarization and militarism are becoming more entrenched in daily life.[4]

At the same time that the costs of war are made to seem more distant, there is seemingly endless discussion of the many horrors, both real and fantastic, that a permanent military and security apparatus exists to defend against. The possibility of North Korean missiles, mass shootings, and serial killers seems ever present even if they never come into our lives. Americans are trained to be virtual soldiers on the home front, militarized to remain vigilant, report unusual people or behavior, and arm themselves so they are ready for anything. Beyond preparation for and conduct of warfare, American consumers have a seemingly insatiable appetite for simulated mass violence. From feature films and television shows to the incredible assortment of first-person shooter games, examples of so-called "militainment" abound.[5] Whether or not one is enlisted, living in a country permanently ready for war means being continually confronted with images of real and virtual violence.

In 2014, with declining American troop numbers in Afghanistan (numbering fewer than 40,000), the Obama administration ordered 275 armed services personnel sent to aid in the offensive against ISIS in Iraq (though two years later this number had increased to as many as 5,000 (Thompson 2016). Also in 2014, approximately 6 million Americans were victims of violent crimes, according to FBI crime statistics. That same year, 16.1 million tuned in to watch the premiere of the fourth season of *Walking Dead*, a popular TV show about a kind of violence—zombie apocalypse—that has never and (most people seem to agree) will never happen.[6] That is only one television show compared with military experiences of warfare and civilian experiences of every kind of real violence. It is quite apparent that imaginary violence far outpaces actual violence for Americans. Put differently, Americans imagine far more violence than happens to them. In all likelihood, there have been far more imaginary than real serial killers, imaginary than real man-eating sharks, imaginary than real interplanetary and intergalactic wars. It is no accident that two of the most prominent American exports involve violent simulacra— Hollywood blockbusters, which invariably contain simulations of cataclysmic destruction, and military weapons ready for any kind of conflict imaginable.

When it comes to national war readiness, history may well regard the contemporary United States as the most prepared of all time. Is it any wonder that in best-selling end-of-the-world fantasies, whether alien invasion or zombie outbreak, all of this excess weaponry suddenly becomes useful? It is as if Americans were waiting for something, anything, to justify the enormous arsenal that they have amassed, ready to mete out violence anywhere, anytime, instantly. Whatever one's personal beliefs about the US military, even when it is not being used to wage war, it is still changing the world. One of those effects might be to intimidate enemies or attract foreign buyers, but another happens on the home front as civilians are confronted with the capacity for great destruction and come to feel and believe things as a result. Perhaps it makes them feel even more as if the world is a dangerous place and being prepared for extraordinary violence is the only possible solution. Perhaps ongoing or occasional war and the occasional mass shooting are, like car accidents, regrettable tragedies watched from a comfortable distance that Americans learn to expect from time to time, that they feel helpless to prevent and maybe a little glad it did not happen to them.

IF YOU CAN DREAM IT. . .

How can a counter-counterinsurgency hope to work in such a militarized environment? It can begin by identifying and challenging the pillars of belief and the streams of profit that support business as usual within the military normal.

—Catherine Lutz (2009, 37)

I want to end this book with some thoughts on identifying and challenging what Lutz calls the military normal. The military normal, as I see it, involves a way of knowing where the distinction between civilians and military collapses altogether. One way to define the military normal is a taken-for-granted way of experiencing the world such that permanent war readiness seems necessary, an end in itself rather than a means to accomplishing peace.[7] This is in line with what C. Wright Mills called a military metaphysic, which he argued was in danger of triumphing "in all areas of life" (1956, 223) as part of the growth of American militarism during the Cold War. The fear, then as now, is that this discourages dissent and imperils democracy. With so few people enlisted, with so many communities economically dependent on manufacturing weapons, and with reduced reliance on policies like conscription, a permanent war economy arguably makes even liberal democracies more prone to war.[8]

Things do not have to be this way.[9] Historically, as we have seen, Americans have had misgivings about new, industrially produced weapons at different times, not only nuclear weapons (Gusterson 1996, 2004) but also aircraft (chapters 1 and 2), ships (chapter 3), antisatellite technology (chapter 4), and guns (chapter 5). They have also worried about the implications of having an international network of bases (chapter 6). In each case there was a struggle over growing the military further, and this was only ever supported with some ambivalence.[10] At the same time, it is important not to blame permanent war readiness wholly on the US state. This is not only because of its commitment to national defense, but because some of its historical militarizing actions have been in response to perceived needs of the American people, whether the fate of merchant sailors (chapter 3), the desires of settler colonists for more land and resources (chapter 5), or the fertilizer needs of farmers (chapter 6). Long before the terrorist attack on New York and Washington, DC, and extended military campaigns in Afghanistan and Iraq, some American civilians helped encourage permanent preparation for war.

Americans debate the military today, as they always have, but there are some things that are rarely up for discussion. In mid-April of 2018, Donald Trump was criticized by some and commended by others for ordering attacks on chemical weapons facilities in Syria. Commentators wonder if he had legal authorization to act without Congressional approval, whether it was a legitimate target, whether Syrian ally Russia was warned in advance, whether more attacks will follow, and so on. No one asks whether the United States ought to have weapons at the ready for such an attack at all times. The American public routinely renders judgments about good or bad, legitimate or illegitimate wars and warriors after the fact.[11] But it is generally agreed that a lot of money should be spent and a lot of firepower should always be available for whoever might want to use it. That is never a matter for political debate, not even among people who routinely encounter and handle military waste.

What Lutz calls the military normal is actually deeply strange. A nation of people who have little experience of war overall, with unmatched military superiority and only geographically distant enemies, has to imagine the world is dangerous enough that a permanent war economy is necessary. The imagination of possible threats and inventive ways to defend against them is only limited by what can be dreamt up. It is partly because of the surrealness of military weaponry in the late twentieth century that Angela Gilliam labeled the culture of US defense a "cargo cult," reversing the anthropological gaze in order to deliberately highlight the barbarous nature of so-called civilized war: "The magical properties of producing death in warfare are such that the more efficiently death can be produced—that is, the more people in the shortest amount of time, and the least currency expended—the more advanced the warfare is considered" (Gilliam 1991, 175). Never before have we been capable of killing one and all in so many creative and horrible ways.

When asked, almost anyone can readily list off various threats, real and imagined, that they think are a danger to the country they live in: Russians, Islamic terrorists, the Chinese, the North Koreans. . . If not for the powerful US military, the assumption goes, nothing would keep those various enemies from descending upon unsuspecting Americans and ending their treasured way of life. This is not only why many people support the military but why some join up and risk their lives in the service. Were it not for general acceptance of the need for military buildup, interminable wars against perceived enemies at home and abroad would not be possible. This helps explain why the US government attempted, in the early years of the War on Terror, to conceal facts about combat-related casualties from the public. This included a prohibition on media coverage of military personnel returning in coffins. Increasingly, only state-approved information about ongoing conflicts is released to the public. These efforts, meant to avoid the public backlash that happened during the Vietnam War, have been at least partly successful.[12] If there is one pillar of belief that sustains the permanent war economy, it might be that the United States must ever be ready for war because the world is a violent place full of people who mean each other harm. Americans routinely worry, then and now, about falling behind real and imagined enemies in war preparation.

But mass death is about simulation as much as reality, in that far more people witness and worry about violence than actually commit violent acts or suffer violent attack.[13] Like any risk perceptions, such worries do not need to be based on fact to be strongly felt. As Barry Glassner (2010, 236) puts it:

> In a worst-case scenario, if a terrorist group were to somehow detonate a nuclear bomb in a major U.S. City, the highest casualty rate is predicted to be around 250,000. As gruesome as that would be, the nation has borne worse. The influenza epidemic of 1918 killed 600,000.

And yet, even when the Ebola epidemic in West Africa was making national headlines, the Center for Disease Control's budget for emergency prepared-ness was being drastically cut back. This was at the same time, of course, that the War on Terror was raising military budgets to new heights.[14] Jennifer Mitzen (2006) convincingly argues that individuals and states fear terrorism not purely due to actual body counts but as a result of what she calls loss of "ontological security." Terrorism, for instance, does not simply threaten physi-cal bodies with harm, but disrupts familiar routines and a sense of "basic trust" in others (one could argue, of course, that car accidents are identical in this respect).[15] More to the point, the United States has been attacked far less than many other countries, countries that spend far less of their GDP on always being ready for war; this fear of enemies and enthusiasm for military strength does not appear to stand up to empirical scrutiny. Whatever the reality of all of these imagined threats, they are critical to the military normal.

Permanent war preparation also means simulating the possibility of vio-lence, whether running exercises, loading up bases with weapons and troops, or circling the globe with ships, satellites, and aircraft ready to strike. As men-tioned in chapter 4, many of the people I interviewed to learn about astron-omy and space debris were employed in some way by the defense industry and DoD, especially by Lockheed Martin or the Defense Contract Management Agency (DCMA). For this reason, discussions about astronomy would occa-sionally turn to military devices, as this was a familiar language for many of the people involved. Not long before I sat down to write this conclusion, an email thread began appearing in my inbox that caught my attention. It was from the local Kopernik Astronomical Society, of which I am a member. Most of the time, these messages are about use of equipment at the Kopernik Observatory, new photos members have taken with their own or Kopernik equipment, and upcoming events they are participating in.

In early April 2018, one of the members sent an email to raise awareness of how President Trump's proposed tariffs on Chinese imports could impact access to astronomical equipment. Though he warned that he was not trying to start a political debate, this conversation soon devolved into a broader discussion about how the tariffs could also impact the permanent war economy. For instance, the M-109 howitzer tank was mentioned, which has been used as artillery from the Vietnam War up to the more recent Syrian Civil War and, it was suggested, may go up in price as it contains many metal and plastic components from China. But that might not matter, since Russia and the United States have both been pursuing drone-like tank divisions that would run with AI. Another person chimed in at that point, writing tongue in cheek, and I reprint this reply with his permission:

> Cool... AI and TANKS!? Maybe this is what Dr Hawking and Elon [Musk] were talking about. . .deadly AI? South Korea recently started using university AI with their defense forces causing many academic AI researchers [to] object, YET, these US researchers <whoever is left in US universities, as most are sucked into $$$,$$$ commercial research at the moment> still take DARPA dollars and I bet they are doing the same sort of AI/DoD research (used to be on some of those contracts..but the AI was not as good then as it is now...cool..think Terminator <pick a number> and Skynet..)
>
> Maybe this will make conventional warfare like nuclear warfare...mutual destruction..so all parties will not use it? This could be a good thing as we get to live our lives and enjoy commerce without ducking flying robotic tanks <drones, swarms of autonomous micro insects with... well, if you can dream it, it's probably under development in a DARPA lab right now.>

This KAS member draws attention to what is exciting and frightening about this new technology, some of which he used to work on previously with Lockheed. On the one hand, it threatens apocalyptic scenarios of the sort famously depicted in the ongoing Terminator film franchise (1984–2015), where a hyperintelligent AI eliminates its human creators by triggering a nuclear war. On the other hand, he imagines that AI weapons might finally be the war machine to end all wars. In doing so, this KAS member draws on mutual deterrence theory (Gusterson 1996, 2004), namely the assumption that with the threat of enough destructive force (in the right hands, of course, usually meaning "Western") it is rational for all parties to avoid conflict.

As I discuss in chapter 2, a form of mutual deterrence thinking predates the nuclear age, which some people associated with the newly invented airplane.

And if this image of permanent peace appears fanciful, it is important to note that so is the image of imminent attack that motivates arms races in the first place. And all of this is fueled, not by actual threats facing the most powerful military in the world, but by fantasy. As the email author concludes, "if you can dream it, it's probably under development in a DARPA lab right now." From imagining the real possibility of a trade war to imagining the unanticipated impact of this on the armed forces, to the promise of new military weapons that sound straight out of the realm of science fiction... If this chain of thoughts is a bit surreal, that is because there is something deeply strange, even phantasmagoric about the military normal and the society with which it is deeply interwoven. Much like the waste industry, its influence on American life is simultaneously obvious and hidden from sight, real yet simulated or screened by fantasy.[16]

This book has reviewed some of the imaginative ways that war machines can be demilitarized or reworlded by artists, curators, docents, divers, ham radio operators, and others, beyond simulation alone. DARPA's well-funded imaginarium may be impressive and world-altering, but does not have the last say on what can be made of the panoply of military leftovers. Looking around the ruins of the rusted gun belt that is New York's Southern Tier, the place I now call home, there is no shortage of good that the billions upon billions of dollars spent on defense could do instead. Such peace dividends, the kind that were promised by world leaders after they divested from the Cold War, might finally return to the places and people abandoned by the creative destruction of the permanent war economy. That might seem like an unlikely solution or an impossible problem to fix, but fixing impossible problems has always driven military spending. If you can dream it, then there are probably experts currently employed in a DARPA lab somewhere that could try and make it happen. Imagine if all of those resources were given to the people in the United States and around the world working amid the ruins of a permanent war economy, trying to rebuild the world instead of planning for its inevitable destruction.

The American military normal is not concealed away in darkened halls of power, but involves relationships between neighbors in a community who think they do the best work they can, which often involves accounting for waste. Military technology does not stay on bases and battlefields, but ends up in the hands of artists and entrepreneurs who remake it on their own terms. Other devices might turn to waste in orbit only to be later reactivated by intrepid space enthusiasts, or they fall from the sky and end up somewhere, probably in Wisconsin, where they inspire a wonderfully weird annual festival. Like military technology, the ideology of militarism does not remain confined to battlefronts, but inspires militias and mass shooters throughout US history, recycled again and again, usually as a means of restoring a sense of white male pride and honor by murdering civilians. Finally, waste can be found woven into the history of American empire, connecting hinterland and homeland through wastelands. This book has shown people struggling to remake and reimagine militaristic materials to new ends, leading to new projects and new stories to tell. There is every reason to think others will emerge, some inspiring and some devastating, as the nation permanently ready for war slouches toward the Polemocene, the uncertain future it helped birth.

NOTES

INTRODUCTION

1. On the environmental destructiveness of war, see Sloterdijk (2009), Machlis and Hanson (2008), and Tucker (2012). For lingering health impacts, see Clarkin (2010, 2012). On the psychological and physical scars left behind, see Sherman (2015), Wool (2015), and Puar (2017).

2. Joseph Masco (2014) makes this argument with respect to scientists involved in the nuclear arms race. In a similar way, Paul Edwards (2010) and David Price (2016) demonstrate how the Cold War US security state helped make possible climatological and anthropological knowledge, respectively, of a non- or antimilitaristic nature. On the peace movement in the United States, see Gusterson (1996), Howlett (2005), Howlett and Lieberman (2008), and Harvey (2014).

3. For different definitions and ethnographic uses of the concept of waste, see Gille (2007), Nagle (2013), Reno (2016), Fredericks (2018), and Millar (2018).

4. For examples of how to study the nonrelational appearance of imperial formations, to expose relational interconnections, see Coronil (1996), Pedersen (2013), and Stoler (2013).

5. The subject of military-civilian relations was of major concern at the start of the Cold War, with intellectual adversaries Samuel P. Huntington (1957) and Morris Janowitz (1960) both presupposing that they were separate spheres to begin with (see Schiff 1995 for an alternative model). More recently, legal scholar and former Pentagon staff member Rosa Brooks (2016) has argued that the modern distinctions between war and peace and between the military and civilian worlds create misunderstanding in national security policy, which risks making everything militarized and war never-ending (see also Fallows 2002; cf. Touhouliotis 2018 and Zani 2019).

6. Thanks to an anonymous reviewer for helping me to clarify this point. The very concept of *militarism* suggests an ontological separation between military and civilian

according to Bernazzoli and Flint (2009). In this book, I discuss both *militarism* and *militarization*, but with each successive chapter I also seek to expose the limitations of both those terms.

7. Following Lutz (2001, 227–46), MacLeish challenges such compartmentalization based on his ethnographic work around the community of Killeen, Texas, and Fort Hood. He finds that "self-conscious talk of inside and outside both points to an awareness of the military's enclosing and totalizing nature, and posits the broader civilian world as a 'normal' baseline against which the particulars of the Army, good and bad, are understood" (2013, 44). Yet, within the "world" of the military, categorical distinctions proliferate that complicate purification from civilian life (49).

8. For this report, see Copp (2018). Military base and military manufacturing closures both tend to leave behind economic and environmental scars. Lindsey Dillon (2014, 2015, 2017, 2018) demonstrates how the redevelopment of military base-conversion projects in the San Francisco Bay Area led to racialized environmental injustice and the slow violence of toxic pollution (see also Gillem 2017).

9. As Cynthia Enloe (2007) argues, demilitarization calls for "more than silencing the cannons. Those working for demilitarization with feminist analytical tools have discovered that ideas about manliness have to be addressed" (126). She adds that demilitarization, like militarization, is a "many-step process" (137). This book is structured around investigating unexpected relationships and experiences arising from permanent war preparation. Insofar as this means questioning some taken-for-granted assumptions, about military-civilian divides for instance, the book draws from the method of feminist curiosity as discussed by Enloe.

10. Calling the United States an "empire" may strike some as unfair or inaccurate. Whether or not this term is used to characterize America's relationship with other countries and the world, today or in the past, depends on how one defines the term. For the purposes of this book, insofar as a state uses the threat of military force to encourage cooperation or subservience from many countries beyond its borders, whatever the justification used, it is an empire or, better said, becoming an imperial formation (see Stoler 2013).

11. This structure also involves some shifts in use of evidence. By the fifth chapter, I rely heavily on research I conducted on school shootings as an undergraduate student, making it more an exercise in rereading and interpreting ethnography than a first-person account. By the final chapter, the slipperiness of silenced imperial histories stretches beyond the limits of conventional ethnography altogether, into historical research and media analysis.

12. See Atlas Obscura (n.d.) for more discussion.

13. On the disposal of nuclear weapons, see Masco (2006) and Custers (2007). On the differential impact of disarmament treaties on the former Soviet Union, the United States, and NATO countries, see Kopte and Wilke (1998).

14. The many nuclear bombs dropped after the conclusion of WWII gave national security states more information than they bargained for about the lasting impact of new weapons. Testing proved how unpredictable and planetary the consequences of

all-out nuclear war would be. For a discussion of how nuclear exchange transforms what war means, see Luke (1989). On the profound impact of "the bomb" on American culture and society generally, see Gusterson (2004); on nuclear testing and remains in the continental United States, see Masco (2006, 2014) and Ialenti (2018). On the impact of nuclear weapons testing on unsuspecting communities living on islands in the Pacific, see Johnston and Baker (2008). There has been less research on Soviet nuclear testing, but see Alexander (2009).

15. As Nordstrom (2007) argues, big and small arms are more likely to be traded and smuggled within unofficial grey and black markets, which have proliferated in recent decades. Selling weapons overseas is a key dimension of the US war economy; see Feinstein (2012).

16. Gusterson (2004, 180–82) refers to the emerging global securityscape of nuclear weapons as a "virtual arms race" in simulating and planning. In this context, he argues, nuclear arms have exchange value rather than use value. This does not conflict with Masco, in my reading, since they seem to be using exchange value in a slightly different way—Gusterson's use is more symbolic and Masco's more economic.

17. More can be read about radioactive dumping by the Navy during the Cold War in Levesque (2013) and Hamblin (2009). The most hazardous and toxic labor of American service members also has a history of being unfairly distributed on the basis of race, with more African Americans losing their lives in preventable accidents (see Arbona 2017).

18. On the history of antibase activism in Vieques, see Barreto (2002) and McCaffrey (2002).

19. On the open-ended character of industrial hazards, see Adam (1998) and Nixon (2011). On an alternative view of contamination as unexpected and emergent multispecies collaboration across difference, see Tsing (2015). For a discussion of ecotoxicology of explosives and the FUDS program, see Sunahara et al. (2009).

20. My goal is not to simply celebrate such unknowability, which Zsuzsa Gille (2013) rightly calls a form of *waste fetishism*. Rather, my goal is to trace some of the unexpected places, people, and processes that American military waste becomes entangled with, beyond familiar accounts of the benefits and costs of war, and to see how they come to matter.

21. Examples of explosive ordnance left behind after war has "ended" can be found throughout the world, including in Bosnia (Henig 2012), Cambodia (Uk 2016), the Korean Demilitarized Zone (Kim 2014, 2018), Laos (Zani 2019), and Lebanon (Touhouliotis 2018). Nuclear arms production can also be integrated into everyday life, as documented hauntingly by Robert Adams's photographs of ordinary Americans living near the Rocky Flats nuclear weapons plant in Denver, Colorado (Adams 2018).

22. Like Zani (2019, 185), I hope to contribute to an emerging anthropology of military waste, which "might approach the broader processes of wasting, endangerment, militarization, and terrorization within and beyond" zones of ordnance clearance.

23. I want to thank an anonymous reviewer for helping me to clarify this point.

24. The easiest to explain, arguably, is the relative age range of participants. All were either retired volunteers in civic organizations or senior enough to be directors or heads of companies, museums, and galleries. This would tend to skew toward middle-aged and older participants.

25. And while some of the artists whose work is discussed are Latin American, they did not agree to an interview.

26. Discussions of gender and racial disparities in STEM fields draw on evidence from those pursuing a STEM-related education (Xu 2008), as well as among professionals (Xu 2015; Ballenger, Polnick, and Irby 2016; Simon, Wagner, and Killion 2017). For a cross-cultural argument about the role of machines and tinkering in gendering social interactions and spaces, see Mellström (2004).

27. There was perhaps an overly materialist emphasis on "following the thing" in my initial approach. As the book progresses, it is harder to detect empirically specific wastes, and this term is more flexibly applied. Instead of discrete things literally disposed of, by chapters 5 and 6, waste is more complex and morally freighted: misused and worthless guns, domestic blowback, the excess of militarized masculinity, wastelands, exhausted soils, plastic oceans, etc. They are no less real for that but, like Haraway's (2016) string figures, are only differently interwoven with the world.

28. For critiques of the HTS, see Network of Concerned Anthropologists (2009), Price (2011), and Forte (2011).

29. On the expansion of American higher education and changes brought by the GI Bill, see Mettler (2005). On Harpur College relying on returning GIs in its beginning years and the community's later transformation, see Klaf, Legette, and Frazier (2010).

30. For an account of this investment by New York State, which other SUNY schools also received, see Melas (2012).

31. On military strategies associated with fighting just and unjust war, see McMahan (2009). For copies of the maps see Masco (2014), pages 53 and 55.

CHAPTER 1. WORTH THE WASTE

1. According to one Pentagon aerospace engineer, "[Lockheed Martin makes] crappy airplanes. The F-35 is a total piece of crap, far worse than the planes it's replacing" (quoted in Feinstein 2012, 336).

2. On Obama's military legacy and its perception within the military, see Altman and Shane (2017).

3. For classic Marxian critiques of the close relationship between the US economy and the military sector, sometimes described as "military Keynesianism" (Custers 2010), see Baran and Sweezy (1966) and Mandel (1999). More recently, Linda Weiss (2014) has argued that investment from the national security state bolstered American innovation during the Cold War but that this was discontinued during the War on Terror. For discussions of the destructive effects of US military spending on the national economy, see Melman (1970a, 1981), Lutz (2001), and Duncan and Coyne

(2013). On the transition from a defense-based economy in the United States and the contested realization of peace dividends, see also Gholz and Sapolsky (1999/2000), and Markusen et al. (2003).

4. Lockheed went by the Scottish spelling Loughhead at the time, which the owners changed, supposedly not to escape accusations of past wrongdoing, but actually after frequent mispronunciations encouraged them to spell it phonetically.

5. Custers begins his unique analysis with the Marxian formula for the ordinary circuit of capital, wherein the investment of money is used to accumulate the capital and employ the labor power needed to produce a salable commodity and earn a financial profit. Custers argues that military production demonstrates the incompleteness of this formula, requiring the further subtraction of unusable by-products that come from the production process, money invested to treat and manage these by-products, and the ultimate lack of utility (or *negative use value*) of the commodity itself.

6. In a polemic against an intellectual rival who supported militarization, Luxemburg argued that military contracts were especially beneficial to industrial manufacturers (1971, 141–42; see also Baran and Sweezy 1966, 207–8, and Custers 2007, 67–69). Military investment represented an artificial injection of state surplus into the economy (Kidron 1967, 1977).

7. Baran and Sweezy go further, arguing that it is rational for American workers to support a permanent war economy because of its absorption of economic surplus, thereby maintaining high profits and employment (1966, 209–10).

8. According to Patrick Vitale (2011), a sense of contribution to the war effort and nationalistic pride can serve as an ideological "wage" among military manufacturers, especially in times of economic precariousness.

9. For a longer explanation of these senses of waste, see Reno (2018b).

10. On the history of the tri-city area and its pollution by IBM, see Little (2014). For IBM's role in SAGE, see Marzec (2016): 51–55.

11. On the uneven occurrence of firm conversion, which instigated corporate consolidation and downsizing, see Atkinson (1993) and Oden et al. (2003). On the concept of military Fordism, see Kaldor et al. (1998). As "the last remaining bastion of the Fordist era," defense-related industries finally caught up to the sweeping changes that had been affecting manufacturing sectors since the 1970s (Kaldor, Albrecht, and Schméder 1998, 2).

12. The entire thread can be found online, and not everyone cared for this assessment: www.city-data.com/forum/new-york/536458-binghamton-ny-really-bad-2.html #ixzz5EbONA3Yq.

13. In some ways, the cuts in military spending only exacerbated shifts that were decades in the making (see Baran and Sweezy 1966). Arguably, rising unemployment and precarity represent a form of *human waste* disposed of by the logic of military capital (Bauman 2004; Yates 2011).

14. Jean-Michel Servet distinguishes between the abstract economic logic thought to characterize market economies and the sociality of customer ties. With customer ties, sellers hope to "generate loyalty and sustain the relationship" with buyers, rather

than take advantage of them: "In contrast to the juridical interpretation of a sales contract, a major part of contemporary sales strategy consists precisely of seeking to ensure that the customer relationship is not severed, but is, rather, renewed and perpetuated" (Servet 2009, 83).

15. Some blame the company for mishandling the project to build a presidential helicopter, for instance, which was canceled by the Obama administration during the push for budget cuts in his first term. The Owego plant was blamed for this loss, employees tell me, which was subsequently "punished" by being placed beneath another division within Lockheed.

16. Taking pleasure in a durable and quality product is somewhat analogous to how some nuclear weapons scientists perceive well-designed technology as beautiful (Gusterson 1996, 119–21) or how they test their own reliability, as scientists, by testing the reliability of weapons (Gusterson 2004, 149). Though none of the Lockheed or DCMA employees I talked to used aesthetic language per se, they most certainly took pride in their work.

17. In this sense, product testing and audit resemble the formalized performativity of ritual; Michael Lambek (2015, 308) argues that these procedures "do not only fulfill responsibility, they produce it." Importantly, Das and Kleinman (2000) and Das (2007) point out that anthropological analysis is capable of mediating and obviating responsibility for violence in similar ways.

18. This is in keeping with what Gusterson found among nuclear weapons scientists, who tended to keep their moral reflections on their work private, unless pressed (1996, 49–53).

19. Broadly speaking, this way of managing the economy is known as "neoliberalism," although there was, as argued by Kean Birch (2015), a large yet typically unacknowledged gap between neoliberal ideas and actual policies during this time.

20. Graeber rightly claims that American supremacy is made possible by ruling the skies. But it is equally dependent on the naval bases that cover much of the globe, which provide convenient access for planes, drones, and missiles and their prospective targets. For more discussion of America's empire of bases, see Lutz (2009).

21. In this way, discourses of military waste reflect what Bear and Mathur characterize as a "yearning for, and imposition of, new public goods within and beyond specific bureaucracies" (2015, 21). It is as if the Pentagon's purpose were too sacred to be corrupted by such negligence and excess. After Weber, many social analyses of corporations, bureaucracies, and similar impersonal institutions became dominantly focused on their ossification and corruption, their surreptitious spread of class injustice and violence under the guise of formal rules and infrastructures (see Graeber 2016). What is missing from "the absolutist moral critique or dismissal of bureaucracy," according to Bear and Mathur (2015, 19), is attention to the various utopian goals and pragmatic moves involved in struggles for private profit and the public good, respectively (see Welker 2014; Alexander and Reno 2014; Bear 2015).

22. As successful as the military industrial complex critique has been, many scholars have noted that it tends to replicate the compartmentalization and totalization that

divides military from civilian worlds (Bernazzoli and Flint 2009). This is why new institutions are routinely added to "military" and "industry" to depict "the complex" and more fully demonstrate the intrusion of militarism into social life.

CHAPTER 2. FLIGHT OR FIGHT

1. Though this and the next chapter were coauthored, we use "I" in order not to deviate from the style of the rest of the book.

2. Strictly speaking, Ingold and Keane disagree over their respective uses of the term affordance, which they both develop from the psychologist J. J. Gibson. For the purposes of my argument in this chapter, their differences are immaterial, but see Ingold (2018) and Keane (2018) for more.

3. For museums as sites of cultural production and contestation, see Karp et al. (1991), Karp et al. (1992), Clifford (1997), and Karp et al. (2006). My own approach is closest to that of Pamela Smart, who focuses on museums as "institutions populated by people who are themselves engaged in critical analysis of their own practices, procedures, and institutional trajectories" (2010, 18).

4. Deacon (2012) argues that it does not make sense to refer to things in the world as iconic, indexical, or symbolic since these describe a cognitive process—that is, three distinct ways that thoughts make connections between things and signs (cf. Kockelman 2005).

5. On repairing as a form of differentiation, see Houston (2017).

6. In Smart's analysis, via Paul Holdengräber and Walter Benjamin, there is actually a "countermodel" whereby museum practitioners rescue and consecrate artifacts, rather than deprive them of utility through recontextualization (2010, 135).

7. Focusing on repair and maintenance involves a methodological decision to examine the world as involving the perpetual threat of breakdown and decay, which Steven J. Jackson (2014) calls "broken world thinking," wherein repair practices can actually be seen to constitute emergent spaces or "repair-scales" (Lepawsky et al. 2017). See also chapter 1, this volume.

8. On the cultural and historical impact of the Russian satellite *Sputnik*, see chapter 4.

9. That being said, restoration and repair are not always opposed. Restored planes may be able to fly again, but if they are only restored for display this is incidental to their functioning.

10. In this way, Pima is similar to businesses run by elites that are located near, and rely upon, military bases and their personnel (see Lutz 2001; Baca 2010).

11. Peircian semiotics, or the study of signs, is useful in this sense, because it provides conceptual clarification as to what kinds of connections to people and stories specific restorations, repairs, and reuses accomplish, i.e., what they make visible or conceal. For more discussion of the semiotic analyses of material objects, see Peirce (1955), Keane (2003), Deacon (2012), and Kohn (2013).

12. John Law (2002, 97–98) describes the role of these absences in the design process of planes, but they also play a role in their later disposal and reuse.

13. According to one Navy pilot who read this chapter, "This is pretty standard in military aviation; we typically order a spare engine when we purchase an aircraft. So, buying an F-16 includes buying the engine that is in the plane and a spare."

14. When asked whether they would ever fly the planes, James said insurance costs would be too high to make that possible. The only time this happened was when an aerospace company located north of the Museum lent a Bell UH-1 Iroquois (aka "Huey") helicopter to the museum and a number of staff were taken for flights in it. Other museums often restore and fly planes with special significance, like P-51s, which are known for their involvement in World War II.

15. This account of planes as extraordinary objects is somewhat analogous to Spelman's discussion of art restoration practices (2003, 15–17, 24–25; see also Smart 2010).

16. They also may discuss the Strategic Arms Limitation Talks (SALT II, 1993) with the Soviets during the Cold War, which required the visible destruction of B-52 Stratotfortresses. It took them awhile to be in compliance with the treaty, which was verified by Russian satellites surveying the Boneyard as massive guillotines sliced whole planes in half.

17. This level of knowledge is relatively common for pilots but had been a passion for him since he was a child, and he acquired a lot of this knowledge out of personal interest.

18. The use of the term "understories" is borrowed from the book of that name by Jake Kosek (2006).

19. To imagine the plane as not yet a weapon, I am taking inspiration from Hugh Gusterson's attempt to look back at the transition from US isolationism to international intervention, associated with the postwar debates around the NATO treaty (2004, 87). In order to imagine that change is possible, it is important to consider historical moments of indecision and uncertainty in the past when things could have been otherwise, prior to the establishment of the current permanent war economy. I do the same thing in other chapters around the creation of the Navy (chapter 3), NASA (chapter 4), a modern military equipped and trained in firearms (chapter 5), and a global empire (chapter 6).

20. Aeronautic enthusiasm was so intense in the interwar period that "People distinguished little between one airplane and another, or between one flight or another. All flying seemed wondrous; all planes miraculous" (Corn 1983, 16). Reverence for planes are also alleged to have infected the writing of a century of historians and historiographers (see Hansen 1989; Pisano 2003b).

21. As Wohl argues, "The force of Wells's novel and its impact on its readers derived from his insight that the rapid development of aeronautical technology would erase the age-old distinction between combatants and civilians" (1994, 74). Moreover, he suggests that European writers nationalized and militarized aviation "long before general staffs were willing to take flying machines seriously as a means of waging war" (89). This was also the case with the submarine (see Donovan 2014). Yet, there was still ambivalence about the militarization of planes after the war (Bilstein 2003, 20).

22. In fact, the bicycle was equally imagined to be a form of modern military technology in the early twentieth century, what one British brigade major described as "this, the [military's] youngest excrescence" (quoted in Miéville 2018, 187). One could well imagine a future where bicycling became as thoroughly militarized in public culture and military practice as did its aerial counterpart.

23. On Mexican spending compared to the United States during World War I, see Holley (1971, 29). According to Vander Meulen (1991), the attempt to use existing approaches to mass production to build planes was to blame for the American aviation deficit. On the Wright Brothers' attempts to sell the airplane as a weapon, both in the United States and abroad, see Wohl (1994, 15–19). In their efforts to expand their business, the Wrights negotiated with a "well-connected financier and arms dealer" named Charles Flint, who would go on to found the company that would become IBM (see chapter 1). According to Wohl, Flint was "a 'merchant of death' then, if ever there was one, who made fortunes from the anxieties generated by a constantly escalating arms race among the world's great and would-be great powers" (1994, 19–20).

24. Many of these companies were relatively new and, partly for this reason, were looked at suspiciously as parasitic enterprises (see Vander Meulen 1991). Echoing the antiwar sentiments of many Americans in the early twentieth century, Congress members publicly condemned these firms for having failed to supply combat planes in the country's time of need, despite being awarded large wartime contracts.

25. On the imagined role of air travel in reducing geographical boundaries separating peoples, see Corn (1983, 38) and Bilstein (2003, 24). On the alt-man that would rise to supremacy as a result of taking to the skies, see Corn (1983, 40–41) and cf. Wohl (1994, 115–22). This also fits with historical and anthropological research by Bhimull (2012, 2014, 2017) on the relationship between the first airlines and imperial expansion and imagination in the colonial West Indies. As she writes, "the airplane in motion signifies the penetration of air bound borders, the outside coming in—bombs, bodies, mail, commodities—and the inside going out—commodities, mail, bodies, bombs" (Bhimull 2014, 131).

26. Bilstein (2003), Moy (2003), and Hartung (2010) offer different accounts of the profitability of airplane manufacturers and their influence on lawmakers in the early twentieth century. Moy (2001) shows how difficult it was to transform military bureaucracy and technology around the threat and promise of long-distance aerial bombardment, particularly during the interwar years.

27. On the history of the bomber gap lie, see Franklin (2003, 340). Wohl describes this through the popular military metaphor of the conquest of the air: "The new empire to be subjugated lay in the sky" (1994, 69).

28. The war machine would consist of an anarchic and creative force captured by the state, yet one that routinely exceeds these limits imposed upon it (see Patton 1984). I do not want to give the impression, however, that artistic practice always runs counter to or resists military control and cooptation. For example, Beyer and Sayles (2015) describe efforts by artists to create simulated "ghost armies" to confuse enemy surveillance in World War II.

29. For a thorough discussion of the history of artistic representations of planes, see Wohl (1994). As Silk puts it, "the altered observation of outer reality that the airplane allows provides clues to understanding a deeper, more profound reality" (2003, 256). This includes, for example, the perceived importance of photographs taken from a plane of the ground, which that plane (and the unique view it offered) had newly transcended and objectified (Weems 2015). Interest in streamlining appeared not only in plane design, but architecture and domestic commodities (Pisano 2003a).

30. According to Velasco (2004, 8), some theaters of World War II were more conducive to nose art than others, because of "an absence of top brass." He further claims that nose art declined in popularity after the end of conscription and was actually officially reintroduced by Strategic Air Command in the late 1980s (2004, 28–29). Valant (1987) argues, by contrast, that nose art began to disappear during the Korean War. However, much of what follows in this section comes from Velasco's text.

31. On the concept of reproducible sameness, derived from Walter Benjamin and Susan Buck-Morss, see Masco (2006) and Reno (2016).

32. On the ability for art and technology to elicit a sense of agentive power, see Gell (1998).

33. This policy may have changed rather recently. The Boneyard has been utilized as of 2017 to help deal with a shortage of aircraft maintainers.

34. As Schaub goes on to argue, DeLillo is focused on "the whatness or objecthood of the past...an improvisation on the theme of waste, insofar as the novel constitutes the remaining 'effects' of memory, here accumulating like a landfill. The novel as dump" (Schaub 2011, 74).

35. As Martucci (2007, 128–29) insists, Klara Sax's project is also significant because the desert landscape, irradiated by nuclear weapons testing, is as significant a choice of gallery space as the planes are a choice of medium. According to Martucci, DeLillo is particularly concerned with the inseparability of destruction of the environment from the destruction of people, what might be called war's hyperwastefulness. Putting the art project in the desert also challenges the normal consumption of art, because there is a need to see it from above (Martucci 2007, 131; Pike 2011, 88; see also chapter 3, this volume). Because the planes can fly, and provide an aerial vision from above, they are not only a product of an artist's vision but a process of perception as destruction: "As art, the B-52s provide some form of aesthetic experience; however, as a source of vision, they are as if a dark underground lifted up into the air" (Pike 2011, 88).

36. Artistic production is not the only way to rescue materials from disposal or loss, nor is museum restoration; there are other means of doing so that will be explained in the next chapter.

CHAPTER 3. SUNK COST

1. For over a century, merchant ships provided the foundation for the colonial economy, chief among them slavers. Insofar as they did employ violence, the slave ship

could be seen as a militant arm of the nation-state and a precursor to the formal navy, see Rediker (2007).

2. For recent overviews of this historical episode, from the American side, see Lunsford (2016) and Slaughter (2016); from the Algerian side, see Maameri (2008).

3. On the national debate over the Navy, see Kitzen (1996), 604.

4. For more on US empire, its origins, global infrastructure, and relationship to waste, see chapter 6.

5. For this reason, various artists have used the shipwreck trope as a way of "recuperating the critical potentiality within the failing, fragmented, and resolutely open-ended" (Cocker 2014, 232; see also Le Juez and Springer 2015). Mentz (2015) uses the shipwreck as a "master trope" to interrogate the natural history of globalization as one of perpetual disaster amid continuity.

6. If any shipwreck is potentially valuable, as a source of materials and goods, then those closer to shore are arguably more so. On urban scavengers of the industrial era, see Pike (2004). According to Jatin Dua (2013), relationships to shipwrecks and maritime piracy are part of a historical struggle for control over oceanic wealth.

7. Tsing (2015) is particularly interested in using nonhuman and human collaborations amid capitalist ruins to counter both a narrative of decline and its opposite—the master trope of Progress in whose name capitalist accumulation ravaged the world and ushered in the era of the Anthropocene.

8. According to Bennett's research, *Conch* was first used as a term for white Bahamians and only later became a general term for any and all Key West residents.

9. For a similar account, see Patrick Laviolette's (2006) analysis of recycled maritime vessels in Cornwall.

10. On the importance of shipwrecks to the history of Key West, see Stebbins (2007) on the nineteenth century and Smith (1988) for the last century.

11. On alternative currencies, see Guyer (2004) and Maurer (2005).

12. On different forms of diving tourism, see Garrod and Gossling (2008) and Merchant (2012).

13. For Tsing, world-making projects are not solely human, but involve nonhuman rhythms and timescales. On dwelling as a perspective on ecological becoming, see Ingold (2000, 2011). On coral reef as a distinct form of animal life, see a wonderful essay by Eva Hayward (2010).

14. As discussed in the first chapter, the cost of the military itself is routinely discussed in terms of dollars. For instance, the legislation around retiring naval ships suggests that they should be disposed of in a way that earns the best return for the taxpayers who financed it.

15. On the timeline and debate surrounding the disposal of American ships, see Puthucherril (2010). On the global market in recycled materials and the Basel Convention in general, see Gregson and Crang (2015); in terms of e-waste, see Lepawsky and McNabb (2011), and Lepawksy (2015a, 2015b).

16. For a reconsideration of the use of *biocapital* or similar neologisms to refer to what are arguably broader processes of capital accumulation, see Birch and Tyfield

(2013). On the distinction between commodity and asset and the general role of asset-ification in contemporary capitalist economies, see Birch (2015).

17. On theories of rentiership that emphasize the social relations they engender, as compared with wages and profits, see Harvey (1982), Coronil (1997), and Birch (2015, 2017).

18. Souvenir salvage is common all over the world. Gregson, Crang, and Watkins (2011) discuss how salvaging souvenirs from great naval ships can help lend material support for "military masculinities." It is unclear how Joe's customers interpret what they salvage, but I would argue that his own way of thinking about it is not reducible to either masculinity or the military.

19. By "world-making," I do not merely mean focus on "the global," but a scaling practice that entails a complex interweaving of what are normally imagined to be distinct "levels." As Amelia Moore puts it, in her ethnography of marine conservation in the Caribbean, "waters and sea life are localized, universalized, and naturalized to legitimate management" simultaneously (2012, 669). On the politics of world-building, specifically as an effort to create new worlds within which to dwell, see Jarrett Zigon (2017).

20. Mote Marine has been more successful recently. It received $500,000 from the state budget in the spring of 2018; see Rutger (2018).

21. If US bases and bombs keep the dollar flowing as the de facto world currency (see chapter 1), then what could seem more appropriate, after warcraft fall into disuse, than recycling them into pure liquid capital and continuing the circuit (C to M)?

CHAPTER 4. THE WRONG STUFF

1. On the history of NASA's creation, see Wang (2008, 88–99). On the use of NASA as part of the cover story for the U2 spy plane, see Brugioni (2010, 346–47).

2. Other posts about *Cassini* took a visual approach to the probe's death dive into Saturn, depicting it as self-conscious yet pitifully unaware of its impending demise, or as a spectral figure that might return to exact its revenge on those who programmed its death. On the interpretive flexibility of space debris and for a detailed account of the early history of satellite identification, see Rand (2016, 33–73). A similarly nuanced view of old and lost space equipment is taken up by some archaeologists of outer space who consider these remains as artifacts and a form of cultural heritage, a position that some national space agencies have adopted as well. See Barclay and Brooks (2009), Capelotti (2004, 2010), Gorman (2005, 2009, 2015, 2017), Idziak (2013), and O'Leary (2006, 2015).

3. Here I follow Susan Lepselter's analysis in *The Resonance of Unseen Things* (2016), which describes what she characterizes as a dominant poetics of the American uncanny. According to Lepselter, conspiracy theories are stories that index social antagonism and existential anxieties: "Though it is never a one-to-one kind of symbol, the accumulated stories that point to a forgotten *something* do suggest what that something might be. There are stories of class and its invisible, unmarked limitations, and

stories of race and gender, and the small, multiple ways that a life is disappointed by master narratives of progress and success" (2016, 19). In their edited volume, Harry G. West and Todd Sanders (2003) are attentive to such sentiments on a global scale, connecting the rise of conspiracy theories to widespread precariousness in what is perceived as a neoliberal New World Order.

4. The militarization of space is also related, historically and practically, to the "defense" against near-Earth objects. This is not the focus of my chapter, but for an excellent discussion see Olson (2018).

5. Myra Hird (2012) describes waste, in general, as an attempt to render determinate the complex processes and encounters that are inherently indeterminate or open-ended in their outcomes and possibilities. For a critique of this position see Gille (2013) and Hecht (2018). For an attempt to find possible middle grounds between these positions, see Hird (2013) and Reno (2018b).

6. For a clear outline of these issues, followed by a proposal for how to clear the orbital environment with the help of robotics, see Aghili (2012). For more on the characteristics of space debris at different altitudes, see Liou et al. (2010).

7. For a related discussion of the power of the ocean itself, see chapter 6.

8. *Panspermia* and *necropanspermia* propose that life may originate from organisms hitching a ride on debris. Whether or not they survive the journey, their chemical makeup may. It is entirely possible that a material-expelling Earth has already done this, with or without human involvement; see Wesson (2010) and Olson (2018).

9. Alice Gorman (2015) describes space debris as an emergent assemblage that takes on new spatio-temporal properties. This is most clearly represented in the idea of the Kessler Syndrome (Kessler and Cour-Palais 1978). This theory predicts a "cascade of random collisions that create so much debris the Earth is enveloped and cut off from space" (Gorman 2015, 42). Gorman points out that it is unclear such a dire situation has emerged or necessarily will. For an account of satellites, usable and wasted, as part of a growing technosphere, one developed from the Marxian ecological criticism of metabolic rifts, see Gärdebo et al. 2017. For more on metabolic rift, see chapter 6.

10. For an explanation of planetary cross-contamination and the risks thereof, see Williamson (2000) and Nicholson et al. (2009).

11. What Dickens and Ormrod term the "humanization of the cosmos" involves the spread of human beings and designs into space. According to them, it brings with it a "cosmic risk society," which creates new threats to life on Earth and in the cosmos (2007, 151–53). On private NewSpace initiatives, see also Dickens (2009), Valentine (2012), Berinstein (2002), and Olson (2018). On the value of geostationary orbit in particular, see Collis (2009).

12. On Point Nemo or "the South Pacific Ocean Uninhabited Area" as a space debris graveyard, see Davies (2016). On the distinct environmental and political problem posed by garbage patches, see De Wolff (2014); on space debris as occupying a similar borderlands, see Rand (2016). For an exploration of the idea of social problems and communities of the affected, see Marres (2012).

13. According to Gärdebo, Marzecova, and Knowles, "Since the 1990s, one policy solution has been to 'clean up space' by pre-programming satellites in LEO to descend after 25 years" (2017, 47).

14. As Rand demonstrates, both space debris and climate change were discovered around the same time in conversation with Cold War experimental science and environmental movements. The difference is that the "orbital tipping point cannot be as alarmingly and effectively illustrated—no charismatic, imperiled polar bears circle the planet, no ice floes encapsulate landscape change in a landless, illegible, invisible environment" (2016, 3; see also Steffen et al. 2015 and Gärdebo, Marzecova, and Knowles 2017). On the importance of "the bomb" to life and imagination in the twentieth and twenty-first centuries, see Gusterson (2004).

15. On the social production and deferral of responsibility and blame, see chapter 1.

16. For a detailed history of the impact of *Sputnik* on military and government policy, see Wang (2008) and McCray (2008). This is strikingly similar to what happened with the second Bush administration, when they pivoted from promising to slash wasteful military spending to increasing it dramatically as part of the War on Terror; see Turse (2008), 83–87.

17. For an account of these developments, see especially Wang (2008).

18. On "black" spy satellites and civilian attempts to track them, see Paglen (2009), 97–125.

19. On space debris emerging alongside space exploration, see Damjanov (2016) and Rand (2016). McCray (2008, 15) points out the connection between *Sputnik* and UFO sightings. As recently declassified government reports indicate, moreover, the Pentagon also engaged in UFO searches during the Cold War and after.

20. This finally occurred in April of 2018, though it happened later than expected (Hui and du Lac 2018). For a detailed account of the history of amateur involvement in raising awareness about the pollution of orbital environments, see Rand (2016, 86–127).

21. On the properties of the orbital environments as involving self-cleaning attributes, see Rand (2016, 150). On the emergence of an ecological perspective on the solar system, see Olson (2018).

22. For an account of Obama's speech and what it means, see Basu (2011). Obama claimed he was unaware of the connection.

23. For a discussion of one consequence of such planning, the Secret War in Laos, see Zani (2019). For Arendt and Morozov, technical expertise makes ideas seem so internally consistent that they can encourage people to forgo common sense. A similar sensibility, skeptical of techno-solutionism, was also promoted by members of the Presidential Scientific Advisory Committee (PSAC) created by Eisenhower after *Sputnik* was launched. For a detailed history of the PSAC, and the shifting boundary between technology, science, and politics, see Wang (2008).

24. On NASA's changing self-representation, see Byrnes (1994, 171–73. Both McCray (2008, 7) and Gabrys (2016, 3) discuss how early satellites gradually fulfilled both civilian and military purposes. For a review and endorsement of the Reagan

administration's position on the militarization of space, see Gray (1982). For a critique of this kind of Cold War reasoning, and the moral justification of the arms race more broadly, see Gusterson (1996).

25. Nonweapon uses of space, for military purposes, include surveillance and reconnaissance, attack warning and assessment, communication, navigation, meteorology, and geodesy; see Gray (1982, 23–44) for a clear breakdown of these uses.

26. Such a scenario is imagined by Deblois et al. (2005, 11) in their review of the potential for war in space.

27. This 2004 report, in which Tyson is listed as coauthor, is titled "A Journey to Inspire, Innovate, and Discover." It was commissioned by the Bush Administration and is available online: http://govinfo.library.unt.edu/moontomars/docs/M2MReport ScreenFinal.pdf/

28. Even those achievements billed as civilian in orientation were primarily about defense concerns. The infamous ARPANET that helped shape the internet was meant to solve the dilemma of information loss after a nuclear attack. At the same time, the internet's creation had a contested and tangled history, and was not solely ARPA's creation; see Rosenzseig (1998).

29. For news of the new telescope, see InnovationNewsDaily Staff (2011) and Yirka (2011).

30. Understanding why the Air Force might think to move the SST to Australia is easier with DARPA's second major orbital space debris initiative in mind. In order not only to see, but to track and potentially capture space debris, a possibility I discuss in the next section, it helps to have the SST on the other side of the world from where other participants are viewing the night sky. For reporting on the SST's movement, see www.revolvy.com/main/index.php?s=Naval%20Communication%20Station%20 Harold%20E.%20Holt&item_type=topic.

31. This analogy came from John T. Mengel, who moved from the Navy to NASA, along with many of his colleagues, in order to establish satellite-tracking capabilities (1956, 755). Mengel's involvement with military and civilian space agencies is recounted on NASA websites: https://www.nasa.gov/audience/forstudents/postsecondary/features /john_mengel_pioneer_prt.htm. For an incredible account of the central role of civilian amateur astronomers in the early days of satellite tracking, which also discusses Mengel and Cold War scientists like him, see McCray (2008).

32. I attempted to enroll the Kopernik observatory in DARPA's SpaceView program, with the permission and assistance of the director. We never received a response from them, despite several attempts to ask for an update on our application status. Nevertheless, DARPA claims that SpaceView is in development and being tested now.

33. Jerome thinks the best solution is probably a tax on all launches to help go toward the cleanup of the debris this causes. For a critique of the Tragedy of the Commons idea and its use to justify colonial and military appropriation, see Marzec (2016).

34. Precisely because amateur astronomers are used to undergoing attunement to terrestrial and cosmic temporalities, they may not answer the call (see also Reno 2018a). Those astronomers whom I have met are skeptical of DARPA's plans (which,

like many proposals to capture and clean up the orbital environments of Earth, have yet to materialize).

35. Online searches for *hammy*/*hammie* in relation to Ham Radio users can bring up results from everywhere from California to South Africa, but the term is not familiar to all users. Thank you to Robin Nagle for pointing this out to me.

36. NASA is capable of recovering objects too, as when it fired the thrusters of the *Voyager* 1 deep space probe which had been drifting debris for thirty-seven years (see SkyNews 2017).

37. Tim Ingold (2014) characterizes attunement as "undergoing" a creative process with nonhuman materials (see also Tsing 2015). Attunement can be seen, in this sense, as the counterpart to material affordances, as discussed in chapter 2.

38. Khalili (2013, 57) points out that while population-centered tactics appear less brutal, they still shape people, places, and social relations in direct and indirect ways, still coerce them and have political impacts. For a critique of population-based counterinsurgency, especially the *Counterinsurgency Field Manual* upon which it is largely based, and its relationship to anthropology, see Network of Concerned Anthropologists (2009).

39. On Rods from God, see Stillwell (2017). On the secretive "space plane" see Wall (2017).

CHAPTER 5. DOMESTIC BLOWBACK

1. For a helpful breakdown of common misconceptions about causes of and solutions to mass shootings, see Fox and DeLateur (2014).

2. This interpretation of the Second Amendment was successfully contested in the early 1980s by members of the National Rifle Association and the New Right, who sought to reframe this as a matter of personal rights, rather than state regulation. On contemporary militarism as a product of the period post-Vietnam, see Bachevich (2013).

3. On violence as involving a trichotomy of perpetrator, victim, and witness, see Riches (1986). For a discussion of witnessing of violence as critical in the formation of subjectivity, see Das (2000).

4. Gun violence can therefore be interpreted using Victor Turner's idea of social drama (Turner 1980). But social dramas in the United States are heavily shaped by racial politics (see Baca 2010), especially when it comes to shootings of black men and boys (see Curry 2017).

5. On the lack of reliability and availability of arms during that same period, see Bellesiles (2000).

6. On the history of Samuel Colt and his business empire, see Hosley (1996).

7. On the shift from little to total war see Weigley (1973); for a critique of Weigley, see Grenier (2005). On changes in cavalry tactics in response to firearms, see Fox (1993, 41–45) and Utley (1973, 69–73).

8. For an account of the transformation in US government policy with Native American groups before and after the Civil War, see Weigley (1973, 153–63) and Utley (1973, 10–36).

9. For an overview of the battle, which compares the historical and archaeological evidence, see Fox (1993). For indigenous accounts of the battle, see Hardorff (1997) and Michino (1997).

10. That being said, there was also widespread criticism of militias when they were more heavily relied on earlier in the nineteenth century; see Bellesiles (1999). When a desire for armed militias was denied by Congress it arguably manifested in organizations like the Ku Klux Klan, which can be seen as a reinvention of the slave patrols of the pre–Civil War era (Dunbar-Ortiz 2018). On the struggle between parties concerning funding the military and the end of Reconstruction, see Utley (1973).

11. On the role of white humiliation in the formation of militias and opposition to the military, see Wyatt-Brown (2014). On the prison-industrial complex as the New Jim Crow, see Alexander (2010).

12. The renewed effort toward professionalization was often more hope than reality; according to Utley, the soldiers at Little Big Horn were just as inexperienced as those at Wounded Knee (1973, 25). On styles of American ways of war as described here, see Weigley (1973), Grenier (2005), and Dunbar-Ortiz (2018). On US censorship associated with of the Battle of Bud Dajo, see Balce (2016, 71–73).

13. Lieutenant Colonel Dave Grossman (2009) documents the increasing efficiency with which soldiers were trained to kill from the world wars to Vietnam, arguing how this was made possible by increasing distance (by means of technology) and othering (by means of dehumanizing the enemy). See also Protevi (2009, 2013).

14. On the production of successful killers, in the military and in popular American culture, see Grossman (2009). Grossman traces the production of killers to the establishment of distance between shooters and targets, both literal and figurative. More recently, Vince Emanuele (a former marine who now works for Progressive Talk Radio) has spoken publicly about the hypermasculinity of military training and a deadening of people to feelings. He connects this to gendered masculinity more broadly.

15. On the invention of the serial killer as a literary trope for industrial mass society and as a made-up person, see Seltzer (1996). The gunfighter, like the serial killer or the superhero (Wolf-Meyer 2003), needn't be a defender of order or the status quo in order to support it through acts of violence. Needless to say, the gunfighter, according to Slotkin, is essentially a militarist: "the world is a hostile place, human motives are rarely good, and outcomes depend not on right but on the proper deployment of might" (1992, 402). This could just as easily be used to diagnose a sociopath.

16. This is where Dunbar-Ortiz (2018) begins her overview, but points out the arbitrary nature of historicizing mass shootings in that way.

17. On the Columbine shooters, especially their performance of distinctiveness from their victims, see Zoba (2000). On masculinity and its role in school violence in particular, see Klein and Chancer (2000).

18. On mass shooting as a form of suicide, see Fast (2008), Langman (2009), and Rocque (2012).

19. A similar example, beautifully depicted in the documentary *Tower* (2016) about the 1966 University of Texas shooting, is the young, red-haired woman who comes to

the aid of the injured, pregnant Claire James, and lies with her in the open, in full view of the shooter, pretending to be dead and keeping her from going into shock.

20. On the established relationship between suicides and the media, see Phillips (1974) and Gould, Jamieson, and Romer (2003). On school shootings as a mass media phenomenon, see Muschert (2007).

21. Jeremy has since been released and last I heard was doing well. We have regrettably lost touch, but I hope that my account is a true reflection of the conversations we had over the years.

22. Despite the apparent artificiality of the interview as a methodological tool, interviews can therefore resemble spontaneous conversation (Koven 2011), where audience-speaker interactions are similarly dynamic (Jakobson 1957; Bauman and Briggs 1990).

23. On school shootings as deliberate political acts that target elite students, those who are perceived as upholding the social order of "popularity," see Larkin (2009).

24. Jeremy claims he told two friends about his plans, but only one—his closest, Mike—knew most of the details. He does not know if they thought he was serious, but they didn't openly discourage him either.

25. In the terminology of semiotics, these embodied affects could be seen as qualisigns of value; see Munn (1986) and Keane (2003). On the role of hierarchical authority in all forms of violence, see bell hooks (1984, 118).

26. On the choice between violence and nonviolence, when both are possible but only one fits with local circumstances, see Coburn (2011) in the context of Istalif, Afghanistan, and Ralph (2014) on gangs in Chicago. For a comparative approach to nonviolence and peace as anthropological phenomena, see Sponsel (2016).

27. This increase in gun purchases also correlated with a spike in accidental gun deaths (Levine and McKnight 2017).

28. Merritt Roe Smith (1981) provides a historical overview of early attempts to create reliable arms manufacturing in early America.

CHAPTER 6. ISLAND ERASURE

1. On the leak and its aftermath, see Jeffery (2013, 302–4; 2014b).

2. On wasteland in American history see Kuletz (1998), Beck (2009), and Voyles (2015). On erasure of island-dwellers and island histories, especially in the Pacific, see Davis (2007, 2015). On the conversion of military sites into wildlife areas, see Havlick (2007) and Kim (2018).

3. On the British attempt to spread enclosure across the globe, see Marzec (2016, 83–96). Beyond the references to waste, Locke's theory of property is notable because it insists that individuals own the products of their own labor, in apparent contradiction with the African slave trade that characterized "the Atlantic of the early modern world economy" (Hart 1990, 46). Paradoxically, Locke's brand of Enlightenment liberalism arguably helped shape the antislavery movement that would eventually bring emancipation to the Chagos and, decades later, to America.

4. It is not only literal places that are discarded, as part of imperial formations, but representations as well. On the circulation and discard of racialized and sexualized images, associated with American imperial abjection in the Philippines, see Balce (2016).

5. Analyzing imperial ruination in process, rather than empires as fixed systems, fits with Stoler's argument in favor of imperial formations rather than empire. Imperial formations are "states of deferral that mete out promissory notes that are not exceptions to their operation but constitutive of them" (2013, 8). For a discussion of the political processes by which certain life-forms are rendered natural or invasive, see Jeffery (2014a) and Moore (2012).

6. The ocean is an entity in its own right that exceeds any and all attempts to bend it to submission or fully predict how it will behave in the short or long term. For an approach that emphasizes the "vitality" of nonliving processes, see Bennett (2009).

7. There is a debate over how much this soil crisis was due to population growth or development, in general, or capitalist production, in particular. According to a critique by Salvatore Engel-Di Mauro (2014), many tend to assume the former without adequately studying the dialectical relationship between soil and society that capitalist farming brings into crisis. For my purposes, it is more important how the crisis was perceived and reacted to by farmers and the US government. According to Engel-Di Mauro (2014, 148) arguments involving global environmental transformation risk obscuring or denying specific socioecological conditions.

8. On the importance of the legal history of the guano islands for American expansion and imperialism, see Burnett (2005).

9. On the close vote in 1901, see Gray (1982, 29). On the Insular Cases as helping to support colonialism legally, see Ramos (1996).

10. On the acquisition of the islands and their role in World War II and the "networked empire" that emerged from it, see Oldenziel (2011), Davis (2015), and Lutz (2017). For an assessment of coral reef and the environmental health of the islands post-occupation, see Vargas-Ángel (2009) and Brainard (2005).

11. Elizabeth M. DeLoughrey (2012) describes the relationship between ecosystem and systems thinking and nuclear testing in the Pacific islands. Barbara Rose Johnston and Holly M. Baker (2008) describe the incredible toll that nuclear testing took on the Marshall Islands and their struggle for recognition. On chemical weapons storage on Johnston Atoll and attempts to decontaminate it, see Creasy et al. (1999). For more on the Smithsonian's bird survey and the resulting controversy, see MacLeod (2001). This is not unlike the use of civilian science for cover in space exploration; see chapter 4, this volume.

12. On the idea of national capitalism and its historical transformation, see Hart (2005, 79–80). Within national capitalism, states become much like the landlord class of a previous era, since they depend so much on rents, see Coronil (1997).

13. On the Chagossian people and their struggle, see Vine (2008, 2011) and Jeffery (2013, 2014a, 2014b).

14. Dan Brockington calls this kind of strategy, which can be found around the world, *fortress conservation*. The irony is that, "if 'dying' areas can be resuscitated, it is because they are resilient and not threatened with imminent destruction. They are continually vulnerable to being saved, recreated and restored to the pantheon of 'last wildnerness' upon which fortress conservation thrives" (2002, 127–28).

15. Alternatives come in the form of sculptures, underwater and aboveground, created by British artist Jason deCaires Taylor in an attempt to advocate for climate justice. See Elizabeth Deloughrey (2017) for a critical appraisal, focusing on Taylor's work and the oceanic turn in the Anthropocene. Thank you to Nancy Reynolds for bringing this to my attention.

16. A parallel effort can be found in the edited collection *Iraq + 100* (Blasim 2017), which invited Iraqi science fiction authors to imagine their country one century after the invasion, a time far enough into the future that one could hope for something new as well as grieve for what has been lost.

17. On the politics of representation associated with vulnerable island-based populations in the Anthropocene, see Barnett and Campbell (2010, 169) and Whyte (2017). On the tendency of the US military to imagine worst-case scenarios with regard to climate change, see Marzec (2015, 43).

18. Coates et al. (2011) point out that relationships between the military and environmental scientists and agencies are not mere greenwashing. That being said, it is important to recognize the interests that these relationships serve; see Havlick (2007), Davis (2007, 2015), and Kim (2018).

19. Thanks again to Laura Jeffery for bringing this to my attention.

20. See Graeber (2001) and Munn (1986) for a take on value that inspires the one I am employing here, one which would connect Chagossian and capitalist values as very different expressions of the same generic substance. On Diego Garcia's role in global positioning, see Vine (2011). On the intermingling of digital communication infrastructure and military histories, see Starosielski (2015).

21. Thanks to Kim De Wolff for helping me to think through gyres as a collection of accumulation zones. For a discussion of ocean plastic as the "apocalyptic twin" of climate change, see Winn (2016).

22. On the relatively less well-known Indian Ocean gyre, see Lebreton, Greer, and Borrero (2012).

23. On technofossils and their relevance for life in the Anthropocene, see Zalasiewicz et al. (2014).

24. This is an extension of how imperial cartography works more broadly—creating abstract geohistorical categories and then systematically denying the geopolitical origins and consequences of their creation, see Coronil (1996). For the story of Bluie East base in Greenland, see Lang (2018). On the importance of documenting even the weakest traces of the imperial archive, see Stoler (2013).

25. On the pollution of nuclear testing in the Pacific impacting military bases and people back on the mainland, see Dillon (2014, 2015).

CONCLUSION

1. According to recent survey research, moreover, public support for wartime casualties changes depending not only on partisan ideology, but enduring "casualty gaps" between groups (Kriner and Shen 2010, 2015).

2. Two years before, Williams had been suspended by NBC for lying about events he claimed to witness on the front lines of the Iraq invasion in 2003.

3. For this story, see Engelhardt (2013) and TomDispatch.com in general.

4. On militarization and militarism in the United States, from an anthropological perspective, see Lutz (2004) and Gusterson (2007). From a critical feminist standpoint, see Enloe (2007).

5. Stahl (2010) and Masco (2014) explore the affects associated with witnessing simulated and real military spectacles. Stahl describes these as militainment: a new social formation offering "opportunities for the citizen to step into the screen and dabble as a virtual soldier on a battlefield playground" (2010, 35). And life is beginning to imitate art. With the increasing implementation of drone technology in warfare, one's military service can be done from a computer monitor relatively detached from the actual carnage of the battlefield; see Chamayou (2015) and Gusterson (2016).

6. That being said, in 2014 it was also reported that the Pentagon had prepared plans in the event of zombie attack; see Crawford (2014). For FBI statistics on crime data, see https://www.bjs.gov/content/pub/pdf/cv14.pdf. For *Walking Dead* viewership, see Hibberd (2013).

7. The militarization of the United States, also known as the garrison state hypothesis (Lasswell 1941, 1962; Regan 1994; Bernazzoli and Flint 2010), suggests that military values and objectives have increasingly come to control and influence American governance and everyday life. One could also look at this from the reverse side, however, as the civilianization of the military.

8. In complementary ways, Rebecca Thorpe (2014) and Jonathan Caverley (2014) argue that aggressive democratic militarism, in the United States in particular, is made possible as a result of the shift from state reliance on social mobilization to military capitalization. It is as if all of this dead labor were working not against but in favor of the living labor of enlisted troops. On the paradoxical status of soldiers' bodies in relation to military equipment, see MacLeish (2012).

9. Human beings have spent the vast majority of their time on this planet without the means for warfare and with little interest in killing one another in large numbers, or worrying about how to spare themselves from such a fate. For an overview of the anthropological record on nonkilling societies, see Sponsel (2009).

10. Early American antimilitarism stemmed in part from opposition to British imperialism and colonialism, but it also can be explained as a result of the young country's isolation from major world conflicts of the nineteenth century and relative distance from any rival states of comparable might (Black 2002). It wasn't until the Spanish-American War of the late nineteenth century that the United States fully

transitioned from relatively decentralized militias to more centralized and profession-alized armed forces (Mills 1956, 179; see also chapter 5, this volume). Even so, Ameri-cans remained generally opposed to armed conflict and dubious about the military service as a profession throughout the interwar years (see Lutz 2001, 36–44).

11. This analysis comes from one of the first anthropologists to systematically evalu-ate the concept of violence, David Riches (1986), who argues that violence implies a tripartite relationship between a perpetrator, a victim, and a real or imaginary witness to validate the victim's interpretation of events. Pacifism could be seen as a form of interpretation that refuses to distinguish between acts of war and other kinds of vio-lence, seeing all as equally illegitimate. For a philosophical defense of this position, see McMahan (2009).

12. The increasing mediation dividing civilian spectators from the actual practice of war led Jean Baudrillard (1991) to provocatively declare that the Gulf War did not take place. At the same time, there are more online sources today that attempt to depict the costs of war for the general public, including *Demonocracy.info* infographics, *TomDis-patch*, and the Watson Institute's *Costs of War* website.

13. On the promotion of American fear in unlikely events, see Glassner (2010). Glassner argues that this has increased since 9/11 and has been promoted by politi-cians and the media.

14. On cuts to the CDC budget, see Stone (2014). For a recent appraisal of the relative investment in US epidemic preparation in contrast to war preparation, see Loria (2018).

15. Security theorists often assume that well-run states are the only way to achieve security. As Barry Buzan puts it, in a widely cited text, "There is no real option of going back, and therefore the security of individuals is inseparably entangled with that of the state" (2009, 51). Mitzen (2006) is critical of realist theorists in international relations who assume that warfare can only be explained by what happens within individual states.

16. Nick Turse (2008) and Rosa Brooks (2016) describe the many ways that the American military pervades all sectors of national and world society in unexpected ways. Lutz (2009) and Vine (2011, 2015) investigate the presence and influence of American bases located abroad, and Lutz (2001) and MacLeish (2013) bases on the home front. The American military is so huge and all-pervasive, in fact, that it is increasingly involved even in many nonviolent projects abroad (Lutz 2001, 217–22), though this is at least partially for the good PR.

REFERENCES

Adam, Barbara. 1998. *Timescapes of Modernity: The Environment and Environmental Hazards*. London: Routledge.

Adams, Robert. 2018. *Hope Is a Risk That Must Be Run*. Stuttgart: Hartmann Books.

Adkins, Brent. 2015. *Deleuze and Guattari's* A Thousand Plateaus: *A Critical Introduction and Guide*. Edinburgh: Edinburgh University Press.

Aghili, Farhad. 2012. "A Prediction and Motion-Planning Scheme for Visually Guided Robotic Capturing of Free-Floating Tumbling Objects with Uncertain Dynamics." *IEEE Transactions on Robotics* 28, no. 3: 634–49.

Ahmed, Sara. 2016. "Interview with Judith Butler. *Sexualities* 19, no. 4: 482–92.

Albini, Joseph L. 2001. "Dealing with the Modern Terrorist: The Need for Changes in Strategies and Tactics in the New War on Terrorism." *International Security Consultant* 12, no. 4: 255–81.

Alexander, Catherine. 2009. "Waste under Socialism and After: A Case Study from Almaty." In *Enduring Socialism: Explorations of Revolution, Transformation and Restoration*, edited by Harry G. West and Parvathi Ramen, 148–68. Oxford: Berghahn Books.

Alexander, Catherine, and Joshua Reno. 2012. *Economies of Recycling: The Global Transformation of Values, Materials and Social Relations*. London: Zed Books.

———. 2014. "From Biopower to Energopolitics in England's Modern Waste Technology." *Anthropological Quarterly* 87, no. 2: 335–58.

Alexander, Michelle. 2010. *The New Jim Crow: Mass Incarceration in the Age of Colorblindness*. New York: The New Press.

Altman, George R., and Leo Shane III. 2017. "The Obama Era Is Over. Here's How the Military Rates His Legacy." *Military Times*, January 8, 2017, www.militarytimes.com/news/2017/01/08/the-obama-era-is-over-here-s-how-the-military-rates-his-legacy/.

Anderson, Joe. 2017. "Gun Owners, Ethics, and the Problem of Evil: A Response to the Las Vegas Shooting." *Hau* 7, no. 3: 39–48.

Andrews, Allen H., Ryuji Asami, Yasufumi Iryu, Donald R. Kobayashi, and Frank Camacho. 2016. "Bomb-Produced Radiocarbon in the Western Tropical Pacific Ocean: Guam Coral Reveals Operation-Specific Signals from the Pacific Proving Grounds." *Journal of Geophysical Research* 121, no. 8: 6351–66.

Appadurai, Arjun, ed. 1986. *The Social Life of Things: Commodities in Cultural Perspective.* Cambridge: Cambridge University Press.

Arbona, Javier. 2017. "Trial by the Bay: Treasure Island and Segregation in the Navy's Lake." In *Urban Reinventions: San Francisco's Treasure Island,* edited by Lynne Horiuchi and Tanu Sankalia, 125–39. Honolulu: University of Hawai'i Press.

Arendt, Hannah. 1958. *The Human Condition.* London: University of Chicago Press.

———. 1970. *On Violence.* Orlando: Harcourt.

Arsenault, Mark. 2017. "In Upstate New York, a Tragedy Eclipsed, but Not Forgotten." *Boston Globe,* November 11, 2017. www.bostonglobe.com/metro/2017/11/11/upstate-new-york-tragedy-eclipsed-but-not-forgotten/CyyINhuYP3QHfBkqzydMeI/story.html.

Atkinson, Robert D. 1993. "Defense Spending Cuts and Regional Economic Impact: An Overview. *Economic Geography* 69, no. 2: 107–22.

Atlas Obscura. n.d. "Wreck of the SS Richard Montgomery." Accessed May 7, 2019. www.atlasobscura.com/places/wreck-of-the-ss-richard-montgomery.

Baca, George. 2010. *Conjuring Crisis: Racism and Civil Rights in a Southern Military City.* New Brunswick, NJ: Rutgers University Press.

Bachevich, Andrew J. 2013. *The New American Militarism: How Americans are Seduced by War.* Oxford: Oxford University Press.

Balce, Nerissa S. 2016. *Body Parts of Empire: Visual Abjection, Filipino Images, and the American Archive.* Ann Arbor: University of Michigan Press.

Ballenger, Julia, Barbara Polnick, and Beverly Irby, eds. 2016. *Women of Color in STEM: Navigating the Workforce.* Charlotte, NC: Information Age Publishing.

Baran, Paul A., and Paul M. Sweezy. 1966. *Monopoly Capital: An Essay on the American Economic and Social Order.* New York: Monthly Review Press.

Barclay, Robert, and Randall Brooks. 2009. "In Situ Preservation of Historic Spacecraft." In *Handbook of Space Engineering, Archaeology, and Heritage,* edited by Ann Garrison Darrin and Beth Laura O'Leary, 679–700. Boca Raton, FL: CRC Press.

Barnett, Jon, and John Campbell. 2010. *Climate Change and Small Island States: Power, Knowledge, and the South Pacific.* London: Earthscan.

Barreto, Amilcar Antonio. 2002. *Vieques, the Navy, and Puerto Rican Politics.* Gainesville: University Press of Florida.

Basu, Moni. 2016. "Obama Will Have a Special Sputnik Moment in Wisconsin Town." *CNN Politics,* January 26, 2011. www.cnn.com/2011/POLITICS/01/26/wisconsin.obama.sputnik/index.html.

Baudrillaird, Jean. 1991. *The Gulf War Did Not Take Place.* Bloomington: Indiana University Press.

Bauman, Richard, and Charles L. Briggs. 1990. "Poetics and Performance as Critical Perspectives on Language and Social Life." *Annual Review of Anthropology* 19: 59–88.

Bauman, Zygmunt. 2004. *Wasted Lives: Modernity and Its Outcasts*. Oxford: Blackwell.

Bear, Laura. 2015. *Navigating Austerity: Currents of Debt along a South Asian River*. Stanford, CA: Stanford University Press.

Bear, Laura, and Nayanika Mathur. 2015. "Remaking the Public Good: A New Anthropology of Bureaucracy." *Cambridge Journal of Anthropology* 33, no. 1: 18–34.

Beck, John. 2009. *Dirty Wars: Landscape, Power, and Waste in Western American Literature*. Lincoln: University of Nebraska Press.

Becker, Avi. 1982. "The Arms-Oil Connection: Fueling the Arms Race." *Armed Forces & Society* 8, no. 3: 419–42.

Beery, Jason. 2016. "Unearthing Global Natures: Outer Space and Scalar Politics." *Political Geography* 55: 92–101.

Bélanger, Pierre, and Alexander Scott Arroyo. 2012. "Logistics Islands: The Global Supply Archipelago and the Topologics of Defense." *Prism* 3, no. 4: 55–75.

Bellesiles, Michael A. 1999. "The Origins of Gun Culture in the United States, 1760–1865." In *Guns in America: A Reader*, edited by Jan E. Dizard, Robert M. Muth, and Stephen P. Andrews, Jr., 17–46. New York: NYU Press.

———. 2000. *Arming America: The Origins of a National Gun Culture*. New York: Alfred A. Knopf.

Bennett, Jane. 2009. *Vibrant Matter: A Political Ecology of Things*. Durham, NC: Duke University Press.

Berinstein, Paula, ed. 2002. *Making Space Happen: Private Space Ventures and the Visionaries Behind Them*. Medford, NJ: Plexus.

Bernhard, Ronald P., Eric L. Christiansen, and Donald J. Kessler. 1997. "Orbital Debris as Detected on Exposed Aircraft." *International Journal of Impact Engineering* 20, no. 1: 111–20.

Bernazzoli, Richelle M., and Colin Flint. 2009. "From Militarization to Securitization: Finding a Concept That Works." *Political Geography* 28: 449–50.

———. 2010. "Embodying the Garrison State? Everyday Geographies of Militarization in American Society." *Political Geography* 29: 157–66.

Beyer, Rick, and Elizabeth Sayles. 2015. *The Ghost Army of World War II*. New York: Princeton Architectural Press.

Bezboruah, Monoranjan. 1977. *U.S. Strategy in the Indian Ocean: The International Response*. New York: Praeger.

Bhimull, Chandra D. 2012. "Caribbean Airways, 1930–32: A Notable Failure." *Journal of Transport History* 33, no. 2: 228–42.

———. 2014. "Passages: Airborne in an African Diaspora." *Anthropology and Humanism* 39, no. 2: 129–44.

———. 2017. *Empire in the Air: Airline Travel and the African Diaspora*. New York: NYU Press.

Bickford, Andrew. 2015. "Anthropology, the Anthropocene, and the Military." *Envirosociety*, January 31, 2015. www.envirosociety.org/2015/01/anthropology-the-anthropocene-and-the-military/.

Billings, Lee. 2017. "Alien Probe or Galactic Driftwood? SETI Tunes In to 'Oumuamua." *Scientific American*, December 11, 2017. www.scientificamerican.com/article/alien-probe-or-galactic-driftwood-seti-tunes-in-to-oumuamua/.

Bilstein, Roger. 2003. "The Airplane and the American Experience." In *The Airplane in American Culture*, edited by Dominick A. Pisano, 16–35. Ann Arbor: University of Michigan Press.

Birch, Kean. 2015. *We Have Never Been Neoliberal: A Manifesto for a Doomed Youth.* Winchester: Zero Books.

———. 2017. "Rethinking Value in the Bioeconomy: Finance, Assetization, and the Management of Value." *Science, Technology, & Human Values* 42, no. 3: 460–90.

Birch, Kean, and David Tyfield. 2013. "Theorizing the Bioeconomy: Biovalue, Biocapital, Bioeconomics or . . . What?" *Science, Technology & Human Values* 38, no. 3: 299–327.

Black, Jeremy. 2002. *America as a Military Power: From the American Revolution to the Civil War*. Westport, CT: Praeger.

Blake, Travis, Michael Sánchez, and Mark Bolden. 2016. "OrbitOutlook: Data-centric Competition Based Space Domain Awareness (SDA)." Unpublished paper presented at the 30th Space Symposium, Colorado Springs, CO.

Blasim, Hassan, ed. 2017. *Iraq + 100*. New York: Tor Press.

Borneman, John, and Joseph Masco. 2015. "Anthropology and the Security State." *American Anthropologist* 117, no. 4: 781–94.

Bower, Amanda. 2001. "Scorecard of Hatred." *Time*, March 19, 2001, 30–31.

Brainard, Rusty et al. 2005. "The State of Coral Reef Ecosystems of the US Pacific Remote Island Areas." In *The State of Coral Reef Ecosystems of the United States and Pacific Freely Associated States*, 338–72. Silver Spring, MD: US Department of Commerce, National Oceanic and Atmospheric Administration, and National Ocean Service.

Bremner, Lindsay. 2015 "Thinking with an Indian Ocean Archipelago." Unpublished paper presented at the Indian Ocean Energies conference, Johannesburg, July 23, 2015.

Bridges, J. C. et al. 2017. "Identification of the Beagle 2 Lander on Mars." *Royal Society Open Science* 4: 170785.

Brockington, Dan. 2002. *Fortress Conservation: The Preservation of the Mkomazi Game Reserve, Tanzania*. Bloomington: Indiana University Press.

Brooks, Rosa. 2016. *How Everything Became War and the Military Became Everything*. New York: Simon and Schuster.

Brugioni, Dino. 2010. *Eyes in the Sky: Eisenhower, the CIA, and the Cold War Aerial Espionage*. Annapolis, MD: Naval Institute Press.

Buchli, Victor. 1999. *An Archaeology of Socialism: The Narkomfin Communal House, Moscow*. Oxford: Berg.

Bui, Julie. 2017. "Body-Worn Cameras: Reducing Citizen Complaints and Improving Relationships." *Themis: Research Journal of Justice Studies and Forensic Science* 5, no. 1. https://scholarworks.sjsu.edu/themis/vol5/iss1/1.

Burbick, Joan. 2006. "Cultural Anatomy of a Gun Show." *Stanford Law and Policy Review* 17, no. 3: 657–70.

Burnett, Christina Duffy. 2005. "The Edges of Empire and the Limits of Sovereignty: American Guano Islands." *American Quarterly* 57, no. 3: 779–803.

Buzan, Barry. 2009. *People, States & Fear: An Agenda for International Security Studies in the Post-Cold War Era*. Colchester: ECPR Press.

Byrnes, Mark E. 1994. *Politics and Space: Image Making by NASA*. Westport, CT: Praeger.

Capelotti, P. J. 2004. "Space: the Final (Archaeological) Frontier." *Archaeology* 57, no. 6: 46–51.

———. 2010. *The Human Archaeology of Space: Lunar, Planetary and Interstellar Relics of Exploration*. Jefferson, NC: McFarland Publishers.

Carr, Summerson. 2009. "Anticipating and Inhabiting Institutional Identities." *American Ethnologist* 36, no. 2: 317–36.

Caverley, Jonathan D. 2014. *Democratic Militarism: Voting, Wealth, and War*. Cambridge: Cambridge University Press.

Chamayou, Gregorie. 2015. *A Theory of the Drone*. New York: The New Press.

Ciufolini, Ignazio, Erricos Pavlis, Federico Chieppa, Eduardo Fernandes-Vieira, and Juan Pérez-Mercader. 1998. "Test of General Relativity and Measurement of the Lense-Thirring Effect with Two Earth Satellites." *Science* 279, no. 5359: 2100–2103.

Clark, Brett, and John Bellamy Foster. 2009. "Ecological Imperialism and the Global Metabolic Rift: Unequal Exchanges and the Guano/Nitrates Trade." *International Journal of Comparative Sociology* 50, nos. 3-4: 311–34.

Clarkin, Patrick F. 2010. "The Echoes of War: Effects of Early Malnutrition on Adult Health." In *The War Machine and Global Health: The Human Costs of Armed Conflict and the Violence Industry*, edited by Merrill Singer and G. Derrick Hodge, 31–58. Lanham, MD: Alta Mira Press.

———. 2012. "War, Forced Displacement and Growth in Laotian Adults." *Annals of Human Biology* 39, no. 1 (January–February): 36–45.

Clastres, Pierre. 1974. *Society against the State: Essays in Political Anthropology*. New York: Zone Books.

Clifford, James. 1997. *Routes: Travel and Translation in the Late Twentieth Century*. Cambridge, MA: Harvard University Press.

Coates, Peter, Tim Cole, Marianna Dudley, and Chris Pearson. 2011. "Defending Nation, Defending Nature? Militarized Landscapes and Military Environmentalism in Britain, France, and the United States." *Environmental History* 16: 456–91.

Coburn, Noah. 2011. *Bazaar Politics: Power and Pottery in an Afghan Market Town*. Stanford, CA: Stanford University Press.

Cocker, Emma. 2014. "Salvaging a Romantic Trope: The Conceptual Resurrection of Shipwreck in Recent Art Practice." In *Shipwreck in Art and Literature: Images and Interpretations from Antiquity to the Present Day*, edited by Carl Thompson, 218–36. New York: Routledge.

Cohen, Jeffrey Jerome. 2015. "Noah's Arkive." *In the Middle* (blog), March 25, 2015. www.inthemedievalmiddle.com/2015/03/noahs-arkive.html.

Collier, Stephen J., and Aihwa Ong, eds. 2005. *Global Assemblages: Technology, Politics, and Ethics as Anthropological Problems*. Oxford: Blackwell.

Collis, Christy. 2009. "The Geostationary Orbit: A Critical Legal Geography of Space's Most Valuable Real Estate." *Sociological Review* 57, no. 1: 47–65.

Connell, R. W., and James W. Messerschmidt. 2005. "Hegemonic Masculinity: Rethinking the Concept." *Gender and Society* 19, no. 6: 829–59.

Consalvo, Mia. 2003. "The Monsters Next Door: Media Constructions of Boys and Masculinity." *Feminist Media Studies* 3, no. 1: 27–45.

Copp, Tara. 2018. "DoD: At Least 126 Bases Report Water Contaminants Linked to Cancer, Birth Defects." *Military Times*, April 26, 2018, www.militarytimes.com /news/your-military/2018/04/26/dod-126-bases-report-water-contaminants -harmful-to-infant-development-tied-to-cancers/.

Corn, Joseph C. 1983. *The Winged Gospel: America's Romance with Aviation, 1900– 1950*. Baltimore: Johns Hopkins University Press.

Coronil, Fernando. 1996. "Beyond Occidentalism: Toward Nonimperial Geohistorical Categories." *Cultural Anthropology* 11, no. 1: 51–87.

———. 1997. *The Magical State: Nature, Money, and Modernity in Venezuela*. Chicago: University of Chicago Press.

Cowen, Deborah. 2014. *The Deadly Life of Logistics: Mapping Violence in Global Trade*. Minneapolis: University of Minnesota Press.

Crawford, Jamie. 2014. "Pentagon Document Lays Out Battle Plan against Zombies." *CNN Politics*, May 16, 2014. www.cnn.com/2014/05/16/politics/pentagon-zombie -apocalypse/index.html.

Creasy, William R. et al. 1999. "Analysis of Chemical Weapons Decontamination Waste from Old Ton Containers from Johnston Atoll Using Multiple Analytical Methods." *Environmental Science and Technology* 33, no. 13: 2157–62.

Creighton, Jolene. 2015. "Space Debris to Collide with Earth Next Month (no, it's not a comet or aliens)." *Futurism*. October 27, 2015. https://futurism.com/space-debris -to-collide-with-earth-next-month-no-its-not-a-comet-or-aliens/.

Cronon, William. 1995. *Uncommon Ground: Rethinking the Human Place in Nature*. New York: W. W. Norton and Company.

Curry, Timothy. 2017. *The Man-Not: Race, Class, Genre, and the Dilemmas of Black Manhood*. Philadelphia: Temple University Press.

Custers, Peter. 2007. *Questioning Global Militarism: Nuclear and Military Production and Critical Economic Theory*. Monmouth, Wales: Merlin Press.

———. 2010. "Military Keynesianism Today: An Innovative Discourse." *Race & Class* 51, no. 4: 79–94.

Damjanov, Katarina. 2016. "Of Defunct Satellites and Other Space Debris: Media Waste in the Orbital Commons." *Science, Technology & Human Values* 42 (1): 166–85.

Das, Veena. 2000. "The Act of Witnessing: Violence, Poisonous Knowledge, and Subjectivity." In *Violence and Subjectivity*, edited by Veena Das, Arthur Kleinman, Mamphela Ramphele, and Pamela Reynolds, 205–25. Berkeley: University of California Press.

———. 2007. *Life and Words: Violence and the Descent into the Ordinary*. Berkeley: University of California Press.

Das, Veena, and Arthur Kleinman. 2000. Introduction. In *Violence and Subjectivity*, edited by Veena Das, Arthur Kleinman, Mamphela Ramphele, and Pamela Reynolds, 1–18. Berkeley: University of California Press.

David, Leonard. 2016. "When Will China's 'Heavenly Palace' Space Lab Fall Back to Earth?" *Space.com*, June 10, 2016. www.space.com/33140-china-tiangong-1-space -lab-falling-to-earth.html.

Davies, Ella. 2016. "The Place Furthest from Land Is Known as Point Nemo." *BBC Earth*, October 5, 2016. www.bbc.com/earth/story/20161004-the-place-furthest -from-land-is-known-as-point-nemo.

Davis, Jeffrey Sasha. 2007. "Military Natures: Militarism and the Environment." *Geojournal* 69: 131–34.

———. 2015. *The Empires' Edge: Militarization, Resistance, and Transcending Hegemony in the Pacific*. Athens: University of Georgia Press.

Deacon, Terrence. 2012. "Beyond the Symbolic Species." In *The Symbolic Species Evolved*, edited by Theresa Schilhab, Frederik Stjernfelt, and Terrence Deacon, 9–37. New York: Springer.

Deblois, Bruce M., Richard L. Garwin, R. Scott Kemp, and Jeremy C Marwell. 2005. "Star Crossed." *IEEE Spectrum*, March 3–11, 2005.

Deleuze, Gille, and Felix Guattari. 1987. *A Thousand Plateaus*. Minneapolis: University of Minnesota Press.

Delgado, James P. 1992. "Recovering the Past of USS Arizona: Symbolism, Myth, and Reality." *Historical Archaeology* 26: 69–80.

DeLillo, Don. 1997. *Underworld*. New York: Scribner.

DeLoughrey, Elizabeth M. 2012. "The Myth of Isolates: Ecosystem Ecologies in the Nuclear Pacific." *Cultural Geographies* 20, no. 2: 167–84.

———. 2017. "Submarine Futures of the Anthropocene." *Comparative Literature* 69, no. 1: 32–44.

Denis, Jérôme, and David Pontille. 2017. "Beyond Breakdown: Exploring Regimes of Maintenance." *continent* 6, no. 1: 13–17.

Desjarlais, Robert, Leon Eisenberg, Byron Good, and Arthur Kleinman. 1995. *World Mental Health: Problems and Priorities in Low-Income Countries*. New York: Oxford University Press.

De Wolff, Kim. 2014. "Gyre Plastic: Science, Circulation and the Matter of the Great Pacific Garbage Patch." PhD diss., University of California, San Diego.

Dickens, Peter. 2009. "The Cosmos as Capitalism's Outside." *Sociological Review* 57, no. s1: 66–82.

Dickens, Peter, and James S Ormrod. 2007. *Cosmic Society: Towards a Sociology of the Universe.* London: Routledge.

Dillon, Lindsey. 2014. "Waste, Race, and Space: Brownfield Re-development and Environmental Justice at the Hunters Point Shipyard." *Antipode* 46, no. 5: 1205–21.

———. 2015. "War's Remains: Slow Violence and the Urbanization of Military Bases in California." *Environmental Justice* 8, no. 1: 1–5.

———. 2017. "Pandemonium on the Bay: Naval Station Treasure Island and the Toxic Legacies of Atomic Defense." In *Urban Reinventions: San Francisco's Treasure Island,* edited by Lynne Horiuchi and Tanu Sankalia, 140–58. Honolulu: University of Hawai'i Press.

———. 2018. "Crossroads in San Francisco: The Naval Radiological Defense Laboratory and Its Afterlives." In *Inevitably Toxic: Historical Perspectives on Contamination, Exposure, and Expertise,* edited by Brinda Sarathy, Vivien Hamilton, and Janet Farrell Brodie, 74–96. Pittsburgh, PA: University of Pittsburgh Press.

Donovan, Stephen. 2014. "What Lies Beneath? The Submarine Shipwreck in Anglo-American Culture, 1880–1920." In *Shipwreck in Art and Literature: Images and Interpretations from Antiquity to the Present Day,* edited by Carl Thompson, 150–70. New York: Routledge.

Douglas, Mary. 1966. *Purity and Danger.* London: Routledge.

Dua, Jatin. 2013. "A Sea of Trade and a Sea of Fish: Piracy and Protection in the Western Indian Ocean." *Journal of Eastern African Studies* 7, no. 2: 353–70.

Dunbar-Ortiz, Roxanne. 2018. *Loaded: A Disarming History of the Second Amendment.* San Francisco: City Lights Books.

Duncan, Thomas K., and Christopher J Coyne. 2013. "The Overlooked Costs of the Permanent War Economy: A Market Process Approach." *Review of Austrian Economics* 26, no. 4: 413–31.

Dunne, Richard P. 2011. "Chagos Islands in Sea-Level Rise Controversy." *New Scientist,* November 23, 2011. www.newscientist.com/article/mg21228403-500-chagos-islands-in-sea-level-rise-controversy/.

Dunne, Richard P., Susana M. Barbosa, Philip L. Woodworth. 2012. "Contemporary Sea Level in the Chagos Archipelago, Central Indian Ocean." *Global and Planetary Change,* 82–83: 25–37.

Edensor, Tim. 2005. "Waste Matter: The Debris of Industrial Ruins and the Disordering of the Material World." *Journal of Material Culture* 10, no. 3: 311–32.

Edwards, Paul. 1997. *The Closed World: Computers and the Politics of Discourse in Cold War America.* Cambridge, MA: MIT Press.

———. 2010. *A Vast Machine: Computer Models, Climate Data, and the Politics of Global Warming.* Cambridge, MA: MIT Press.

Eikenberry, Karl W., and David M. Kennedy. 2013. "Americans and Their Military, Drifting Apart." *New York Times,* May 26, 2013. www.nytimes.com/2013/05/27/opinion/americans-and-their-military-drifting-apart.html?_r=0.

Engel-Di Mauro, Salvatore. 2014. *Ecology, Soils, and the Left: An Ecosocial Approach.* New York: Palgrave Macmillan.

Engelhardt, Tom. 2013. "'Bride and Boom!' We're Number One…In Obliterating Wedding Parties." *TomDispatch*, December 20, 2013. www.tomdispatch.com/blog/175787/tomgram%3A_engelhardt,_washington%27s_wedding_album_from_hell/.

Enloe, Cynthia. 2007. *Globalization and Militarism: Feminists Make the Link.* Lanham, MD: Rowman and Littlefield.

Evans, David H. 2006. "Taking Out the Trash: Don DeLillo's Underworld, Liquid Modernity, and the End of Garbage." *Cambridge Quarterly* 35: 106–32.

Fallows, James. 2002. "The Military Industrial Complex." *Foreign Policy* 133: 46–48.

Fast, Jonathan. 2008. *Ceremonial Violence: A Psychological Explanation of School Shootings.* New York: Overlook Press.

Feinstein, Andrew. 2012. *The Shadow World: Inside the Global Arms Trade.* New York: Farrah, Straus and Giroux.

Franklin, H. Bruce. 2003. "'Peace Is Our Profession': The Bombers Take Over." In *The Airplane in American Culture*, edited by Dominick A. Pisano, 333–56. Ann Arbor: University of Michigan Press.

Forte, Maximilian C. 2011. "The Human Terrain System and Anthropology: A Review of Ongoing Public Debates." *American Anthropologist* 113, no. 1: 149–53.

Fox, James Alan, and Monica J. DeLateur. 2014. "Mass Shootings in America: Moving beyond Newtown." *Homicide Studies* 18, no. 1: 125–45.

Fox, Richard Allan, Jr. 1993. *Archaeology, History, and Custer's Last Battle: The Little Big Horn Reexamined.* Norman: University of Oklahoma Press.

Fredericks, Rosalind. 2018. *Garbage Citizenship: Vital Infrastructures of Labor in Dakar, Senegal.* London: Duke University Press.

Froelich, Amanda. 2015. "Mexican Artist Melts 1,527 Guns, Makes Shovels to Plant Trees." *Pocho*, December 11, 2015. www.pocho.com/chilango-artist-melts-1527-guns-makes-shovels-to-plant-trees/.

Gabrys, Jennifer. 2016. *Program Earth: Environmental Sensing Technology and the Making of a Computational Planet.* Minneapolis: University of Minnesota Press.

Gärdebo, Johan, Agata Marzecova, and Scott Gabriel Knowles. 2017. "The Orbital Technosphere: The Provision of Meaning and Matter by Satellites." *Anthropocene Review* 4, no. 1: 44–52.

Garrod, Brian, and Stefan Gossling. 2008. *New Frontiers in Marine Tourism: Diving Experiences, Sustainability, Management.* London: Elsevier.

Gell, Alfred. 1998. *Art and Agency.* Oxford: Oxford University Press.

Gholz, Eugene, and Harvey M. Sapolsky. 1999/2000. "Restructuring the U.S. Defense Industry." *International Security* 24, no. 3: 5–51.

Gidwani, Vinay. 2013. "Six Theses on Waste, Value, and Commons." *Social and Cultural Geography* 14, no. 7: 773–83.

Gidwani, Vinay, and Rajyashree Reddy. 2011. "The Afterlives of 'Waste': Notes from India for a Minor History of Capitalist Surplus." *Antipode* 43, no. 5: 1625–58.

Gille, Zsusza. 2007. *From the Cult of Waste to the Trash Heap of History*. Indianapolis: Indiana University Press.

———. 2013. "Is There an Emancipatory Ontology of Matter? A Response to Myra Hird." *Social Epistemology Review and Reply Collective* 2, no. 4: 1–6.

Gillem, Mark L. 2017. "Visions of Reuse: The Legacy of the Bay Area's Military Installations." In *Urban Reinventions: San Francisco's Treasure Island*, edited by Lynne Horiuchi and Tanu Sankalia, 159–86. Honolulu: University of Hawai'i Press.

Gilliam, Angela. 1991. "Militarism and Accumulation as Cargo Cult." *Decolonizing Anthropology*, edited by Faye V. Harrison, 170–91. Arlington, VA: Association of Black Anthropologists and American Anthropological Association.

Glassner, Barry. 2010. *The Culture of Fear: Why Americans Are Afraid of the Wrong Things*. New York: Basic Books.

Gleason, Paul. 2002. "Don DeLillo, T.S. Eliot, and the Redemption of America's Atomic Waste Land." In *UnderWords: Perspectives on Don Delillo's* Underworld, edited by Joseph Dewey, Steven G. Kellman, and Irving Malin, 130–43. Newark: University of Delaware Press.

Gorman, Alice. 2005. "The Cultural Landscape of Interplanetary Space." *Journal of Social Archaeology* 5, no. 1: 85–107.

———. 2009. "The Archaeology of Space Exploration." *Sociological Review* 57, no. 1 (supp): 132–45.

———. 2015. "Robot Avatars: The Material Culture of Human Activity in Earth Orbit." In *Archaeology and Heritage of the Human Movement into Space*, Beth Laura O'Leary and P.J. Capelotti, 29–47. Switzerland: Springer.

———. 2017. "Comet Quest: How the Rosetta Mission Created a New Archaeological Site in Space." *Anthropology News* 58, no. 1, e63–70.

Gould, Madelyn, Patrick Jamieson, and Daniel Romer. 2003. "Media Contagion and Suicide among the Young." *American Behavioral Scientist* 46, no. 9: 1269–84.

Graeber, David. 2001. *Towards an Anthropological Theory of Value: The False Coin of Our Own Dreams*. New York: Palgrave MacMillan.

———. 2011. *Debt: The First 5000 Years*. New York: Melville House.

———. 2016. *The Utopia of Rules: On Technology, Stupidity and the Secret Joys of Bureaucracy*. New York: Melville House.

Graham, Stephen, and Nigel Thrift. 2007. "Out of Order: Understanding Repair and Maintenance." *Theory, Culture & Society* 24, no. 3: 1–25.

Gray, Colin S. 1982. *American Military Space Policy: Information Systems, Weapon Systems, and Arms Control*. Cambridge, MA: Abt Books.

Gregson, Nicky, and Mike Crang. 2015. "From Waste to Resource: The Trade in Wastes and Global Recycling Economies." *Annual Review of Environment and Resources* 40: 151–76.

Gregson, Nicky, Mike Crang, and Helen Watkins. 2011. "Souvenir Salvage and the Death of Great Naval Ships." *Journal of Material Culture* 16, no. 3: 301–24.

Grossman, Dave. 2009. *The Psychological Cost of Learning to Kill in War and Society*. New York: Open Road.

Grenier, John. 2005. *The First Way of War: American War Making on the Frontier, 1607–1814.* Cambridge: Cambridge University Press.

Günel, Gökçe. 2019. *Spaceship in the Desert: Energy, Climate Change and Urban Design in Abu Dhabi.* Durham, NC: Duke University Press.

Gustafsson, Anders, Javier Iglesias Camargo, Håkan Karlsson, and Gloria M. Miranda González. 2017. "Material Life Histories of the Missile Crisis (1962): Cuban Examples of a Soviet Nuclear Missile Hangar and US Marston Mats." *Journal of Contemporary Archaeology* 4, no. 1: 39–58.

Gusterson, Hugh. 1996. *Nuclear Rites: A Weapons Laboratory at the End of the Cold War.* Berkeley: University of California Press.

———. 2004. *People of the Bomb: Portraits of America's Nuclear Complex.* Minneapolis: University of Minnesota Press.

———. 2007. "Anthropology and Militarism." *Annual Review of Anthropology* 36: 155–75.

———. 2013. "Making a Killing." *Anthropology Today* 29, no. 1: 1–2.

———. 2016. *Drone: Remote Control Warfare.* London: MIT Press.

Guyer, Jane. 2004. *Marginal Gains: Monetary Transactions in Atlantic Africa.* London: University of Chicago Press.

Hamblin, Jacob Darwin. 2009. *Poison in the Well: Radioactive Waste in the Oceans at the Dawn of the Nuclear Age.* New Brunswick, NJ: Rutgers University Press.

Hansen, James R. 1989. "Aviation History in the Wider View." *Technology and Culture* 30, no. 3: 643–56.

Haraway, Donna J. 2016. *Staying with the Trouble: Making Kin in the Chthulucene.* Durham, NC: Duke University Press.

Hardorff, Richard G. 1991. *Lakota Recollections of the Custer Fight: New Sources of Indian-Military History.* Lincoln: University of Nebraska Press.

Harman, Graham. 2009. *Prince of Networks: Bruno Latour and Metaphysics.* Melbourne: Re.Press.

Hart, Keith. 1990. "Blacks in the World Economy." *Cambridge Journal of Anthropology* 14, no. 2: 43–56.

———. 2005. *The Hitman's Dilemma: Or, Business, Personal and Impersonal.* Chicago: Prickly Paradigm Press.

Hartigan, John Jr. 1999. *Racial Situations: Class Predicaments of Whiteness in Detroit.* Princeton: Princeton University Press.

Hartung, William. 2010. *Prophets of War: Lockheed Martin and the Making of the Military-Industrial Complex.* New York: Nation Books.

Harvey, David. 1982. *The Limits to Capital.* New York: Verso.

Harvey, Kyle. 2014. *American Anti-Nuclear Activism, 1975–1990: The Challenge of Peace.* New York: Palgrave Macmillan.

Havlick, David. 2007. "Logics of Change for Military-to-Wildlife Conversions in the United States." *Geojournal* 69: 151–64.

Hayward, Eva. 2010. "Fingereyes: Impressions of Cup Corals." *Cultural Anthropology* 25, no. 4: 577–99.

Hecht, Gabrielle. 2018. "Interscalar Vehicles for an African Anthropocene: On Waste, Temporality, and Violence." *Cultural Anthropology* 33, no. 1: 109–41.

Helmreich, Stefan. 2008. "Species of Biocapital." *Science as Culture* 17, no. 4: 463–78.

Henig, David. 2012. "Iron in the Soil: Living with Military Waste in Bosnia-Herzegovina." *Anthropology Today* 28, no. 1: 21–23.

Hibberd, James. 2013. "'The Walking Dead' Season 4 Premiere Ratings Enormous." *Entertainment Weekly*, October 14, 2014. http://ew.com/article/2013/10/14/the-walking-dead-returns-to-record-viewership/.

Hird, Myra. 2012. "Knowing Waste: Towards an Inhuman Epistemology." *Social Epistemology* 26, nos. 3–4: 453–69.

———. 2013. "Is Waste Indeterminacy Useful? A Response to Zsuzsa Gille." *Social Epistemology Review and Reply Collective* 2, no. 6: 28–33.

Hirschkind, Charles. 2015. "Religion." In *Keywords in Sound*, edited by David Novak and Matt Sakakeeny, 165–74. Durham, NC: Duke University Press.

Holley, I. B. Jr. 1971. *Ideas and Weapons*. Hamden, CT: Archon Books.

hooks, bell. 1984. *Feminist Theory: From Margin to Center*. Boston: South End Press.

Hosley, William N. 1996. *Colt: The Making of an American Legend*. Boston: University of Massachusetts Press.

Houston, Lara. 2017. "The Timeliness of Repair." *continent* 6, no. 1: 51–55.

Houston, Lara, Daniela K. Rosner, Steven J. Jackson, and Jamie Allen. 2017. "Letter from the Editors." *continent* 6, no. 1: 1–3.

Howlett, Charles F., ed. 2005. *History of the American Peace Movement, 1890–2000: The Emergence of a New Scholarly Discipline*. Lewiston, NY: Edwin Mellen Press.

Howlett, Charles F., and Robbie Lieberman. 2008. *A History of the American Peace Movement from Colonial Times to the Present*. Lewiston, NY: Edwin Mellen Press.

Hui, Mary, and J. Freedom du Lac. 2018. "China's 9 1/2-Ton Space Lab Will Soon Crash to Earth. No One Knows Where It Will Hit." *Washington Post*, January 4, 2018. www.washingtonpost.com/news/speaking-of-science/wp/2017/10/16/chinas-first-space-station-will-soon-crash-to-earth-no-one-knows-where-itll-hit/?utm_term=.dcd2dd39ac55.

Huntington, Samuel P. 1957. *The Soldier and the State: The Theory and Politics of Civil-Military Relations*. Cambridge, MA: Harvard University Press.

Ialenti, Vincent. 2018. "Waste Makes Haste: How a Campaign to Speed Up Nuclear Waste Shipments Shut Down the WIPP Long-Term Repository." *Bulletin of the Atomic Scientists*, June 28, 2018. https://thebulletin.org/2018/06/waste-makes-haste-how-a-campaign-to-speed-up-nuclear-waste-shipments-shut-down-the-wipp-long-term-repository/.

Idziak, Luke A. 2013. "Cultural Resources Management in Outer Space: Historic Preservation in the Graveyard Orbits." *Synesis* 4, no. 1: G61–75.

Ingold, Tim. 2000. *The Perception of the Environment: Essays on Dwelling, Livelihood and Skill*. London: Routledge.

———. 2011. *Being Alive: Essays on Movement, Knowledge and Description*. New York: Routledge.

———. 2014. "The Creativity of Undergoing." *Pragmatics & Cognition* 22, no. 1: 124–39.

———. 2018. "Back to the Future with the Theory of Affordances." *HAU* 8, nos. 1–2: 39–44.

InnovationNewsDaily Staff. 2011. "DARPA Wants Telescopes to Protect Military Satellites from Space Junk. *NBC News*, April 17, 2011. www.nbcnews.com/id/4263 4299/ns/technology_and_science-space/t/darpa-wants-telescopes-protect-mili tary-satellites-space-junk/#.Wl-qWpM-fpA.

IPCC. 2014. *Climate Change 2014: Impacts, Adaptation, and Vulnerability. Part A: Global and Sectoral Aspects.* New York: Cambridge University Press.

Jackson, Stephen J. 2014. "Rethinking Repair." In *Media Technologies: Essays on Communication, Materiality, and Society,* edited by Tarleton Gillespie, Pablo J. Boczkowski, and Kirsten A. Foot, 221–39. Cambridge, MA: MIT Press.

Jakobson, Roman. 1957. *Shifters, Verbal Categories, and the Russian Verb.* Cambridge, MA: Harvard University Russian Language Project.

Janowitz, Morris. 1960. *The Professional Soldier: A Social and Political Portrait.* New York: Free Press.

Jecu, Marta. 2015. *Architecture and the Virtual.* Chicago: University of Chicago Press.

Jeffery, Laura. 2013. "'We Are the True Guardians of the Environment': Human-Environment Relations and Debates about the Future of the Chagos Archipelago." *Journal of the Royal Anthropological Institute* 19: 300–18.

———. 2014a. "Ecological Restoration in a Cultural Landscape: Conservationist and Chagossian Approaches to Controlling the 'Coconut Chaos' on the Chagos Archipelago." *Human Ecology* 42, no. 6: 999–1006.

———. 2014b. "Neither Confirm Nor Deny." *Anthropology Today* 30, no. 3: 9–13.

Johnson, Kevin. 2017. "Trump Lifts Ban on Military Gear to Local Police Forces." *USA Today,* August 27, 2017. www.usatoday.com/story/news/politics/2017/08/27/trump-expected-lift-ban-military-gear-local-police-forces/606065001/.

Johnson, Nicholas, and Heiner Klinkrad. 2009. "The International Space Station and the Space Debris Environment: 10 Years On." *Orbital Debris Quarterly News* 13, no. 2. https://ntrs.nasa.gov/archive/nasa/casi.ntrs.nasa.gov/20090004997.pdf.

Johnston, Barbara Rose, and Holly M. Baker. 2008. *Consequential Damages of Nuclear War: The Rongelap Report.* Walnut Creek, CA: Left Coast Press.

Jones, Toby Craig. 2012. "America, Oil, and War in the Middle East." *Journal of American History* 99, no. 1: 208–18.

Kaldor, Mary, Ulrich Albrecht, and Geneviève Schméder. 1998. *The End of Military Fordism: Restructuring the Global Military Sector,* vol. 2. London: Bloomsbury.

Karp, Ivan, ed. 1991. *Exhibiting Cultures: The Poetics and Politics of Museum Display.* Washington, DC: Smithsonian.

Karp, Ivan. 1992. *Museums and Communities: The Politics of Public Culture.* Washington, DC: Smithsonian.

Karp, Ivan, Corinne A. Kratz, Lynn Szwaja, and Tomás Ybarra-Frausto. 2006. *Museum Frictions: Public Cultures/Global Transformations.* Durham, NC: Duke University Press.

Keane, Webb. 2003. "Semiotics and the Social Analysis of Material Things." *Language & Communication* 23, nos. 3–4: 409–25.

———. 2016. *Ethical Life: Its Natural and Social Histories*. Princeton, NJ: Princeton University Press.

———. 2018. "Perspectives on Affordances, or the Anthropologically Real. *HAU* 8, no. 1: 27–38.

Kessler, Donald J., and Burton G. Cour-Palais. 1978. "Collision Frequency of Artificial Satellites: The Creation of a Debris Belt." *Journal of Geophysical Research* 83, no. A6: 2637–46.

Khalili, Laleh. 2013. *Time in the Shadows: Confinement in Counterinsurgencies*. Stanford, CA: Stanford University Press.

Kidron, Michael. 1967. "A Permanent Arms Economy." *International Socialism* 28: 8–12.

———. 1977. "Two Insights Don't Make a Theory." *International Socialism* 100: 4–9.

Kilgore, De Witt Douglas. 2003. *Astrofuturism: Science, Race and Visions of Utopia in Space*. Philadelphia: University of Pennsylvania Press.

Kim, Eleana. 2014. "Toward an Anthropology of Landmines: Rogue Infrastructure and Military Waste in the Korean DMZ." *Cultural Anthropology* 31, no. 2: 162–87.

———. 2018. "Locating Landmines in the Korean Demilitarized Zone." In *Ethnographies of U.S. Empire*, edited by Carole McGranahan and John F. Collins, 313–32. Durham, NC: Duke University Press.

King, James. 2015. "The Deadliest Mass Shooting Everyone Forgot." *Vocativ*, December 10, 2015. www.vocativ.com/258994/the-deadliest-mass-shooting-everyone-forgot/.

Kitzen, Michael. 1996. "Money Bags or Cannon Balls: The Origins of the Tripolitan War, 1795-1801." *Journal of the Early Republic* 16, no. 4: 601–24.

Klaf, Suzanna, Karima Legette, and John W. Frazier. 2010. "Diversity Comes to a Small City: The Case of Binghamton, NY." In *Multicultural Geographies: The Changing Racial/Ethnic Patterns of the United States*, edited by John W. Frazier and Florence M. Margai, 207–18. Albany, NY: SUNY Press.

Klein, Jessie, and Lynn S. Chancer. 2000. "Masculinity Matters: The Omission of Gender from High-Profile School Violence Cases." In *Smoke and Mirrors: The Hidden Context of Violence in Schools and Society*, edited by Stephanie Urso Spina, 129–62. Lanham, MD: Rowman and Littlefield Publishers.

Klinkrad, Heiner. 2010. "Space Debris." *Encyclopedia of Aerospace Engineering* (online). New York: John Wiley and Sons. https://doi.org/10.1002/9780470686652.eae325.

Kockelman, Paul. 2005. "The Semiotic Stance." *Semiotica* 157, no. 157: 233–304.

Kohn, Eduardo. 2013. *How Forests Think: Toward an Anthropology Beyond the Human*. Berkeley: University of California Press.

Koistinen, Paul A.C. 2012. *State of War: The Political Economy of American Warfare, 1945–2011*. Lawrence: University Press of Kansas.

Kopte, Susanne, and Peter Wilke. 1998. "Disarmament and the Disposal of Surplus Weapons: A Survey of the Dismantling, Destruction and Transfer of Surplus Weapons and Ammunition." In *The End of Military Fordism: Restructuring the*

Global Military Sector, vol. 2, edited by Mary Kaldor, Ulrich Albrecht, and Geneviève Schméder, 67–100. London: Pinter.

Kosek, Jake. 2006. *Understories: The Political Life of Forests in Northern New Mexico.* Durham: Duke University Press.

Koven, Michele. 2011. "Comparing Stories Told in Sociolinguistic Interviews and Spontaneous Conversation." *Language in Society* 40, no. 1: 75–89.

Kraska, Peter, ed. 2001. *Militarizing the American Criminal Justice System: The Changing Roles of the Armed Forces and the Police.* Boston: Northeastern University Press.

Kraska, Peter. 2007. "Militarization and Policing—Its Relevance to 21st Century Police." *Policing* 1, no. 4: 501–13.

Kriner, Douglas L., and Francis X. Shen. 2010. *The Casualty Gap: The Causes and Consequences of Wartime Inequalities.* Oxford: Oxford University Press.

Kriner, Douglas, and Frances X. Shen. 2015. "Conscription, Inequality, and Partisan Support for War. *Journal of Conflict Resolution* 60, no. 8: 1419–45.

Kuletz, Valerie. 1998. *Tainted Desert: Environmental Ruin in the American West.* New York: Routledge.

Lambek, Michael. 2015. *The Ethical Condition: Essays on Action, Person, and Value.* Chicago: University of Chicago Press.

Lang, Hannah. 2018. "See the Abandoned WWII Base on Greenland Leaking Toxic Waste." *National Geographic,* January 12, 2018. https://news.nationalgeographic .com/2017/07/greenland-abandoned-military-base-spd/.

Langlie, BrieAnna. 2018. "Building Ecological Resistance: Late Intermediate Period Farming in the South-Central Highland Andes (CE 1100-1450)." *Journal of Anthropological Archaeology* 52: 167–79.

Langman, Peter F. 2009. *Why Kids Kill: Inside the Minds of School Shooters.* New York: Palgrave Macmillan.

Larkin, Ralph W. 2009. "The Columbine Legacy: Rampage Shootings as Political Acts." *American Behavioral Scientist* 52: 1309–26.

Lasswell, Harold D. 1941. "The Garrison State." *American Journal of Sociology* 46: 455–67.

———. 1962. "The Garrison State Hypothesis Today." In *Changing Patterns of Military Politics,* edited by Samuel P. Huntington. New York: Free Press of Glencoe.

Latour, Bruno. 2005. *Reassembling the Social.* Oxford: Oxford University Press.

Laviolette, Patrick. 2006. "Ships of Relations: Navigating through Local Cornish Maritime Art." *International Journal of Heritage Studies* 12, no. 1: 69–92.

Law, John. 2002. *Aircraft Stories: Decentering the Object in Technoscience.* Durham, NC: Duke University Press.

Lebreton, L. C-M, S. D. Greer, and J. C. Borrero. 2012. "Numerical Modelling of Floating Debris in the World's Oceans." *Marine Pollution Bulletin* 64: 653–61.

Leifer, Larry J., and Martin Steinert. 2011. "Dancing with Ambiguity: Causality Behavior, Design Thinking, and Triple-Loop-Learning." *Information Knowledge Systems Management* 10, nos, 1–4): 151–73.

Le Juez, Brigitte, and Olga Springer. 2015. *Shipwreck and Island Motifs in Literature and the Arts.* Leiden: Brill Rodopi.

Lemoine, Bret. 2016. "'What Is That?!' Unidentified, Unexplained Large Object Damages Man's Van on Milwaukee's North Dide." *Fox6Now*, December 22, 2016. http://fox6now.com/2016/12/22/what-is-that-unidentified-unexplained-large-object-damages-mans-van-on-milwaukees-north-side/.

Lenin, Vladimir I. 1917. *Imperialism: The Highest Stage of Capitalism*. Sydney: Resistance Books.

Lepawsky, Josh. 2015a. "Are We Living in a Post-Basel World?" *Area* 47, no. 1: 7–15.

———. 2015b. "The Changing Geography of Global Trade in Electronic Discards: Time to Rethink the E-waste Problem." *Geographical Journal* 181, no. 2: 147–59.

Lepawsky, Josh, Max Liboiron, Arn Keeling, and Charles Mather. 2017. "Repairscapes." *continent* 6, no. 1: 56–61.

Lepawsky, Josh, and Chris McNabb. 2010. "Mapping International Flows of Electronic Waste." *Canadian Geographer* 54, no. 2: 177–95.

Lepselter, Susan. 2016. *The Resonance of Unseen Things: Poetics, Power, Captivity, and UFOs in the American Uncanny*. Ann Arbor: University of Michigan Press.

Levesque, William R. 2013. "USS Calhoun County Sailors Dumped Thousands of Tons of Radioactive Waste into Ocean." *Tampa Bay Times*, December 20, 2013. http://tampabay.com/news/military/veterans/the-atomic-sailors/2157927.

Levine, Phillip B., and Robin McKnight. 2017. "Firearms and Accidental Deaths: Evidence from the Aftermath of the Sandy Hook School Shooting." *Science* 358, no. 6368: 1324–28.

Liou, J.-C., Nicholas L. Johnson and N. M. Hill. 2010. "Controlling the Growth of Future LEO Debris Populations with Active Debris Removal." *Acta Astronautica* 66, no. 5: 648–53.

Lioy, Paul J. 2009. *Dust: The Inside Story of Its Role in the September 11th Aftermath*. New York: Rowman & Littlefield.

Little, Peter. 2014. *Toxic Town: IBM, Pollution, and Industrial Risks*. New York: NYU Press.

Lockheed Martin. 2019. "Lockheed Reports Fourth Quarter and Full Year 2018 Results." January 29, 2019. https://news.lockheedmartin.com/2019-01-29-Lockheed-Martin-Reports-Fourth-Quarter-and-Full-Year-2018-Results.

Loria, Kevin. 2018. "Bill Gates Thinks a Coming Disease Could Kill 30 Million People within 6 Months—And Says We Should Prepare for It as We Do for War." *Business Insider*, April 27, 2018. www.businessinsider.com/bill-gates-warns-the-next-pandemic-disease-is-coming-2018-4.

Luhrmann, Tanya, and Rachel Morgain. 2010. "Prayer as Inner Sense Cultivation: An Attentional Learning Theory of Spiritual Experience." *Ethos* 40, no. 4: 359–89.

Luke, Timothy. 1989. "On Post-War: The Significance of Symbolic Action in War and Deterrence." *Alternatives* 14: 343–62.

Lunsford, Virginia W. 2016. "The American War for Independence at Sea." In *America, Sea Power, and the World*, edited by James C. Bradford, 11–25. Malden, MA: Wiley Blackwell.

Lutz, Catherine. 2001. *Homefront: A Military City and the American Twentieth Century*. New York: Beacon Press.

——. 2004. "Militarization." In *A Companion to the Anthropology of Politics*, edited by David Nugent and Joan Vincent, 318–31. Oxford: Blackwell.

——, ed. 2009. *The Bases of Empire: The Global Struggle against U.S. Military Posts*. New York: NYU Press.

——. 2017. "How Did Guam Become a Target of North Korean Missiles?" *Common Dreams*, August 18, 2017, www.commondreams.org/views/2017/08/18/how-did -guam-become-target-north-korean-missiles.

Luxemburg, Rosa. 1971. *Selected Political Writings*. New York: Modern Reader.

Maameri, Fatima. 2008. "Ottoman Algeria in Western Diplomatic History with Particular Emphasis on Relations with the United States of America, 1776–1816." PhD diss., University Mentouri, Constantine.

Machlis, Gary E., and Thor Hanson. 2008. "Warfare Ecology." *BioScience* 58, no. 8: 729–36.

MacLeish, Kenneth T. 2012. "Armor and Anesthesia: Exposure, Feeling, and the Soldier's Body." *Medical Anthropology Quarterly* 26, no. 1: 49–68.

——. 2013. *Making War at Fort Hood: Life and Uncertainty in a Military Community*. Princeton, NJ: Princeton University Press.

MacLeod, Roy. 2001. "'Strictly for the Birds': Science, the Military, and the Smithsonian's Pacific Ocean Biological Survey Program, 1963–1970." *Journal for the History of Biology* 34: 315–52.

Mandel, Ernest. 1999. *Late Capitalism*. New York: Verso.

Markusen, Ann, Sean DiGiovanna, and Michael C. Leary, eds. 2003. *From Defense to Development? International Perspectives on Realizing the Peace Dividend*. London: Routledge.

Markusen, Ann, Peter Hall, Scott Campbell, and Sabina Deitrick. 1991. *The Rise of the Gunbelt: The Military Remapping of Industrial America*. New York: Oxford University Press.

Markusen, Ann, and Joel Yudken. 1992. *Dismantling the Cold War Economy*. New York: Basic Books.

Marres, Nortje. 2012. *Material Participation: Technology, the Environment and Everyday Publics*. New York: Palgrave Macmillan.

Martucci, Elise A. 2007. *The Environmental Unconscious in the Fiction of Don DeLillo*. New York: Routledge.

Marzec, Robert. 2016. *Militarizing the Environment: Climate Change and the Security State*. Minneapolis: University of Minnesota Press.

Masco, Joseph. 2006. *The Nuclear Borderlands: The Manhattan Project in Post–Cold War New Mexico*. Princeton, NJ: Princeton University Press.

——. 2014. *The Theater of Operations: National Security Affect from the Cold War to the War on Terror*. Durham, NC: Duke University Press.

Massanari, Adrienne. 2017. "#Gamergate and The Fappening: How Reddit's Algorithm, Governance, and Culture Support Toxic Technocultures." *New Media & Society* 19, no. 3: 329–46.

Maurer, Bill. 2005. *Mutual Life, Limited: Islamic Banking, Alternative Currencies, Lateral Reason.* Princeton, NJ: Princeton University Press.

McCaffrey, Katherine T. 2002. *Military Power and Popular Protest: The U.S. Navy in Vieques, Puerto Rico.* New Brunswick, NJ: Rutgers University Press.

McCall, Grant. 1976. "European Impact on Easter Island: Response, Recruitment and the Polynesian Experience in Peru." *Journal of Pacific History* 11, no. 2: 90–105.

McCray, W. Patrick. 2008. *Keep Watching the Skies! The Story of Operation Moonwatch and the Dawn of the Space Age.* Princeton, NJ: Princeton University Press.

McMahan, Jeff. 2009. *Killing in War.* Oxford: Oxford University Press.

Melas, Emily. 2012. "Stenger Presents NYSUNY 2020 Plan to Cuomo." *Pipe Dream* (at Binghamton University), April 27, 2012. www.bupipedream.com/news/9902/nysuny 2020/

Mellström, Ulf. 2004. "Machines and Masculine Subjectivities: Technology as an Integrated Part of Men's Life Experiences." *Men and Masculinities* 6, no. 4: 368–82.

Melman, Seymour, ed. 1970a. *The Defense Economy: Conversion of Industries and Occupations to Civilian Needs.* New York: Praeger.

———. 1970b. *Pentagon Capitalism: The Political Economy of War.* New York: McGraw Hill.

———. 1981. *From Military to Civilian Economy: Issues and Options.* Los Angeles: Center for the Study of Armament and Disarmament.

Mengel, John T. 1956. "Tracking the Earth Satellite, and Data Transmission, by Radio." *Proceedings of the IRE* 44, no. 6: 755–60.

Mentz, Steve. 2015. *Shipwreck Modernity: Ecologies of Globalization, 1550–1719.* Minneapolis: University of Minnesota Press.

Merchant, Stephanie. 2012. "Submarine Geographies: The Body, the Senses and the Mediation of Tourist Experience." PhD diss., University of Exeter.

———. 2014. "Deep Ethnography: Witnessing the Ghosts of SS *Thistlegorm*." In *Water Worlds: Human Geographies of the Ocean*, edited by Jon Anderson and Kimberley Peters, 119–134. Farnham, UK: Ashgate.

Messeri, Lisa. 2016. *Placing Outer Space: An Earthly Ethnography of Other Worlds.* Durham, NC: Duke University Press.

Mettler, Suzanne. 2005. *Soldiers to Citizens: The G.I. Bill and the Making of the Greatest Generation.* Oxford: Oxford University Press.

Michino, Gregory F. 1997. *Lakota Noon: The Indian Narrative of Custer's Defeat.* Missoula, MT: Mountain Press.

Miéville, China. 2018. *October: The Story of the Russian Revolution.* New York: Verso.

Millar, Kathleen. 2018. *Reclaiming the Discarded: Life and Labor in Rio's Garbage Dump.* London: Duke University.

Miller, Daniel. 1987. *Material Culture and Mass Consumption.* Oxford: Basil Blackwell.

———, ed. 2005. *Materiality.* Durham: Duke University Press.

———. 2010. *Stuff.* Cambridge, UK: Polity Press.

Mills, C. Wright. 1956. *The Power Elite.* Oxford: Oxford University Press.

Mitchell, Timothy. 2011. *Carbon Democracy.* New York: Verso.

Mitchell. W. J. T. 2005. *What Do Pictures Want? The Lives and Loves of Images*. Chicago: University of Chicago Press.

Mitzen, Jennifer. 2006. "Ontological Security in World Politics: State Identity and the Security Dilemma." *European Journal of International Relations* 12, no. 3: 341–70.

Miyazaki, Hirokazu. 2006. *The Method of Hope: Anthropology, Philosophy, and Fijian Knowledge*. Stanford, CA: Stanford University Press.

Molloy, Patricia. 2002. "Moral Space and Moral Panics: High Schools, War Zones and Other Dangerous Places." *Culture Machine* 4. http://svr91.ednsi.com/~culturem /index.php/cm/article/viewArticle/274/259.

Moore, Amelia. 2012. "The Aquatic Invaders: Marine Management Figuring Fishermen, Fisheries, and Lionfish in the Bahamas." *Cultural Anthropology* 27, no. 4: 667–88.

Moore, Jason W. 2017. "The Capitalocene, Part 1: On the Nature and Origins of Our Ecological Crisis." *Journal of Peasant Studies* 44, no. 3: 594–630.

Morozov, Evgeny. 2013. *To Save Everything, Click Here: The Folly of Technological Solutionism*. New York: Public Affairs.

Moskalenko, Sophia and Clark McCauley. 2011. "The Psychology of Lone-Wolf Terrorism." *Counselling Psychology Quarterly* 24, no. 2: 115–26.

Moy, Timothy. 2001. *War Machines: Transforming Technologies in the U.S. Military, 1920-1940*. College Station: Texas A&M University Press.

———. 2003. "Transforming Technology in the Army Air Corps, 1920-1940: Technology, Politics, and Culture for Strategic Bombing." In *The Airplane in American Culture*, edited by Dominick A. Pisano, 299–332. Ann Arbor: University of Michigan Press.

Munn, Nancy. 1986. *The Fame of Gawa: A Symbolic Study of Value Transformation in a Massim (Papua New Guinea) Society*. Durham, NC: Duke University Press.

Muschert, Glenn W. 2007. "Research in School Shootings." *Sociology Compass* 1, no. 1: 60–80.

Nagle, Robin. 2013. *Picking Up: On the Streets and Behind the Trucks with the Sanitation Workers of New York City*. New York: Farrar, Straus and Giroux.

Navaro-Yashin, Yael. 2012. *The Make Believe Space: Affective Geography in Postwar Policy*. Durham, NC: Duke University Press.

Neitschmann, Bernard. 1987. "The Third World War." *Cultural Survival Quarterly* 11, no. 3: 1–16.

Network of Concerned Anthropologists. 2009. *The Counter-counter Insurgency Manual*. Chicago: Prickly Paradigm Press.

Nicholson, Wayne L, Andrew C. Schuerger, and Margaret S. Race. 2009. "Migrating Microbes and Planetary Protection." *Trends in Microbiology* 17, no. 9: 389–92.

Nisbett, Richard E. 1996. *Culture of Honor: The Psychology of Violence in the South*. Boulder, CO: Westview Press.

Nixon, Rob. 2011. *Slow Violence and the Environmentalism of the Poor*. Cambridge, MA: Harvard University Press.

Nordstrom, Carolyn. 2007. *Global Outlaws: Crime, Money, and Power in the Contemporary World*. Berkeley: University of California Press.

Oden, Michael, Laura Wolf-Powers, and Ann Markusen. 2003. "Post-Cold War Conversion: Gains, Losses, and Hidden Changes in the US Economy." In *From Defense to Development? International Perspectives on Realizing the Peace Dividend*, edited by Ann Markusen, Sean DiGiovanna, and Michael C. Leary, 15–42. London: Routledge.

O'Donnell, Dan. 1993. "The Pacific Guano Islands: The Stirring of American Empire in the Pacific Ocean." *Pacific Studies* 16, no. 1: 43–66.

Oldenziel, Ruth. 2011. "Islands: The United States as a Networked Empire." In *Entangled Geographies: Empire and Technologies in the Global Cold War*, edited by Gabrielle Hecht, 13-42. Cambridge, MA: MIT Press.

O'Leary, Beth Laura. 2006. "The Cultural Heritage of Space, the Moon and Other Celestial Bodies." *Antiquity* 80, no. 307. www.antiquity.ac.uk/projgall/oleary/.

———. 2015. "'To Boldly Go Where No Man [sic] Has Gone Before': Approaches in Space Archaeology and Heritage." In *Archaeology and Heritage of the Human Movement into Space*, edited by Beth Laura O'Leary and P.J. Capelotti, 1–12. Switzerland: Springer.

Olson, Valerie. 2018. *Into the Extreme: U.S. Environmental Systems and Politics Beyond Earth*. Minneapolis: University of Minnesota Press.

O'Neill, Ian. 2008. "Project Lucifer: Will Cassini Turn Saturn Into a Second Sun?" (Part 1). *Universe Today*, July 24, 2008. www.universetoday.com/15905/project-lucifer-will-cassini-turn-saturn-into-a-second-sun-part-1/.

Paglen, Trevor. 2009. *Blank Spots on the Map: The Dark Geography of the Pentagon's Secret World*. New York: New American Library.

Paoletta, Rae. 2017. "A Few Last Words on the Best Spacecraft of Our Lives, Before It Dies." *Gizmodo*, September 13, 2017. http://gizmodo.com/a-few-last-words-on-best-spacecraft-of-our-lives-befor-1803889697.

Patton, Paul. 1984. "Conceptual Politics and the War-Machine in 'Mille Plateaux.'" *SubStance* 13, nos. 3–4: 61–80.

Pedersen, David. 2013. *American Value: Migrants, Money, and Meaning in El Salvador and the United States*. Chicago: University of Chicago Press.

Peirce, Charles S. 1955. *Philosophical Writings of Peirce*. New York: Dover.

Perrino, Sabina. 2007. "Cross-chronotope Alignment in Senegalese Oral Narrative." *Language & Communication* 27, no. 3: 227–44.

Phillips, David P. 1974. "The Influence of Suggestion on Suicide: Substantive and Theoretical Implications of the Werther Effect." *American Sociological Review* 39, no. 3: 340–54.

Pike, David L. 2004. "Sewage Treatments: Vertical Spaces and Waste in Nineteenth-Century Paris and London." In *Filth: Dirt, Disgust, and Modern Life*, edited by William A. Cohen and Ryan Johnson, 51–77. Minneapolis: University of Minnesota Press.

———. 2011. "*Underworld* and the Architecture of Urban Space." In *Don DeLillo: Mao II/Underworld/Falling Man*, edited by Stacey Olster, 83–98. London: Continuum.

Pisano, Dominick A. 2003a. "The Airplane and the Streamline Idiom in the United States." In *Aerospace Design: Aircraft, Spacecraft and the Art of Modern Flight*, edited by Anthony M. Springer, 40–51. London: Merrell.

———. 2003b. "New Directions in the History of Aviation." In *The Airplane in American Culture*, edited by Dominick A. Pisano, 1–15. Ann Arbor: University of Michigan Press.

Platsky, Jeff. 2016. "Demolition: Mammoth Shoe Factory to Come Down." *Press Connects*, April 26, 2016, www.pressconnects.com/story/news/2016/04/26/former-ej -victory-plant-demolished/83547428.

Povinelli, Elizabeth. 2016. *Geontologies: A Requiem to Late Liberalism*. London: Duke University Press.

Price, David. 2008. *Anthropological Intelligence: The Deployment and Neglect of American Anthropology in the Second World War*. Durham, NC: Duke University Press.

———. 2011. *Weaponizing Anthropology: Social Science in Service of the Militarized State*. Oakland, CA: AK Press.

———. 2016. *Cold War Anthropology: The CIA, the Pentagon and the Growth of Dual-Use Anthropology*. Durham, NC: Duke University Press.

Protevi, John. 2009. *Political Affect: Connecting the Social and the Somatic*. Minneapolis: University of Minnesota Press.

———. 2013. *Life, War, Earth: Deleuze and the Sciences*. Minneapolis: University of Minnesota Press.

Puar, Jasbir K. 2017. *The Right to Maim: Debility/Capacity/Disability*. Durham, NC: Duke University Press.

Puthucherril, Tony George. 2010. *From Shipbreaking to Sustainable Ship Recycling: Evolution of a Legal Regime*. Leiden: Martinus Nijhoff Publishers.

Quinn, Kelly, and Kati Phillips. 2001. "Student Charged in Bomb Scare at Southside." *Star Gazette*, February 15, 2001. Ralph, Laurence. 2014. *Renegade Dreams: Living through Injury in Gangland Chicago*. Chicago: University of Chicago Press.

Ramos, Efrén Rivera. 1996. "The Legal Construction of American Colonialism: The Insular Cases (1901–1922)." *Revista Jurídica de la Universidad de Puerto Rico* 65, no. 2: 225.

Rand, Lisa Ruth. 2016. "Orbital Decay: Space Junk and the Environmental History of Earth's Planetary Borderlands." PhD diss., University of Pennsylvania.

Raphael, T.J., and Todd Zwillich. 2016. "How Old Guns are Turned into Beautiful New Jewelry." *PRI*, June 15, 2016. www.pri.org/stories/2016-06-15/how-old-guns -are-turned-beautiful-new-jewelry.

Rediker, Marcus Buford. 2007. *The Slave Ship: A Human History*. New York: Viking Penguin.

Regan, Patrick M. 1994. *Organizing Societies for War: The Process and Consequences of Societal Militarization*. Westport, CT: Praeger.

Reno, Joshua. 2016. *Waste Away: Working and Living with a North American Landfill*. Oakland: University of California Press.

———. 2018a. "Making Time with Amateur Astronomers and Orbital Space Debris: Attunement and the Matter of Temporality." *Journal of Contemporary Archaeology* 5, no. 1: 4–18.

———. 2018b. "What Is Waste?" *Worldwide Waste Journal* 1, no. 1. http://doi.org /10.5334/wwwj.9.

Riches, David. 1986. *The Anthropology of Violence*. Oxford: Blackwell.

Robertson, Jennifer. 2002. "Reflexivity Redux: A Pithy Polemic on 'Positionally.'" *Anthropological Quarterly* 75, no. 4: 785–92.

Rocque, Michael. 2012. "Exploring School Rampage Shootings: Research, Theory, and Policy." *Social Science Journal* 49: 304–13.

Rosenzweig, Roy. 1998. "Wizards, Bureaucrats, Warriors, and Hackers: Writing the History of the Internet." *American Historical Review* 103, no. 5: 1530–52.

Rutger, Hayley. 2018. "Mote-Led Initiative Will Restore Resilient Corals Across 130 Acres Thanks to New Grant." *Mote Marine Laboratory & Aquarium*, November 9, 2018. https://mote.org/news/article/mote-led-initiative-will-restore-resilient-corals-across-130-acres-thanks-t.

Sand, Peter H. 2009a. "Diego Garcia: British-American Legal Black Hole in the Indian Ocean?" *Journal of Environmental Law* 21, no. 1: 113–37.

———. 2009b. "Diego Garcia Legal Black Hole—A Response to Sheppard et al." *Journal of Environmental Law* 21, no. 2: 295–98.

Saunt, Claudio. 2014. *West of the Revolution: An Uncommon History of 1776*. New York: W. W. Norton.

Schaub, Thomas Hill. 2011. "Underworld, Memory, and the Recycling of Cold War Narrative." In *Don DeLillo: Mao II/Underworld/Falling Man*, edited by Stacey Olster, 69–82. London: Continuum.

Schiff, Rebecca L. 1995. "Civil-Military Relations Reconsidered: A Theory of Concordance." *Armed Forces and Society* 22, no. 1: 7–24.

Scoles, Sarah. 2017. "The Space Junk Problem Is About to Get a Whole Lot Gnarlier." *Wired*, July 31, 2017, www.wired.com/story/the-space-junk-problem-is-about-to-get-a-whole-lot-gnarlier/.

Seaburn, Paul. 2016. "Object Falls from Sky Right before Christmas and Smashes Van." *Mysterious Universe*, December 27, 2016, http://mysteriousuniverse.org/2016/12/object-falls-from-sky-right-before-christmas-and-smashes-van/.

Seltzer, Mark. 1996. *Serial Killers: Death and Life in America's Wound Culture*. New York: Routledge.

Servet, Jean-Michel. 2009. "Toward an Alternative Economy: Reconsidering the Market, Money, and Value." In *Market and Society: The Great Transformation Today*, edited by Chris Hann and Keith Hart, 72–90. Cambridge: Cambridge University Press.

Sherman, Nancy. 2015. *After War: Healing the Moral Wounds of Our Soldiers*. Oxford: Oxford University Press.

Shore, Cris, and Susan Wright. 2000. "Coercive Accountability: The Rise of Audit Culture in Higher Education." In *Audit Cultures: Anthropological Studies in Accountability, Ethics and the Academy*, edited by Marilyn Strathern, 57–89. New York: Routledge.

Silk, Gerald. 2003. "'Our Future is in the Air': Aviation and American Art." In *The Airplane in American Culture*, edited by Dominick A. Pisano, 250–96. Ann Arbor: University of Michigan.

Simon, Richard M., Ashley Wagner, and Brooke Killion. 2017. "Gender and Choosing a STEM Major in College: Femininity, Masculinity, Chilly Climate, and Occupational Values." *JRST* 54, no. 3: 299–323.

SkyNews. 2017. "NASA Fixes Voyager 1 Deep Space Thrusters Not Used in 37 Years." *Sky News*, December 2, 2017. https://news.sky.com/story/nasa-fixes-voyager-1 -deep-space-probe-by-firing-thrusters-not-used-in-37-years-11152505.

Slaughter, Joseph P. 2016. "Genesis of the US Navy, 1785-1806." In *America, Sea Power, and the World*, edited by James C. Bradford, 26–41. Malden, MA: Wiley Blackwell.

Sloterdijk, Peter. 2009. "Airquakes." *Environment and Planning D: Society and Space* 27, no. 1: 41–57.

Slotkin, Richard. 1992. *Gunfighter Nation: The Myth of the Frontier in Twentieth-Century America*. New York: Atheneum.

Smart, Pamela G. 2010. *Sacred Modern: Faith, Activism, and Aesthetics in the Menil Collection*. Austin: University of Texas Press.

Smith, Merritt Roe. 1981. "Military Entrepreneurship." In *Yankee Enterprise: The Rise of the American System of Manufactures*, edited by Otto Mayr and Robert C. Post, 63–102. Washington, DC: Smithsonian Institution Press.

Smith, Roger C. 1988. "Treasure Ships of the Spanish Main: The Iberian-American Maritime Empires." In *Ships and Shipwrecks of the Americas: A History Based on Underwater Archaeology*, edited by George F. Bass, 85–106. London: Thames and Hudson.

Snider, Jill D. 2003. "'Great Shadow in the Sky': The Airplane in the Tulsa Race Riot of 1921 and the Development of African American Visions of Aviation, 1921–1926." In *The Airplane in American Culture*, edited by Dominick A. Pisano, 105–46. Ann Arbor: University of Michigan Press.

Soar, Daniel. 2017. "The Most Expensive Weapon Ever Built." *London Review of Books* 39, no. 7: 3–5.

SpeculumPaper WorldNews. 2014. "Flooded Island Nations Relocate to Pacific Garbage Patch." *Speculum*, February 24, 2014. https://speculumnewspaper.wordpress .com/2014/02/24/flooded-island-nations-relocate-to-pacific-garbage-patch/.

Spelman, Elizabeth V. 2003. *Repair: The Impulse to Restore in a Fragile World*. New York: Beacon Press.

Sponsel, Leslie E. 2009. "Reflections on the Possibilities of a Nonkilling Society and a Nonkilling Anthropology." In *Toward a Nonkilling Paradigm*, edited by Joám Evans Pim, 35–72. Honolulu, Hawaii: Center for Global Nonkilling.

———. 2016. "The Anthropology of Peace and Nonviolence." *Diogenes* 61, nos. 3–4: 30–45.

Stahl, Roger. 2010. *Militainment, Inc.: War, Media, and Popular Culture*. New York: Routledge.

Starosielski, Nicole. 2015. *The Undersea Network*. Durham, NC: Duke University Press.

Stebbins, Consuelo E. 2007. *City of Intrigue, Nest of Revolution: A Documentary History of Key West in the Nineteenth Century*. Gainesville: University Press of Florida.

Steffen, Will, Wendy Broadgate, Lisa Deutsch, Owen Gaffney, and Cornelia Ludwig. 2015. "The Trajectory of the Anthropocene: The Great Acceleration." *Anthropocene Review* 2, no. 1: 81–98.

Stillwell, Blake. 2017. "These Air Force 'Rods from God' Could Hit with the Force of a Nuclear Weapon." *We Are the Mighty*, September 6, 2017. http://www.wearethe mighty.com/articles/these-air-force-rods-from-god-could-hit-with-the-force-of-a -nuclear-weapon.

Stoler, Ann Laura, ed. 2013. *Imperial Debris: On Ruins and Ruination*. Durham, NC: Duke University Press.

Stoler, Ann Laura, with Carole McGranahan. 2018. "Disassemblage: Rethinking U.S. Imperial Formations." In *Ethnographies of U.S. Empire*, edited by Carole McGrana-han and John F. Collins, 477–90. London: Duke University Press.

Stone, Judy. 2014. "Ebola in the U.S.: Politics and Public Health Don't Mix." *Scientific American*, October 6, 2014. https://blogs.scientificamerican.com/molecules-to -medicine/ebola-in-the-u-s-politics-and-public-health-don-t-mix/.

Sunahara, Geoffrey I., Guilherme Lotufo, Roman G. Kuperman, and Jalal Hawari. 2009. *Ecotoxicology of Explosives*. Boca Raton, FL: CRC Press.

Susman, Tina. 2015. "In New York State, Fracking Ban Fuels Secession Talk. *LA Times*, March 26, 2015, www.latimes.com/nation/la-na-ny-fracking-secession-2015 0326-story.html.

Taussig, Michael. 2011. *I Swear I Saw This: Drawings in Fieldwork Notebooks, Namely, My Own*. Chicago: University of Chicago Press.

Thacker, Eugene. 2011. *In the Dust of This Planet: Horror of Philosophy*, vol. 1. Alresford, Hants, UK: Zero Books.

Thompson, Carl. 2014. Introduction. In *Shipwreck in Art and Literature: Images and Interpretations from Antiquity to the Present Day*, edited by Carl Thompson, 1–26. New York: Routledge.

Thompson, Mark. 2016. "Number of U.S. Troops in Iraq Keeps Creeping Upward." *Time*, April 18, 2016. http://time.com/4298318/iraq-us-troops-barack-obama-mosul-isis/.

Thompson, Michael. (1979) 2017. *Rubbish Theory: The Creation and Destruction of Value*. New edition. London: Pluto Press.

Thorpe, Rebecca U. 2014. *The American Warfare State: The Domestic Politics of Military Spending*. London: University of Chicago Press.

Touhouliotis, Vasiliki. 2018. "Weak Seed and a Poisoned Land: Slow Violence and the Toxic Infrastructures of War in South Lebanon." *Environmental Humanities* 10, no. 1: 86–106.

Tsing, Anna Lowenhaupt. 2015. *The Mushroom at the End of the World: On the Possibil-ity of Life in Capitalist Ruins*. Princeton, NJ: Princeton University Press.

Tucker, Richard P. 2012. "War and the Environment." In *A Companion to Global Envi-ronmental History*, edited by J.R. McNeill and Erin Stewart Mauldin, 319–39. Oxford: Wiley-Blackwell.

Turner, Victor. 1980. "Social Dramas and Stories about Them." *Critical Inquiry* 7, no. 1: 141–68.

Turse, Nick. 2008. *The Complex: How the Military Invades Our Everyday Lives*. New York: Metropolitan Books.

Uk, Krisna. 2016. *Salvage: Cultural Resilience among the Jorai of Northeast Cambodia*. Ithaca, NY: Cornell University Press.

Utley, Robert M. 1973. *Frontier Regulars: The United States Army and the Indian, 1866-1891*. New York: Macmillan.

Valant, Gary M. 1987. *Vintage Aircraft Nose Art*. Osceola, WI: Motorbooks.

Valentine, David. 2012. "Exit Strategy: Profit, Cosmology, and the Future of Humans in Space." *Anthropological Quarterly* 85, no. 4: 1045–68.

Vander Meulen, Jacob A. 1991. *The Politics of Aircraft: Building an American Military Industry*. Lawrence: University of Kansas Press.

Vargas-Ángel, Bernardo. 2009. "Coral Health and Disease Assessment in the U.S. Pacific Remote Island Areas." *Bulletin of Marine Science* 84, no. 2: 211–27.

Velasco, Gary. 2004. *Fighting Colors: The Creation of Military Aircraft Nose Art*. Paducah, KY: Turner Publishing Company.

Veblen, Thorstein. (1904) 1976. *The Theory of Business Enterprise*. New Brunswick, NJ: Transaction Books.

Verdery, Katherine. 2018. *My Life as a Spy: Investigations in a Secret Police File*. Durham, NC: Duke University Press.

Vine, David. 2008. "Taking on Empires: Reparations, the Right of Return, and the People of Diego Garcia." *Souls* 10, no. 4: 327–43.

———. 2011. *Island of Shame: The Secret History of the U.S. Military Base on Diego Garcia*. Oxford: Princeton University Press.

———. 2015. *Bases of Empire: How U.S. Bases Abroad Harm America and the World*. New York: Metropolitan Books.

———. 2018. "Islands of Imperialism: Military Bases and the Ethnography of U.S. Empire." In *Ethnographies of U.S. Empire*, edited by Carole McGranahan and John F. Collins, 249–69. London: Duke University Press.

Virilio, Paul. 1997. *Pure War*. New York: Semiotext(e).

———. 2007. *The Original Accident*. Cambridge, UK: Polity Press.

Vitale, Patrick. 2011. "Wages of War: Manufacturing Nationalism during World War II." *Antipode* 43, no. 3: 783–819.

Voyles, Traci Brynne. 2015. *Wastelanding: Legacies of Uranium Mining in Navajo Country*. Minneapolis: University of Minnesota Press.

Wall, Mike. 2017. "Secretive X-37B Military Space Plane Marks 7 Days in Orbit." *Space.com*, April 19, 2017. www.space.com/36518-x-37b-military-space-plane-700-days.html?utm_source=sp-newsletter&utm_medium=email&utm_campaign=20170419-sdc.

Walley, Christine J. 2013. *Exit Zero: Family and Class in Postindustrial Chicago*. Chicago: University of Chicago Press.

Wang, Zuoyue. 2008. *In Sputnik's Shadow: The President's Science Advisory Committee and Cold War America*. New Brunswick, NJ: Rutgers University Press.

Webber, Julie A. 2003. *Failure to Hold: The Politics of School Shooting*. Boulder, CO: Rowman & Littlefield.

Weems, Jason. 2015. *Barnstorming the Prairies: How Aerial Vision Shaped the Midwest.* Minneapolis: University of Minnesota Press.

Weigley, Russel Frank. 1973. *The American Way of War: A History of United States Military Strategy and Policy.* Bloomington: University of Indiana Press.

Weiss, Linda. 2014. *America Inc.? Innovation and Enterprise in the National Security State.* Ithaca, NY: Cornell University Press.

Welker, Marina. 2014. *Enacting the Corporation: An American Mining Firm in Post-Authoritarian Indonesia.* Berkeley: University of California Press.

Wesson, Paul. 2010. "Panspermia, Past and Present: Astrophysical and Biophysical Conditions for the Dissemination of Life in Space." *Space Science Reviews* 156, nos. 1–4: 239–52.

West, Harry G., and Todd Sanders, eds. 2003. *Transparency and Conspiracy: Ethnographies of Suspicion in the New World Order.* Durham, NC: Duke University Press.

Wezeman, Simon T. 2014. "The Global Arms Trade after the Cold War." In *The Global Arms Trade: A Handbook,* edited by Andrew T. H. Tan, 193–207. New York: Oxford University Press.

Whyte, Kyle. 2017. "Indigenous Climate Change Studies: Indigenizing Futures, Decolonizing the Anthropocene." *English Language Notes* 55, nos. 1–2: 153–62.

Williamson, Mark. 2000. "Planetary Spacecraft Debris: The Case for Protecting the Space Environment." *Acta Astronautica* 47, nos. 2–9: 719–29.

Wilson, Tom. 2001. "Threats to United States Space Capabilities." Prepared for the Commission to Assess United States National Security Space Management and Organization. https://fas.org/spp/eprint/article05.html.

Winn, Patrick. 2016. "Climate Change, Meet Your Apocalyptic Twin: Oceans Poisoned by Plastic." *PRI,* December 13, 2016. www.pri.org/stories/2016-12-13/climate-change-meet-your-apocalyptic-twin-oceans-poisoned-plastic.

Wohl, Robert. 1994. *A Passion for Wings: Aviation and the Western Imagination 1908–1918.* New Haven, CT: Yale University Press.

Wolf-Meyer, Matthew. 2003. "The World Ozymandias Made: Utopias in the Superhero Comic, Subculture, and the Conservation of Difference." *Popular Culture* 36, no. 3: 497–517.

Wood, J. P. 1999. *Nose Art: 80 Years of Aviation Artwork.* New York: Barnes and Noble Books.

Woodward, Rachel. 2001. "Khaki Conservation: An Examination of Military Environmentalist Discourse in the British Army." *Journal of Rural Studies* 17: 201–17.

———. 2004. *Military Geographies.* Oxford: Blackwell.

Wool, Zoë H. 2015. *After War: The Weight of Life at Walter Reed.* Durham, NC: Duke University Press.

Wyatt-Brown, Bertram. 2014. *A Warring Nation: Honor, Race, and Humiliation in America and Abroad.* Charlottesville: University of Virginia Press.

Xu, Yonghong. 2008. "Gender Disparity in STEM Disciplines: A Study of Faculty Attrition and Turnover Intentions." *Research in Higher Education* 49, no. 7: 607–24.

————. 2015. "Focusing on Women in STEM: A Longitudinal Examination of Gender-Based Earning Gap of College Graduates." *Journal of Higher Education* 86, no. 4: 489–523.

Yates, Michelle. 2011. "The Human-As-Waste, the Labor Theory of Value and Disposability." *Antipode* 43, no. 5: 1679–95.

Yirka, Bob. 2011. "DARPA Unveils New Telescope to Protect Satellites from Space Debris." *Phys.org*, April 25, 2011. https://phys.org/news/2011-04-darpa-unveils-telescope-satellites-space.html.

Yoneyama, Lisa. 2016. *Cold War Ruins: Transpacific Critique of American Justice and Japanese War Crimes.* Durham, NC: Duke University Press.

Zalasiewicz, Jan, Mark Williams, Colin N. Waters, Anthony D. Barnosky, and Peter Haff. 2014. "The Technofossil Record of Humans." *Anthropocene Review* 1, no. 1: 34–43.

Zani, Leah. 2019. *Bomb Children: Life in the Former Battlefields of Laos.* Durham, NC: Duke University Press.

Zhan, Mei. 2009. *Other-Worldly: Making Chinese Medicine through Transnational Frames.* Durham, NC: Duke University Press.

————. 2011. "Worlding Oneness: Daoism, Heidegger, and Possibilities for Treating the Human." *Social Text* 29, no. 4: 107–28.

Zigon, Jarrett. 2017. "A Politics of Worldbuilding." Member Voices, Society for Cultural Anthropology, December 5, 2017, https://culanth.org/fieldsights/1249-a-politics-of-worldbuilding.

Žižek, Slavoj. 2010. *Living in the End Times.* New York: Verso.

Zoba, Wendy Murray. 2000. *Day of Reckoning: Columbine and the Search for America's Soul.* Grand Rapids: Brazos Press.

INDEX

activism, 2, 84; anti-base 10, 200.
See also Chagossians; civil rights;
Diego Garcia
Advanced Research Projects Agency.
See Defense Advanced Research Projects
Agency
affordance, 49, 50–52, 61–62, 69, 70–73, 82, 87,
202. See also Boneyard; nose art; planes;
repair; restoration
agriculture. See guano
amateur astronomers, 13–17, 24, 109, 113, 120,
121–123, 127–128, 131–132, 133–134, 136, 137,
229n34–230n34. See also Cold War; Defense
Advanced Research Projects Agency; ham
radio operators; orbital space debris; space
race
Anthropocene, 188–192, 200–201; critiques of,
104. See also climate change; Polemocene;
sea-level
antisatellite weapons, 119, 129. See also orbital
space debris
arms sales, 20–22, 170; international, 23, 28–29,
105. See also Lockheed Martin
artificial reefing, 88–90, 91–94, 95–98, 102–104;
rent and, 98–102; SINKEX program,
94–96; See also demilitarization; rent;
USNS Vandenberg
attunement, 112–113, 128, 133–136, 202;
affordances and, 50, 230n37.
See also amateur astronomers;
ham radio operators; orbital space
debris

automobile accidents, 85; compared with
military waste, 203–210

Basel Convention, 95; Basel Action Network
(BAN), 95–97. See also environment
Binghamton: Binghamton University, 17–19.
See also International Business Machines;
Mass Shooting; Southern Tier, New York
Boneyard, 50, 51–59, 61–63, 65, 68–69, 74,
77–80. See also planes; repair; scrap
Boneyard Project, 61, 69–70, 72–77, 81–82.
See also demilitarization; nose art

Central Intelligence Agency (CIA), 49, 84, 128,
141; anthropology and, 15–16. See also Cold
War; securitization
Chagossians, 174–175, 184–188, 191–192, 195,
198, 200–201. See also Diego Garcia; empire
civilian-military relations, 3–4, 4–7, 14–15, 18,
20, 22, 48, 51–52, 72–73, 80, 111, 112, 123–127,
144, 203–208; economics of, 27, 104–106,
141–143, 146, 149, 170–171, 172–173; militias
and, 142, 154; science and, 84, 118–120,
128–132, 137, 191–192, 197
civil rights, 128, 150; gun rights considered to
be, 6, 170. See also nonviolence
climate: change 103–104, 176, 187, 188–198;
science, 117, 131, 191–192, 197, 228n14.
See also civilian-military relations; ocean;
Polemocene
Cold War, 1, 4, 6, 8, 48, 55–56, 93, 108, 111, 112,
117, 120, 124–125, 137, 139, 152, 182–185, 208;

Cold War (*continued*)
    economics of, 3, 15–16, 22–23, 26–29, 105,
      212; remains of, 19, 54, 56, 80–81, 95. *See*
      also Eisenhower, Dwight D.; war; military
Columbine school shooting, 153, 155, 156, 160,
    164–165, 168. *See also* mass shooting; school
    shooting
commodities, 71, 77, 184; contrasted with assets,
    98–102; guns as, 170–171; military products
    as, 8–9, 44, 105, 219n5. *See also* economics;
    Marxism; rent; value
conservation, 6, 11, 100–103, 174–175, 186, 199
conspiracy theory, 45, 110–113, 226n3–227n3
contamination. *See* waste

Defense Advanced Research Projects Agency
    (DARPA), 5, 32–33, 129–133, 136, 138,
    211–212; See also Department of Defense;
    military; National Aeronautics and Science
    Administration; orbital space debris;
    techno-solutionism; weapons testing
defense contracts, 4, 14–15, 18, 20, 24, 26, 28,
    132–133, 138, 157, 210–211; critique of, 21–23
    219n6; negotiation surrounding, 29–33,
    37–39, 42–43
demilitarization, 5–6, 14, 49, 59–65, 70, 74, 94,
    119–120, 141, 212, 216n9. *See also* mass shoot-
    ings; nose art; orbital space debris; planes;
    USNS Vandenberg
Department of Defense (DoD), 2, 4, 10, 21,
    25–26, 29–31, 36, 41, 43, 44, 46, 77, 91, 113,
    118–119, 127, 130, 131, 142, 189, 191, 206,
    210–211. *See also* Cold War; Lockheed
    Martin; military
Diego Garcia, 174–175, 177, 184–188, 191–193,
    196–197, 198. *See also* Chagossians; empire;
    islands
divers, 5, 85–86, 88–94, 99–102, 103–104,
    105–106, 212; death dive of satellites,
    109–111, 226n2

Eisenhower, Dwight D., 21–23, 118, 137, 228n23.
    See also Cold War; Defense Advanced
    Research Projects Agency; military-indus-
    trial complex; space race
empire, 23, 136, 145, 147, 189; American, 1, 6, 11,
    15, 19, 55–56, 84, 104, 116, 145, 150, 166, 172,
    174–201, 204, 213, 216n10; British, 83, 175,
    184–185; difficulty with studying, 176–178,
    215n4, 233n4; Japanese, 67; Spanish, 89.
    See also Diego Garcia; military; settler-
    colonialism

environments: government regulation of, 84–85,
    95–98, 175–176, 184, 193–194; marine, 6,
    87–91, 93–94, 99–105; military destruction
    of, 4, 8–11, 186–187, 192, 201; orbital, 112–117,
    127–132, 137–139; perceptions of, 187–188,
    197–201; pollution of, 86–87, 105–106, 117,
    128, 139, 178–180. *See also* climate change;
    conservation; waste; wilderness
ethics, 26, 39–44, 47, 50, 112–113, 128, 143–145,
    158–169, 173; conspiracy theories and,
    110–111; waste avoidance and, 24, 33–39,
    175–176. *See also* attunement; nonviolence;
    violence

fertilizer. *See* guano
fetishism. *See* commodities; value
fossil fuel, 104, 178, 179, 188; carbon democracy
    and, 183–185. *See also* Anthropocene; climate
    change; guano; Polemocene; sea level

garbage. *See* rubbish; waste
gender, 13–14, 15, 16–17, 58–59, 72, 93, 126, 173;
    guns and, 151–155, 158, 160. *See also* mass
    shooting; methodology
Ghost Fleet, 84–85, 94–95
guano: soil exhaustion crisis and, 11, 14,
    177–186, 188, 190, 196, 198
guns, 5, 6, 12, 112, 140–144, 154, 157, 158–163, 167,
    169–172; gunfighter mythos, 151–153,
    155–156, 160, 169; United States history of,
    145–151. *See also* mass shooting; school
    shooting

ham radio operators, 109, 128, 131, 134–136.
    See also amateur astronomers; orbital space
    debris

indigenous people, 11, 54, 87, 142, 145, 150, 154,
    175–176, 181, 186, 197, 204; Sioux, 147–149.
    See also Chagossians; race; settler-colonial-
    ism
International Business Machines (IBM),
    13, 18–19, 26–29, 37, 115, 122–123.
    See also military-industrial complex
islands, 2, 6, 10, 87–88, 122, 126, 174–188,
    191–197, 199–201. *See also* Chagossians;
    climate change; Diego Garcia; guano;
    ocean; sea-level

Key West, 5, 85, 90–94, 98–104; history of,
    87–89. *See also* artificial-reefing; ruins;
    shipwrecks

language. *See* semiotics; storytelling
Lockheed Martin, 4, 13, 17, 19, 20–22, 24–26,
29–44, 47–49, 91, 94, 138, 206, 210–211,
218n1. *See also* planes; weapons testing

mass shooting, 2, 5, 6, 14, 141–145, 147, 150–173,
203, 206, 213. *See also* Columbine; guns;
school
Marxism: critique of militarization and, 23–26,
34, 44, 199, 218n3. *See also* commodities;
rent
materiality. *See* affordance; metabolic rift;
ocean; semiotics
metabolic rift, 11, 177–178, 188, 190–197. *See also*
climate change; environments; fossil fuel;
Marxism
methodology, 13–19, 143–145, 176. *See also*
microworlds
microworlds, 3–6, 21, 39, 47, 112, 202. *See also*
methodology
military: militarism, 14, 72, 140–173, 208, 213;
militarism and militarization compared, 3,
5–6, 52, 141, 145–153, 199, 206, 215n6;
militarization, 2–5, 9–10, 19, 24, 58, 65, 68,
105, 108, 111, 113, 117–121, 124, 128–132, 137,
147, 150, 165, 170–173, 193, 200, 207–213. *See
also* civilian-military relations; demilitarization; military-industrial complex
military-industrial complex, 14–15, 18, 23–26,
42, 47–48, 118, 142, 199; defined, 21–22. *See
also* civilian-military relations; Eisenhower,
Dwight D.; military; Mills, C. Wright
Mills, C. Wright, 3, 9, 21–22, 208, 235n10–236n10.
See also military-industrial complex
museums, 4–5, 13, 28, 47, 50–65, 77, 79, 81, 86,
88, 90, 91–94, 101, 124–126. *See also*
demilitarization; semiotics; storytelling

National Aeronautics and Space Administration (NASA), 2, 28, 108–111, 113, 115–116,
118–119, 122, 128–129, 132–135, 138. *See also*
amateur astronomers; Cold War; Defense
Advanced Research Projects Agency;
military; orbital space debris; space race
National Reconnaissance Office (NRO), 2, 111,
119–120
nature. *See* conservation; environments;
wilderness
New York. *See* Southern Tier, New York
nonviolence, 142, 156–159, 166–169, 173, 232n26;
pacifism, 16, 138. *See also* mass shooting;
military; school shooting; violence

nose art, 52, 69–73, 81, 224n30. *See also*
demilitarization; planes
nuclear weapons, 8–9, 11, 23, 31, 34, 48, 54, 56,
67, 92, 110–111, 119, 137, 152, 182–183, 208, 210;
pollution from, 186–187, 201; and war, 19,
117, 198–199, 211. *See also* Cold War; war

Obama, Barack, 21, 23, 48, 125, 154; guns and,
170–171, 194, 206
ocean, 35, 89, 121; empire and, 174–201; in-itself,
6, 178, 188–197; pollution of, 1, 5, 9, 12,
94–98, 102–106, 116, 182–183, 186–187, 201.
See also climate change; island
orbital space debris, 5, 6, 14, 24, 108–139, 141,
210. *See also* amateur astronomers; Defense
Advanced Research Projects Agency; ham
radio operators; National Aeronautics and
Space Administration
outerspace. *See* National Aeronautics and Space
Administration; orbital space debris; space
race

permanent war readiness, 1–8, 11–12, 14–19, 44,
51, 68, 86, 108, 112, 126–127, 141–142,
149–150, 166, 182, 202–213; critiques of,
20–24, 46–48; economy of, 26–29, 38–39,
46, 49, 54, 57, 83, 106–107, 170–172, 199,
209, 211. *See also* civilian-military relations;
military; military-industrial complex
planes, 1, 4, 12, 14, 21–24, 44, 46, 49–82, 84, 85,
94, 101, 119–120, 125, 131, 134, 138, 141, 142,
146, 203, 211–212. *See also* nose art
plastic, 58–59, 62, 80–81, 211; pollution, 116, 178,
188, 193–198, 200. *See also* Anthropocene;
climate change; metabolic rifts
police, 54, 73, 79, 124, 125, 140–141, 143–144, 151,
155–157, 161–165, 170–173
Polemocene, 9–10, 104, 195–201, 213. *See also*
Anthropocene; climate change

race. *See* indigenous people; methodology;
settler colonialism; white supremacy
Reagan, Ronald, 20, 94–95, 129, 137, 228n24–
229n24. *See also* Cold War; space race
recycling, 5, 12, 57, 69, 81–82, 106, 158, 171–172,
194, 196, 213; compared with preservation,
92, 94–102, 132–134, 136–137. *See also*
rubbish; scrap; waste
reflexive practice, 11, 25–26, 29–44. *See also*
Lockheed Martin; weapons testing
rent, 98–102. *See also* commodities; economics;
value

repair, 49–56, 61–65, 73, 78, 101, 133, 190;
repair-scape, 58, 61, 86. *See also* Boneyard;
planes; restoration

restoration: environmental, 89–90, 97, 102–104,
178; industrial, 27–28, 52–56, 58–63, 69, 73,
79–80, 101; organizational, 129; of social
hierarchy, 149, 152–153, 213. *See also* planes;
repair; rubbish; waste

rubbish, 7–8, 11, 50–51, 55, 68, 111–112, 136, 202,
206. *See also* waste

ruin, 15, 99–101, 103–104, 212; empire and,
176–177, 179, 196, 198; ruinscape, 85–87, 102,
105. *See also* rent; shipwrecks

school, 28, 89, 123, 142–145, 155, 156–169, 170,
187; G.I. Bill, 17; hidden curriculum, 145,
165–169. *See also* mass shootings

scrap (or scrapping), 5, 12, 28, 44–45, 53–57, 61,
78–80, 82, 92–93, 95–102, 105–106, 171;
scrapyard, 29, 51, 54–55, 56, 60, 68–70,
74–75, 77, 91, 101. *See also* Boneyard;
recycling; rubbish; ruin; waste

sea-level, 178, 188–193, 195, 198, 200. *See also*
Chagossians; climate change; Diego Garcia;
ocean

securitization, 15–16, 27, 47, 48–49, 65–68, 78,
84, 86, 108, 117, 120–121, 125, 128, 141, 156,
182–183, 189, 199, 204–206, 208–210. *See
also* military

semiotics, 50–52, 60–65, 68, 77, 80, 86–87,
105–106, 143–145, 221n11. *See also*
storytelling

service members, 9, 20, 27, 43, 47, 68, 71–72, 80,
132, 141, 151, 170, 173, 203–206, 209;
generals, 21, 32–33, 72, 79. *See also* veterans

settler-colonialism, 5, 11, 140, 142–143, 145–153,
172, 176, 178–182, 198, 208. *See also* guns;
indigenous people; mass shooting; race;
United States

shipwrecks, 11, 85–89, 91, 94, 112

simulation, 28–29, 62, 79–80, 91; of warfare, 10,
19, 38–39, 206–207, 210–212. *See also*
semiotics; service members

social movements. *See* activism

Southern Tier, New York, 4, 13–19, 24, 26–29,
34, 109, 115, 134, 145, 212

space race, 112, 118–120, 124, 131, 137, 139;
Sputnik, 108, 118, 120, 121, 124–126, 131. *See
also* Cold War; National Aeronautics and
Space Administration

storytelling, 5, 52, 63–64, 81, 86–87, 92–97, 111,
120, 143–145, 148–156, 158–169, 173, 180, 196,

225n7; tropes of, 7, 72, 153, 155–156, 158,
165–166, 172, 195, 225n5. *See also* military;
semiotics

techno-solutionism, 5, 113, 126–127, 130–132, 136,
138. *See also* Defense Advanced Research
Projects Agency

transvaluation, 11, 81, 108, 111, 145, 158, 172–173,
180, 202

Trump, Donald, 21–23, 27, 46–48, 129, 137–138,
144, 171, 208–209, 211

USNS Vandenberg, 85, 89–104. *See also*
artificial reefing; Key West; rent; ruin;
shipwrecks; world-making

value, 3, 11–12, 16, 23–24, 26, 31, 33–39, 51, 55, 62,
66, 85–86, 87–89, 112–113; economic, 7–9,
29, 34, 46, 90, 100–102, 105, 116, 153, 170;
politics of, 69, 74, 94–104, 149, 175, 179–188,
192–193. *See also* commodities; Marxism;
rubbish; transvaluation; waste

veterans, 51, 56–60, 68, 90–94, 151, 169, 205;
Veterans Affairs, 46–47. *See also* service
members

violence, 12, 17, 70, 79, 141–146, 151–173, 180–181,
198–199, 206–213. *See also* Columbine; mass
shootings; nonviolence; school shootings;
war

war, 1–4, 7–8, 10–12, 14, 17; Barbary Wars,
83–84; Vietnam, 22, 27, 69, 128, 142, 196, 203,
209, 211; violence of, 40, 44, 46, 49, 65–66,
106, 145–151; War on Terror, 21, 27, 65, 66, 68,
86, 121, 140, 152, 204–205, 208–210; World
Wars, 1, 8, 9, 14, 22, 26, 54, 55, 57, 58, 64, 67,
69, 71, 92–104, 137, 147, 169, 182, 184, 198, 203,
204. *See also* permanent war readiness

waste: definitions and uses of, 2, 7–12, 24, 29,
33–35, 37, 100, 112, 123, 151, 169–170, 175–176,
202, 215n3; military spending and, 20–24,
26, 46–48, 59–60, 66–67, 82; open-endedness of, 7, 9–11, 50, 54, 73, 86–87, 105–107,
111, 136, 201, 202, 217n20, 225n5; toxicity of,
1, 4, 7, 9–11, 84, 95–96, 104–105, 119, 157,
183, 186–187, 196, 201, 217n19. *See also*
rubbish; wasteland

wasteland, 6, 11, 50, 175–189, 191, 194–198, 201,
202, 213. *See also* empire; guano; wilderness

weapons testing, 4–5, 8, 24–26, 33–44, 112, 119,
129, 183, 201. *See also* antisatellite weapons;
Lockheed Martin; Marxism

white supremacy, 67, 140, 142–143, 145, 147–150, 154, 171. *See also* indigenous people; settler-colonialism

wilderness, 2, 10, 175–177, 183, 185–186, 191, 197–198, 203

world-making, 11, 86–87, 94–98, 106–107, 202, 212. *See also* microworlds

Founded in 1893,
UNIVERSITY OF CALIFORNIA PRESS
publishes bold, progressive books and journals
on topics in the arts, humanities, social sciences,
and natural sciences—with a focus on social
justice issues—that inspire thought and action
among readers worldwide.

The UC PRESS FOUNDATION
raises funds to uphold the press's vital role
as an independent, nonprofit publisher, and
receives philanthropic support from a wide
range of individuals and institutions—and from
committed readers like you. To learn more, visit
ucpress.edu/supportus.

Printed in Great Britain
by Amazon

21142358R00162